WHAT
IT TAKES

WHAT IT TAKES

. . . TO LIVE AND LEAD WITH PURPOSE, LAUGHTER, AND STRENGTH

Zahra Al-harazi

with Sarah J. Robbins

Collins

Published by Collins, an imprint of HarperCollins Publishers Ltd

First edition

HarperCollins Publishers Ltd
Bay Adelaide Centre, East Tower
22 Adelaide Street West, 41st Floor
Toronto, Ontario, Canada
M5H 4E3

www.harpercollins.ca

Library and Archives Canada Cataloguing in Publication information is available upon request.

ISBN 978-1-4434-4308-1

Printed and bound in the United States of America

LSC/H 9 8 7 6 5 4 3 2 1

For the ones that matter:
my parents, my children, and the love of my life

Between stimulus and response is our greatest power—
the freedom to choose.
—STEPHEN R. COVEY,
The Seven Habits of Highly Effective People

IT TAKES AN INTRODUCTION

I am a girl from Yemen.

For me, this simple sentence holds endless complexity. You likely have already formed some opinion, about me, about this book. I will tell you, though, that whatever you first imagined me to be, I am also the opposite.

I am East *and* I am West—and every single damn thing in between. From obedient Muslim daughter to one of Canada's most powerful women. From dutiful housewife to independent business-woman. From not being allowed to drive to getting my very own motorcycle. From a twenty-year-old married woman with children to a forty-something wild child. I am a million conflicted contra-dictions rolled into one uncomplicated, complicated person.

I spent much of my life bending myself into thousands of dif-ferent shapes in order to be the person I thought I had to be. Ulti-mately, I learned that what I needed was not the ability to fit in, but the freedom and the courage to step away.

This is a story about what happens when the ideals to which you cling most tightly begin to slip from your grasp: what that openness feels like, beyond the fear that without those definitions there is no you. This book is about what it takes to build a life that is your own—to free your mind from its many ugly demons and to walk into the future without the chains that hold you back.

Bookstores are crammed with books full of formulas for success, for happiness, for wealth, health, and fulfillment. Magazines, courses, and websites by the thousands claim to show you how to follow your passion and your desires. They claim to help you define who you think you need to be and draw a picture for you about what life should look like.

Here is the truth: There is no magic bullet, formula, or rule book. And there is not one single template.

I will tell you what it takes: it takes everything you have . . . and then some more.

It takes your experiences, your hard work, your talent, and your perseverance. It takes history and community. It takes opportunities and doors that are open and some that are closed. It takes those you love and the values for which you are willing to sacrifice . . . and sometimes, it simply takes luck and being in the right place at the right time.

It takes legacy that has nothing to do with your ability.

Researchers have found evidence that your ancestors' childhoods or adventures might affect your personality, gifting you with anxiety or resilience. Along with my great grandmother's Burmese nose, my mother's Indian skin, and my father's Yemeni forehead, I inherited a series of advantages and benefits from those who came before me. My fundamental, unchangeable self has been shaped by generations and entire worlds of tradition.

Yours has too.

I wrote *What It Takes* to show you that everything you need to live your best life is already in you. It begins with acknowledging your roots. You can pull the nourishment of your history from the earth.

And you should let it serve you, even as you acknowledge the pain and regrets you still carry.

Acknowledge and accept setbacks that will knock you to your knees and conflicts that will shake your most fundamental beliefs.

Because what it takes is more than simply overcoming the hurdles that arrive in your life without warning or apology: it takes the humility to learn how to embrace them.

It will take joy. Delight in the journey, as rocky as it is, and gratitude for the opportunities we have to share the road.

In this book I share my understanding of identity and the ideas that help me—and, I hope, may help you—stay grounded through life's challenges. These themes are the filter through which I consider every decision, approach, and opinion—and a raft when I have (frequently) thrown myself into deep, uncharted water.

What these themes are *not* are the things other people will tell you that you have to find. Yes, you need typical things like resilience, strength, passion, courage, and motivation, and you need them in spades; however, those are simply table stakes. They are non-negotiable, set in stone. If you don't have them, you won't survive.

The themes in this book are much simpler. They are the small things that fix the big things. The baby steps that lead to winning the long game.

Our body of experience forms a unique prism through which we each see the world and its potential. The longer we live—with every breath, blink, and sound—the more facets we acquire.

Like everyone else, my prism is what I see the world through. For years, I felt owned by it. I made predictable decisions, looking in one boring direction. I was defined by a single angle. Trapped. Stuck.

So I learned how to turn the damn thing around.

I considered new possibilities that swung open new doors and blew open my mind with bold new perspectives. Just like that, I was undefined, unstuck, and liberated by my very own life experience.

Knowing who you are is incredibly hard, I've learned. So I've spent a lot of time figuring out who I'm not. When I feared I'd drown in the depth of a situation, I've found comfort in the shallows. And in so doing, I have come to understand that the circumstances in my life may actually be less important than how much control I have over them.

None of this makes me exemplary. I learn every day. But now, when I am challenged, I have faith that my true power lies not in how much I adapt but in the fact that, no matter what life throws at me, I am, at my core, still the same person. And that I *will* be okay.

This is a story about discovering you can live a life that reflects the hopes of those who love you, and who have loved you. No matter how you differ, there is a best version of yourself that you can give them in return for this love: someone who is content, challenged, focused, and free.

You can be all the contradictory things that inspired you to open this book. And you can thrive.

What it takes, above all, is all of the above . . . and then some more.

CHAPTER ONE

Zahra, no. Zahra, don't do that. Zahra, get away from there. There were many rules to keep track of, and so many people to warn me not to break them.

"You can't talk to boys, Zahra," said the headmistress, as she pulled out her dreaded cane.

"Her mother is not from here," whispered my father's relatives. "That's why she's such a wild child."

"The devil eats with the left hand, Zahra," scolded my aunt's father, tying my left hand behind my back at lunchtime. "Your left hand is for wiping your bottom, not for eating."

I was born into a society of rigid rules, and I often felt like I was breaking them all.

Not one thing about me fit into the world that I lived in. Not the way I looked, not the way I behaved, not even the hand that instinctively reached out for my food before it was slapped away.

The more I tried to fit in, the more I remained an outsider, and the more the spirit of defiance was fed within me.

I began to question the rules. The answer I heard most often was "because it is *haram*"—forbidden by God.

When my children were young and one of them did something wrong, the other kids would threaten to tell the teacher. When I was young, there was no need for someone to tell on me. God was watching—and, in case there was any question, he was keeping score.

If my mother burned the rice, she would say, "Kids that eat the burned rice go to heaven." If I didn't want to eat my food, she would say, "Kids that don't eat their food go to hell." That's how my parents got us to do what they wanted.

I struggled to understand: if we were all God's children to be loved equally, then why did he give me a wild streak that constantly got me into so much trouble . . . that and my father's flat feet?

Even my passport breaks the rules: it says my birthplace is Yemen, but I was actually born in Uganda, like my father before me. When we arrived in Yemen, penniless refugees rejected by the nation of our birth, the passport official told my parents that making the change would save me from discrimination. It didn't . . . not then and especially not today.

Uganda, the country that I first called home, was the opposite of what popular Western media often mistakenly projected Africa to be. Full of contagious smiles, creativity, resiliency, and rhythm, Uganda had a vibrancy. It was richly colorful, chaotic, and diverse. The earth was rolling and green. The crowded markets were stuffed with the sweetest fruits, the loudest chickens, and the most fascinating treasures. Shops like my grandfather's teemed with wild, brightly patterned fabrics imported from all over Africa.

My grandfather, Rizq, was born in the mountain village of Haraz in Yemen, about three and a half hours outside Sana'a, the nation's capital. My last name, Al-harazi, means "of Haraz," a place that for generations has been filled with hundreds of first, second, and third cousins, aunts, and uncles.

Every time someone says my last name, I'm reminded of where I come from. Loyalty is everything in Yemen, and it is given first to your family.

In my grandfather's time, leaving home was considered a

betrayal of tribe and family. Children do not set off in pursuit of adventure or fortune, and families stay together. My grandfather, the first Al-harazi rebel, was an illiterate child who had never left his mountain village when he decided, at fifteen, that his destiny was not to be a sheepherder for the rest of his life.

One morning soon after the end of World War Two, he walked away from everything he knew with just pennies in his pocket. For four months he traveled to the coast, working along the way to pay for shelter and food. In Aden, the capital city of South Yemen, he reached the sea.

With adventure in his heart, he boarded the first boat leaving Yemen. My grandfather arrived on the island of Zanzibar, where he worked on the docks for a few months. He then continued on to Uganda—living for a while first in Jinja, a beautiful city on the coast of Lake Victoria, and then in Kampala, the capital city, filled with people who had come from every corner of the world to find their fortune as he had come to find his.

My grandfather had a thirst for learning, but the local schools in Kampala refused to admit him because his skin was brown. In those days, Ugandan society was deeply divided along ethnic lines, and schools were segregated into black, white, and Asian. He created his own opportunities instead, learning English by listening to the BBC, Swahili from the locals, Gujarati from his customers— and teaching himself to read and write in all three languages.

He opened his first shop by saving every single penny he made, and he filled it with imported African fabrics because he knew how popular they were.

He never intended to leave Yemen behind, and he returned to Haraz every few years, distributing his hard-earned money to both his family and the village poor. Each trip home was almost as complicated as the trip away, with weeks of traveling by road, rail, and sea.

During one of these visits, he married a beautiful young woman in the village, with bright, dark eyes, and skin so tight and smooth she would forever look decades younger than she was. My grandmother, Mohsina.

Arabic is a lyrical language that conveys a depth of meaning and emotion unmatched by many languages. There are at least eleven words for "love," each of which describes a different stage of love.

My favorite Arabic word is *alazima*, which means pride, with a mix of strength, determination, and poise. In my mind, *alazima* is my mother, my grandmother, and every woman who came before them. She might have little, but her back is straight and proud. She is a fierce protector and loyal defender of those she loves. She will do what it takes—to survive, to thrive, and to persevere.

When my grandparents married, my grandmother was fifteen years old, completely illiterate, and in some ways completely provincial. She spent her days climbing up and down the craggy mountainside to fetch firewood and water. She was meticulous: each of her dresses had a similar cut and a matching headscarf that she carefully pinned over a neat braid. She was also a pioneer: the first girl from our village ever to leave it.

Considering that in those days every third child died before she was five years old, it is remarkable that my fiercely independent grandmother had twelve children, all of whom survived but one, who died at birth.

My grandmother learned to speak fluent Swahili, with which she navigated the bustling markets with ease and directed the servants in no uncertain terms. She raised her family with all the fierce protection of a mama bear.

That drive and grit is what my grandparents passed on to their own children, who began working in the shop when they were young, stocking fabrics, chatting with customers, and widening their own world views.

I, too, was raised in a world that was a collision of cultures—from food to politics, fashion to religion, language to skin color. And because of the diversity that has always surrounded me, I do not look at people and see differences. I look at them and see similarities.

I know we all have the same dreams, the same amount of love for our children, and the same fears that keep us up at night. That mindset hasn't changed over the years as I navigate country after country.

But when my father was growing up in Uganda, no amount of hard work or determination could convince the nation's Africans that his Yemeni family were a valuable part of their society. One of only two Arab families in their community, they were grouped—dismissively—with the Asians, the descendants of the mostly Indian workers that British colonialists brought to Uganda as indentured servants, to build the country's railways.

Over time, this Asian minority had ascended into a class of relatively well-off merchants, like my grandfather. Asians controlled most of the country's economy, which was threatening to many Africans.

Unlike his parents, my father, Anwar, and his siblings were able to attend the primary and secondary schools reserved for Asians. Those opportunities ended, however, when it came to higher education; universities in Kampala did not admit non-Africans.

My father had a number of friends from high school who had gone on to study in India, which was relatively inexpensive. Since he spoke Gujarati and Hindi, he began to think about how he, too, could travel abroad in pursuit of a better future.

He graduated from secondary school in 1962 while my grandfather was on one of his regular pilgrimages to Yemen, leaving his brother, my great-uncle, to mind the shop and the family in Kampala.

While my grandfather was away, Yemen's leader was suddenly overthrown by Egyptian-backed revolutionaries, who declared the country the Yemen Arab Republic. Saudi Arabia intervened on behalf of the leader, and the country—and, it seemed, the whole region—was at war. Communication, slow in and around Yemen during the best of times, was now nonexistent.

The family waited for word, and my father worried about their future—and his own. One afternoon, he found the courage to ask his uncle about the money that had been put aside for his education. My great-uncle took seriously his responsibilities to the family; he was not going to make a decision this big.

He told my father in no uncertain terms that as the oldest son, his place was in the store, especially when my grandfather was away, and that he needed to forget about university. But like my grandfather, my father had adventure in his heart and an even bigger thirst for learning. And like my grandfather, my father also decided he was going to take his chances in this world.

He packed in secret, filled with guilt about leaving his family. As he lay staring at the ceiling in the middle of the night, my grandmother walked into his room quietly. He sat up in surprise and fear and waited for her to tell him that she knew what he planned and he should not go.

Instead, my grandmother pulled off her neatly arranged scarf and reached into the corner where she always tied anything she didn't want to lose, like the house keys. "I know that you need to go," she said sadly.

This is what his father would have wanted, she told him, as she handed over a roll of bills. She had sold her jewelry and the jewelry she'd been saving for his sisters' dowries, and she gave him the proceeds along with all the money she had squirreled away over the years.

Speechless, he took the money from her hand and held her tight, tears slipping down his face, knowing the sacrifice she was making for him. He promised to return as soon as he could and use his education to take care of them all. When the early dawn appeared, he left the house quietly and tried not to look back.

Weeks later, my father finally arrived in Pune, about ninety miles southeast of Mumbai. One of the region's intellectual capitals, Pune is so steeped in language and literature that it's sometimes called "the Oxford of the East." At Wadia College, the school most of the non-Indian students went to, he studied zoology, chemistry, and botany. He was handsome, smart, and athletic, the captain of the tennis team and the cricket team.

Although he excelled at school and was happy there, the money his mother had given him eventually ran out. He stopped paying his rent and survived on tea and bread, which he bought on credit from the owner of the restaurant he lived above, his landlord. He borrowed from friends every once in a while, to pay his creditor when he got too impatient with my father.

When the landlord gave him a final ultimatum, my father decided to go home, too proud to ask anyone else for help. As he was packing to leave, he heard banging on the door. Afraid it was his landlord, he ignored it until he heard a voice calling his name in Arabic.

The old man at the door, after looking at my father's passport to make sure it was him, gave him an envelope full of money and a letter from his father. "I am back," it said. "Here is some money for your education. Be well, my son." My father wept tears of joy and relief.

He paid his landlord and his friends and invited them all to the restaurant downstairs for a meal. Amid a great party and well-deserved celebration, that night they were all arrested for being too rowdy and had to sleep in the local police station.

I guess I come by my rebellious nature honestly.

My parents met in the early 1960s, at a dance at the college where my mother, Fatema, was also a student. She recognized the boy that her friends referred to as "the African," but since he was there with another date, she refused to dance with him.

My handsome father was not used to hearing no. Intrigued, he pursued her, first as a challenge, and by the end of the night as the woman he wanted to marry.

My mother fell in love with him long before she gave in to his courtship, but she waited to tell him because he already had an ego that was larger than she liked.

Though they were both Muslim, and both from the same sect of Islam, they worried that their relationship could be doomed by their differences. Their parents' reaction confirmed it.

"You've already been promised to your cousin," my grand-mother told my father. "You can't marry an Indian; she is not one of us." It was the first my father had ever heard of these plans, and he was shocked: his cousin was more like a sister to him. My mother, too, had also been spoken for, said her father.

My mother appealed to the imam, the religious head of the sect. He had a soft spot for this quiet young woman, who rarely asked for anything. She told him how much she loved my father and what a good person he was. The imam asked to meet him.

My parents didn't want to go during the day, as there were always lots of people around the imam, so he reserved time after evening prayers to see them. Travel was difficult in 1965: India and Pakistan were at war, and there was a curfew after dark. They went with a close friend and took back roads to avoid the soldiers, navigating the five miles by night to meet the high priest.

Realizing, as he talked to them, that these two young people were truly in love and that life was not going to be easy for them, he wrote a letter in Arabic, sealed it, and gave it to my father to send home.

My father sent the letter to Kampala, along with a stack of photographs of my mother. My grandfather told my father he didn't need to read the letter: "If this is the girl you love, then you must marry her." My grandmother, on the other hand, was not moved by the photographs or my father's tales of his beloved's generous heart and quick mind.

The letter from the imam, however, was what convinced her. With tears in her eyes, she looked at my grandfather and said, "Tell him to do what he wants to do."

My mother was a shy and admittedly pampered only child. She had been raised by her father and was the apple of his eye. Her mother, the grandmother I never knew, knelt to pray one Friday and simply never got up. If you believe the scripture, that means she went straight to heaven.

Marrying my father and moving with him to Uganda meant leaving the only home she had ever known and adjusting to a new culture in Africa. It also meant instantly inheriting ten brothers and sisters. She was not used to the rough and tumble of an Arab family, who argue as way of conversation. In her new house, the only ones heard were those who spoke the loudest. It took her many years to learn Arabic, which she still hasn't mastered—though to be fair, neither have I.

Most Yemenis married only within their families, or within their tribes. Anybody outside that unit was an outsider. Despite her kindness and poise, and the fact that she had given my father permission to marry the woman he loved, my grandmother did not take kindly to his Indian wife, and for a short while, she threw something at her new daughter-in-law—a broom, a coffee cup, or whatever she had in her hand—when she walked by.

My grandmother claimed it was because they didn't speak the

same language and she wanted to get my mother's attention. I luckily never saw this exchange between my mother and grandmother. By the time I was old enough to observe my family, all I saw was the enormous love and respect that was cemented between these women until the day my grandmother died.

Like Uganda, the south of Yemen is a former British protectorate; as many as a hundred thousand Indians are said to live there today. And, as in Uganda, many people from Yemen's northern villages, including Haraz, perceived Indian people as a lower class.

"The Indian," my father's six brothers teasingly called my mother, who did all that she could to fit in without notice. Two of the brothers had married Arab women who had fit more handily into the family unit. It was not that they were trying to be discriminatory, but the tribe was simply so tight that if you came from the outside, you were forever an outsider, a *mukhraja*, a term I didn't come to understand until many years later.

When my parents found out they were expecting their first baby, my father encouraged my mother to deliver in the large hospital in Kampala. She told him she much preferred the area's smaller, missionary-run Catholic hospital, where she would be under the care of nuns. That, she said, would give her a comforting feeling of home.

When my mother was growing up in India, the best schools were the Catholic schools, and she had attended a very well-regarded convent school in Pune, where she, a Muslim, had learned the catechism straight from the mouths of the nuns and attended mass daily.

To this day she carries a photo of the Virgin Mary and a cross in her wallet, and she cannot walk by any church without going in to pray. For her, religion is less about being Muslim, Jewish, or Christian and more about faith and goodness—belief in a loving

God who cares for all His children, no matter where they are from and how they worship Him.

My parents were overjoyed to welcome a healthy baby boy, Anees, into the world. In both Arab and Indian families, boys are particularly prized, especially a firstborn son. As an only child, my mother had no experience with babies, so when the nuns suggested that my mother and Anees stay in the hospital for a few days to get acclimated, she accepted with relief. She wasn't certain what kind of help she'd receive in her chaotic home.

One of the nuns brought a newborn baby from a nearby village and put him in the nursery. That baby had cholera, and by the next morning my brother and all the other babies in the room were also infected.

That night, my mother dreamed Anees was sleeping between her and my father. Then, as she watched helplessly, he flew away. She woke up the next day knowing that Anees was gone. The hospital did not need to tell her. He died along with six other children. She was inconsolable. She was convinced it was all her fault, and no one could tell her otherwise. Her decision, she said, cost them something they could never replace. Her decision left her with no final goodbye to her first born. Fifty years later, my mother is still inconsolable on Anees' birthday and on the day he died.

Regret is always so much easier to find than self-forgiveness.

My mother couldn't look at the clothes and bedding she had spent months sewing and knitting during her pregnancy, and she asked my father's sister Rukiya to take them away.

"Sue the hospital," everyone said.

Would suing the hospital bring back my brother? Would money ease her pain? Would revenge bring her peace? "No," said my mother.

With the loss of their son, a great, heavy sadness wedged its way between my parents. They began to drift apart, my father burying himself in his research and my mother sliding into a deep depression, gaining an extraordinary amount of weight, and refusing to leave her room.

Seeing her daughter-in-law racked with grief and guilt, and hurting deeply herself for the loss of her first grandchild, my grandmother finally softened toward my mother and became the mother that mine so desperately needed.

My mother, resilient creature that she was, slowly came back to life, lost the weight, and bridged the valley between herself and my father.

A little more than a year later, I was born. My parents bundled me up and took me home as fast as they could. My overprotective mother boiled everything that came within a yard of my cradle, and whenever she fed or bathed me, she wanted her favorite sister-in-law, my aunt Rukiya, beside her, to be sure she was doing it right.

My father wasn't permitted to so much as change a diaper. I was the focal point of the whole house. No matter where I was as a child, if I cried, not only were my parents right by my side, but so were my grandparents, my aunts, and my uncles.

CHAPTER TWO

In Uganda, my family were all outsiders. Or, more pointedly, "bloodsuckers," according to Idi Amin, the country's ruthless dictator who rose to power just a few months after I was born.

The military coup that he led in 1971, which ousted Uganda's first president, turned what had long been a tense situation for my family and so many others into total chaos.

Because of the racist rhetoric of government propaganda, Indians were stereotyped and attacked as "greedy" and "conniving" people without any loyalty to Uganda. In the 1970s, Uganda and other East African nations implemented racist policies that targeted the Asian population of the region.

A former soldier who stood over six feet tall, Idi Amin was someone you saw coming—and someone from whom you ran. Notorious for its sheer brutality and oppressiveness, Amin's rule was characterized by rampant human rights abuses, political repression, ethnic persecution, extrajudicial killings, nepotism, corruption, and gross economic mismanagement.

He had many names for himself, including "His Excellency, President for Life, Field Marshal Al Hadji Doctor Idi Amin Dada, VC, DSO, MC, Lord of All the Beasts of the Earth and Fishes of the Seas and Conqueror of the British Empire in Africa in General and Uganda in Particular," in addition to his officially stated claim of being the uncrowned King of Scotland.

The name that stuck, however, was the one the people gave him: the Butcher of Uganda.

Once he came to power, the streets were no longer safe for non-Africans, who often heard "Go back to where you came from" when they dared to leave their homes. People we knew were robbed at gunpoint, their cars and property taken away. The local gossip was punctuated with home raids, attempted rapes, and the frightening theatrics of Amin's soldiers, who were rumored to walk around Kampala with Asian heads mounted on spears. In neighborhoods like my family's, the once-bustling streets were deserted after sunset.

My parents were just beginning to come into their own. My dad had a good job at one of Uganda's biggest universities, and my mom worked for a private company; they had me, almost two years old, happy and healthy. On August 4, 1972, just days after they had bought their first new car, they heard on its radio the voice of Amin, saying God had come to him in a dream and commanded him to rid the nation of its Asians. He gave Uganda's sixty thousand Asian residents ninety days to leave the country.

The next day, my mother and I were in the car, waiting to pick up my father from his regular squash game. When my mother saw a group of Indian students whom we knew standing on a street corner, she rolled down the windows. "What do you think of the decree?" she called.

Panicked, one of the students gestured in the opposite direction, toward an approaching motorcade—a sign that Amin himself was passing through. They stood up straight, smiling and waving as the dictator's car drove by. Still sitting in the car, my mother was too stunned to follow their lead. She simply froze.

"He's going to come after you now," said one of the kids, in a quiet voice. "You didn't wave at him; your family needs to be careful."

When my father emerged from the gym with his racket in hand, my mother had worked herself into a frenzy of worry. "I'm taking Zahra and going home to India," she told him as she slid over so he could drive. Surely Amin would not hunt her down just for failing to smile, my father reassured. We were Arabs, not Indians, and she was his wife. We would be fine, he said through his worry: he did take the threat seriously.

A few days later, my father and one of his professor friends were invited to attend a reception with His Excellency, who was also the chancellor of the university. My father politely declined, having no desire to attract Amin's attention.

Concerned that my father didn't fully understand the urgency of the situation, his friend pressed him to go: meeting Amin face to face might give him more clarity on the question of whether to stay or leave the country. My father agreed, and the two friends went to stand in the long line waiting to greet Amin. Approaching my father, the dictator looked at him with narrowed eyes. "You are Indian," he said, frowning.

"No," said my father. "I am an Arab."

"You are Arab?" Amin asked, a wide smile breaking out on his face. Then, slapping my father on the back, he said, "You are my brother! You don't have to worry; you don't leave this country. Arabs are going to stay."

Looking around to make sure no one could hear, my father's friend whispered, "Don't believe him." But my father already knew: the look in the dictator's eyes, and the power of his hatred, rendered the seemingly reassuring words meaningless. In that moment, my father decided his family was never going to be safe.

He had never before felt any pull to Yemen. The one visit he'd made to his homeland, right after my birth, had been so difficult and alienating that upon his return he had informed my grandfather that his country was for barbarians and donkeys—and that he would not be going back.

But fear changes everything.

Uganda's relationship with Britain meant that England was a potential refuge for our family. Yet my father couldn't bear to think of his own parents forced to start over again—to fit into a culture and a language they didn't understand. He began making arrangements to move to Yemen. My mother, two of his sisters, and I would go to India immediately.

My father and my grandfather would fly to Egypt and then onward to Yemen. They'd find a place for the family to live in Sana'a, Yemen's capital. The rest of the family—including my grandmother—would go by car to Kenya, where they would stay with relatives until my father sent for them.

I am from Yemen; we are from Yemen. It became a goal, and later a mantra. My father told himself that if you do not share the nationality of the country where you live, you will never be secure. Sadly, around the world, that idea seems to be only more powerful today.

Within a week, my mother, my aunts, and I were in Kampala's airport, carrying only baby food, dried milk, and my cloth diapers. Everything of value had been hastily loaded into boxes that would be stowed underneath the plane: my mother's wedding saris, as well as her mother's saris—many made with gold thread—all expensive and precious. The tiniest baby clothes, the most prized toys. Framed photos, long-passed-down trinkets. Anything and everything that was dear and precious—boxes of memories of a life well lived.

I had refused to let go of my father at the airport, and I was still fussing. My mother and aunties tried their best to soothe me.

They held themselves strong and resolute, despite their uncertainty about leaving everything behind, including the men in our family and their many friends who had decided to remain in order to protect their wealth and the only lives they had ever known.

When we got to customs, my mother asked the customs official if she could use the bathroom while her hand luggage was being scrutinized and weighed. She surrendered me to my aunts. Then she closed herself in a small restroom, put her hands over her face, and let go, for just a minute, the tears of loneliness, disappointment, and fear.

My mother fought so hard to remain strong. Even as the world crushed her every hope, and all her protections were stripped away, she still would not break down in front of me.

When she composed herself and walked back to customs, she found bags that were a lot lighter than when she'd left them there and the defiant faces of officials that dared her to say anything. She simply held me tight and walked away.

Many years later, when I asked my typically feisty, justice-seeking mother why she had not protested, she told me, "You were the only precious thing I had. As long as I could leave with you, they were welcome to everything else."

As happy as she was to be back in her father's cozy flat in Pune, my mother hated being cut off from her life in Uganda. All she could do was send a telex to my father via the neighbor's phone number, knowing it would take a while to arrive—and that, even after it did, her calls with him would be few and far between.

While in India, we spent many afternoons at my mother's beloved convent school, where I was able to play in the small grotto or join in the preschool classes held by the nuns. We visited with her childhood friends, who called me "Zahra the Menace," after the popular American television show about a mischievous little boy named Dennis.

The name was well earned. Even as a child, I was a brat—stubborn and demanding, knowing what I wanted and wanting it now. That may be the one thing about me that has never changed.

It was my first trip abroad, and my mother wanted to give me a bit of freedom to roam. Life as she had known it was slipping through her fingers; she spent too much time worrying about my father and our insecure future to notice all the trouble I was getting into. That was the first time I learned the lesson reinforced throughout my childhood: travel was freedom, travel was escape, travel was life.

Once we had been in India for a few months, my mother felt strong enough to unpack some reminders of the life she had shared with my father. She stood in the storage room at the airport surrounded by the heavy wooden boxes she'd packed in haste in Kampala, memories of a life gone forever flooding her eyes.

She hadn't thought much of how dirty the boxes seemed. With excitement and sadness, she opened the first box, eager for a glimpse of something familiar—only to find filthy, smelly wet grass.

Every time I think of my mother sitting there, opening those boxes, my heart breaks for her, for that moment, for their life. Just like that, gone were my family's valuables: proof of traditions, of milestones, of life and death. My mother gathered me up, along with the shreds of the memories of the life and the husband she'd left behind. She turned to her father, who was watching her with tears in his eyes, and asked him calmly to take us home.

Uganda's military police had taken it all. Until everyone in the family could leave, they still controlled our fates. And as far as they were concerned, we were worth about as much as the dirt they'd shoveled into the boxes.

• • •

Back in Kampala, my father lived in the slowly emptying flat for six months longer. Many of the family's possessions, including their furniture and the fabric stocked in their store, had to be sold or left behind. He tried not to think about the military police rifling through their personal belongings; before their long journey to Yemen, they had sewn some gold jewelry and money into the lining of his and my grandfather's jackets.

Along the twenty-one-mile route from our home to Kampala's airport, my father and grandfather were stopped and searched several times. Usually one soldier would hold up a gun while the others ripped apart their bags and went through their clothes, taking anything of value they could find. To refuse was impossible; people had been shot dead for less. When they arrived at the airport, my father nodded wearily at the soldiers standing guard and tried to keep a steady arm around his father's sagging shoulders. They were searched again in case they had anything of value left. The soldiers took the family's documents: deeds, birth certificates, and bank statements.

When my mother had left the country, only a few months earlier, the soldiers had stolen covertly. Now, they did it openly.

They boarded the plane with nothing but the clothes on their backs, and my father put his head back and sighed. How were they going to survive? Had his mother made it safely to Kenya? Did they still have any money? He wearily slipped off his shoes, and there he found seven dollars he had folded under the toe, which the guards had somehow missed.

My father started crying, asking himself, "Is this what we have come to?" My grandfather patted his knee and told him it was going to be okay, with the same conviction he had used for months.

They arrived in Cairo for their layover, and my father turned to my grandfather and invited him to breakfast. He spent the seven dollars on what he still calls the best meal he has ever had. With nothing left to lose, he put all his worries down and enjoyed the food. Coffee, pita bread, *foul mudammas*, and roasted lamb. When they were finished, they felt so much better: fortified, balanced, even optimistic.

And after breakfast, my father went to the restroom. *I am from Yemen; we are from Yemen* echoed in his head as he flushed his British passport down the toilet. His homeland was all he had left to believe in as they began the final leg of their journey to Yemen. He could no longer question his decision to return.

Their plane landed in Hodeidah, a port city on Yemen's west coast, and my father stepped out the door and saw . . . nothing. No real airport, no paved runway. Then he turned his head and saw a crowd of men in traditional Yemeni dress, singing and dancing the *bara'a*, a dance that involves waving guns and daggers in the air. "Welcome home! Welcome!" they sang.

He started looking around, wondering who those men were there for. Meanwhile, behind him, my grandfather beamed: warm, bright, watery light spilled from his eyes whenever he saw his family.

Unbeknownst to my father, my grandfather had sent a telegram ahead to let extended family know about their arrival. Now here was his tribe, celebrating our family's return. My grandfather was well known for his generosity—so much so that my grandmother rarely trusted him with money, knowing he'd give it away, including his day's earnings, before he walked back in the door from the market. People knew him by now, and they lay in waiting with their stories, knowing he would not let them leave empty-handed.

But no one—not even my grandmother—knew that he was also a savvy investor. In 1949, when Yemen's Jews were moving, in large numbers, to the new state of Israel, my grandfather purchased five of their homes at a very reasonable price. In addition to these four- and five-story houses, he owned an entire mountain that he was growing coffee on. He'd also bought shares in Yemeni businesses ranging from transportation, tobacco, and electricity to the local match factory. When he traveled back to pay his taxes, and to give money to the local families who most needed help, he was also investing in his country. He was still the patriarch in our village.

"What's all this?" asked my father.

My grandfather smiled. And as some of our tribesmen drove the two men inland to Sana'a, my father heard about all the investments. His surprise turned to disbelief, then relief. It seemed the confidence my grandfather had displayed over the past few months had been more than just an elder's reassurance.

"We didn't need all the money in Uganda," he explained to my father, "so I gave what I could to families in need. They are now here to repay us." While they were living far away, he hadn't wanted to speculate on how these investments would work out, and he hadn't wanted to involve my father in business dealings that neither of them could have much influence over. But now that they were here, they would act.

My grandfather wasn't always forthcoming with details. It may be a genetic trait, this habit of "I'm going to keep it to myself until I know how to tackle it." I do it too—everyone in my family does—whether the unknown is a career opportunity, a medical diagnosis, or anything else.

When you put something out in the world, you'd better be ready to deal with it. Before then, it's not worth concerning other people—especially those you love the most.

Together, my grandfather and father sold the investment properties and put some of the money toward renting a house in Sana'a's Old City that could, with some creativity, sleep all of us.

Then they sent wires south and east, to Kenya and India, and the rest of the family began our long journeys across land and sea to our new home.

As our small plane hovered over Sana'a, my mother looked down at the valley's strange terrain in amazement. India and Uganda are lush and rich with flowering plants and greenery, but Yemen is a barren landscape, where everything is brown as far as your eye can see. She felt my small head, hot and heavy, pressed to her chest as I slept. "*Alhamdulillah*," she whispered.

Alhamdulillah is still a constant echo in my head. We say it when something bad happens, and we say it when something good happens. When we sit down to eat and when we are full. When we are exasperated, when we are sad, and when we are over the moon with happiness. *Alhamdulillah*. It means "Thank God." Bear with me, though, because this has nothing to do with religion.

You see, when I was a child, I was never allowed to complain. If I persisted, then my grandmother's very quick wooden spoon would come out, and I would regret my stubbornness. What she was trying to teach me in her own way was to be grateful for everything I have. She wanted me to understand that complaining was not a way to live.

My family, my health, my life, my friends, my limbs, my sight, the food on the table, my intelligence, my faith . . . the list would go on forever. All the blessings I had in my life that I kept taking for granted, she would not let me forget.

Today, my wiser, older self understands that *Alhamdulillah* means much more than giving thanks. The lesson I learned from my grandmother was to believe in my own good faith—not to concern myself with how full the glass is, but with my ability to fill it up again.

There were no customs officials in Sana'a, no long lines—not even a proper tarmac. Our few bags landed on the dirt with a heavy thud. My mother, like my father before her, saw a crowd of strangers. Then, from the chaos, appeared the face of my father and next to him his father, both crying with joy as they ran head-long toward us.

Alhamdulillah.

CHAPTER THREE

One of my mother's first impressions of Yemen was standing in line at the post office to buy stamps for letters she wanted to send to friends and family. A man ahead of her in line bargained for the postage stamps! She couldn't believe her ears . . . or her eyes: everywhere she looked the men wore white skirts that fell above their knees, while the women were covered up completely, trying to not be seen.

Before the 1962 coup that led to the founding of the Yemen Arab Republic, the country had been ruled by imams, and education was nonexistent. The Quran was the only reading sanctioned by the government, and the gates of Sana'a were locked daily from six in the evening to six the next morning: no one was allowed in or out.

We arrived a few years after the end of a civil war; the newly united republic's infrastructure and social services were still in a shambles. Sana'a had poor water distribution, and we bought tankers of water to fill our water tanks. When the tanks were empty, we bought more.

We got one clean bucket of water to take a bath once a week, usually on Fridays. Into that I would plunge an electrical heating rod, holding it still until the water was warm enough to use.

I hated washing my thick, curly hair with that one bucket of water, crouching down on the bathroom floor with a ladle, trying not to waste a drop. It was never enough to wash all the shampoo out, let alone to afford the luxury of conditioning my hair.

Today, no matter where I am in the world, I love to have my hair washed and styled in a salon twice a week. It is a healing desire, and I succumb to its demands with gratitude.

My family lived together in a small house—one tiny room for my parents, one for my grandparents, and a living room where we all sat around a tiny TV in the evenings. That room was also the bedroom for my four aunts, my six uncles, and me. When it was mealtime, we laid a plastic sheet on the floor, and that room became our dining room. I lived the experience of being raised by a village, and I am so lucky for it. Those nights were full of family, stories, love, and a great deal of laughter.

My parents had arrived in Yemen with little other than their very rare university degrees. My mother, who majored in English literature, immediately found a good job as an administrative assistant with the United Nations; after a few months, she traded up to a better job at the U.S. embassy. She was, I am so proud to say, one of the first women to work in the country and also one of the first to drive.

My father had a bit of a tougher time; his background in zoology and laboratory work didn't translate as well to what was needed in Yemen. Luckily, a well-educated friend of our family suggested that my father meet with the Central Planning Organization. Its head was Dr. Abdul-Karim, who had a PhD from Yale University.

After several tries, my father finally got an interview. He sat anxiously outside the office for hours, waiting for Dr. Abdul-Karim's meeting with the Russian ambassador to end. Finally, the office door opened, and the Russian ambassador walked out. My father stood, only to be informed that the American ambassador was coming in five minutes. "Please," he said, "then let me have the five minutes."

Face to face with the tiny, bald-headed man whose bright, kind eyes shone behind oversized glasses, my father drew on his reserves of self-confidence, explaining his schooling and his work experience. He was rattling off names of fellowships when Dr. Abdul-Karim interrupted him. "When can you start?" he asked.

"Right away," said my father, surprised and elated. He walked out knowing only that he would return to start work the next day at 7:30 a.m.

My father's hard-fought-for education was paying off. Imagining that Yemen's most urgent needs did not involve dissecting tigers, he pushed aside both his worries about abandoning his academic career for government work and his trepidation about stepping into a nerve center of Yemen's political machine. An opportunity, he knew, was just that.

On his first day of work, my father learned his title: officer of development projects. All the desks in his new office were occupied, so he pulled a chair over to a nearby windowsill, balanced a piece of paper on its edge, and got to work. On his second day, he arrived early so he would have his choice of desks. On his third day, he learned that his salary would be the equivalent of $160, a king's ransom.

Thus began decades of eight-day work weeks, during which my father established himself as one of the people most integral to rebuilding Yemen's infrastructure after many years of civil war and political stalemate. He believed that the country of twenty-four million people—a larger population than Saudi Arabia—was still stuck in the Middle Ages, and that he and his team could help bring it into the present.

In order to succeed, my father learned to be unassailably likable at work, whether he was navigating a landmine-infested war zone, evaluating a village's water, education, and medical needs, or holding court in a boardroom to secure development funding through partnerships with China, Japan, European nations, and the United States. In time, my father and his team built over four thousand projects—schools, hospitals, universities, roads—most being the first in the country.

He led meetings while hiding the fact that he couldn't read or write Arabic—and that he could barely speak it. He was considered one of the best negotiators for projects with foreign governments. Traveling abroad and meeting government dignitaries became part of his life. While we were glued to the TV set watching his adventures, my father dined at the White House twice, was invited to meet the Pope at the Vatican, and met many heads of state and even royalty.

His tenacity more than made up for his lack of fluency. He simply listened to what the people around him were saying and echoed it until he understood how to communicate in a professional context. He also joined the other government employees when they chewed *qat*.

This popular drug is a leaf. *Qat* chewers hold the leaves in the corner of their jaws, like chewing tobacco. They suck out the juice and then spit out the *qat* at the end of the night. Alcohol is forbidden, but *qat* is chewed daily in Yemen and across much of the Arab and African world; it's a troublesome thread woven through the fabric of Yemeni society. The crop was in such demand that farmers ensured a high yield by using "miracle" pesticides—including DDT—that caused serious long-term health consequences.

My father, unlike many of his colleagues who chewed daily, only chewed on Thursdays. He had to: most deals were made in the *qat* room. If you didn't go, you didn't work, and if you didn't chew, you embarrassed your host. Thursdays, my father would come home at night with shining eyes, filled with inspiration and a sense of possibility.

It didn't take long for me to realize that if I wanted to ask my father for something, I should do it after the office *qat* chew. He never said no . . . and I slept happily with my win until the next morning, when the answer became no again.

In so many ways, the "African" from Uganda was exactly what everyone wanted him to be: a Yemeni by blood who understood the republic's ways and lived to serve its best interests. A worldly, well-educated diplomat known for his hospitality. A prodigal son who returned home for good, and a father who has never failed me.

We have a saying in Arabic, *Rigal Mali Hudumeh*—"a man who fills his clothes"—which means one who walks the Earth full of pride. My father filled his clothes with strength, ease, and grace.

The only barriers my father had were the women in his life. Most of our relatives and neighbors in Yemen couldn't make sense of the fact that my mother worked and that, when she did, she wore Western clothes: tailored shirts and skirts, with heels. On the weekends, she wore jeans and gold heels.

My parents knew they were not traditional, and they responded to eyebrows, questions, or even outright criticism coolly but kindly. Still, as I grew and became more influenced by images of what it meant to be a woman in Yemen, my mother worked to dispel ideas that she did not accept to be true.

One evening, when we were still relatively new to the country, my family entertained a group of about fifty members of my father's tribe who had come for a visit. My mother brought out platter after platter of lamb, rice, savory yogurt salads, pancakes, and honey-soaked pastries. My aunts, on the other hand, knew better than to go among the men. And at the end of the meal, as she cleared away the platters, the leader of the tribe looked at my father and asked, "Anwar, did you bring your wife with you?"

My father apologized to the sheikh for his lack of formality. He gestured toward the kitchen, where she and my aunts were still cleaning, out of sight. "The woman serving you is my wife, Fatema."

"Her? And without a head scarf?" asked the sheikh, jumping to his feet. He had figured that my mother, wearing jeans and a T-shirt, was the maid. "What is this?" he asked with anger at the disrespect he thought my father was showing my mother—and that she was showing to the tribe.

"She is an educated woman," my father said, "and she makes her own decisions. I told her she should choose whether she wants to cover herself or not."

The sheikh frowned, everyone else in the room went silent, and my mother listened from the kitchen. "It's not right," said the sheikh.

"I understand," said my father, "but Fatema is a different woman. She is working; she wears Western clothes at her job."

"No woman in our tribe has ever worked outside the house," said our sheikh. "This is unacceptable."

Ever the diplomat, my father also understood enough of the traditions to know he could not offend an elder, especially not one who was a guest in his house. After letting the sheikh rant for a while, my father calmly said, "Sheikh, listen, please. We are new. I have a big family—many people to feed each day. My father is not earning money; neither are my brothers. My salary is not enough. Fatema is helping. That's why she is working. We *need* for her to work."

The sheikh creased his brow and looked angry at my father's suggestion of prioritizing necessity over tradition. "This is an abomination, Anwar," he said.

Keeping an even tone, my father said, "Because you are in my house, I am giving you respect and listening. I understand your point of view. But I do not share it. She is my wife and I am going to ask you to respect her."

The sheikh's disapproving squint was met with my father's calm gaze. "She will not cover her head but will be decently dressed," said my father. "My wife will lead her life as she feels fit to do, but she will not cross boundaries." Then, he calmly asked if anyone would like tea or dessert.

The Sheikh brought the lion back out of my defeated father's heart. And by putting my mother in charge of her own destiny, my father was finally back in charge of his.

My mother was a pivotal part of the vibrant community of expats in Sana'a, with whom she would speak Gujarati, Arabic, English, Urdu, and Hindi. In that way, she had third, fourth, and fifth jobs— volunteering in the women's prison and at the Mother Teresa home, and organizing bazaars that raised funds for the school for the blind. She was an artist, painting and selling for charity; she wrote two of her own cookbooks. She created a full life for us with many friends and family, parties, and people always over for meals and laughter.

While my mother was working at the American embassy, she decided to have her first Thanksgiving party. The embassy had imported turkeys and gave her one for the party. My mother did not know what to do with the monster chicken, so she and my aunts decided to cut it into small pieces and make a turkey curry with Indian spices.

Twenty-five people came over for dinner, including the ambassador and his wife. We all sat in our hallway on the floor, Yemeni style, eating turkey curry. Nobody said anything to my mother.

It was years before she found out how to properly cook a Thanksgiving turkey.

When I was nine, my mother planned a visit to India. She had not been home in years and said that something in her heart had been telling her for weeks to go see her father. He was growing old and was alone.

One morning not long after, her cousin sent a telegram suggesting she should come home to see her father, as he was ill. My parents still did not have a lot of money and had just built a new house, but my mother didn't want to wait. We drove her to the airport and waved excitedly as she got on the plane.

Two hours after my mother left, and while she was still in the air, we got a telegram from India. We stared at the yellow envelope, knowing that nothing good ever came in a telegram. It said that my grandfather had passed away.

I could not sleep, thinking of my mother's excitement when she left, and the harsh realization that she was going to arrive in time for his funeral.

My mother arrived in Bombay, and her uncle drove her home to Pune without saying a word. It was only when she got home that she found out she had missed not only seeing her father, but also his funeral, which had happened that morning. In Muslim tradition, a burial must happen within twenty-four hours of a death.

When we finally had a chance to talk to her, she told us she already knew—she felt his loss in every fiber of her being. She came home quiet, sad, and very lonely. I was still too young to know how to help my mother, so I pretended nothing had happened.

We all did.

On Fridays, my mother's only day out of the office, she would volunteer alongside the nuns at the Mother Teresa home in Sana'a. What had started as an orphanage had turned into a home for the unwanted, young and old alike. My mother worked tirelessly alongside her beloved nuns, trying to feed and bathe the sick and mentally ill. She often came home exhausted. She would also spend hours on the phone, working to get her friends to donate time, goods, and money.

Every so often, she took me with her. One day, as I was walking up a dark, dirty back stairwell, I was startled by a scream and a rattle. A six-year-old boy was hidden in the shadows, chained to hooks on the wall. He lunged at me.

My mother pulled me away and explained that when the boy was not restrained, he hurt himself and others. With their very limited resources, the orphanage had no choice but to keep him chained. After that, I tried my best to avoid the home: those kids were too dirty, too scary, too damaged. I was afraid I would get swallowed up by that place. I begged my mother to leave me behind when she went. The nightmares I had, which kept all of us awake at night, convinced her.

When I was nine, Mother Teresa herself came to Yemen and made a surprise visit (for security reasons) to the home. Shocked to see her role model before her eyes, my mother fell to her knees. During the few days Mother Teresa spent at the home, my mother was by her side as she bathed some of the heaviest patients and checked the supplies of medications and toiletries. My mother came home to pick me up, and despite many protests, she took me to meet the woman who had inspired her own generosity.

That is when I first discovered there are many different ways to do what it takes. You can be like the mild, soft-spoken Mother Teresa the world saw, or you can be forceful and compelling, as Mother Teresa really was. A formidable woman who barked orders, she got things done with speed and efficiency and strength you wouldn't believe. I watched her carry an old man to his bed by herself. "Mama," I asked when we arrived home from the orphanage, "why was that old lady so angry all the time?"

My mother looked down at the two small medals Mother Teresa had given her, along with the blessing of *May God always keep you safe*. "She has to be that way to get anything done—and there are good reasons why she has done what she has in her life," my mother said. "She is the only hope those people have."

"But she was so *angry*," I said.

My mother reached over and took my hand. "Sometimes it is really hard work to change the world, Zahra," she said in a weary voice. "Sometimes people get tired of the burden they chose to bear. Sometimes they are not sure that they want it, and sometimes they have to do it anyway."

I squeezed her hand back, wondering, for just a minute, if we were still talking about Mother Teresa.

My mother's work connections, with people like the American ambassador, and her incredible persuasiveness, changed the course of my life. One day, she spoke with the administrative officer at the American embassy about how worried she was about my education and the quality of the schools in Yemen. By the next morning, I had a scholarship to attend the American School, a school for the expats and foreign community.

Most schools in Yemen were rudimentary and spare, but my new international school had art on the walls—posters and children's drawings. We had music and dance classes and performances our parents came to watch. The classrooms had individual desks that moved around so they could be in small groupings or semicircles. They were well stocked with supplies like coloring books, crayons, construction paper, and scissors.

But despite the abundance, there was only one pair of left-handed scissors in my first-grade class, and only one left-handed kid: me. One day, about a month after my first day, a boy named Fred decided to ignore a full basket of right-handed scissors and to go instead for the pair I considered mine.

"Give them back to me," I said quietly. "They're mine." It didn't dawn on me that Fred was sweet on me and just wanted my attention, but it wouldn't have changed my mind. With each answer of no, my frustration escalated. Finally, I punched him, grabbed *my* pair of scissors, and calmly sat down to finish my work.

Fred was not going to let awkward, gangly six-year-old me get away with that. I was no match for a tall American boy like him, nor for my teacher, Mr. Anderson, a six-foot-six former football player who had seen what was happening and came quickly over to break up the ongoing fight. While he was trying to separate us, I punched him too. It was an accident, honestly, but one with a big side of *let me at him.*

Mr. Anderson knew better than anyone the challenges I had as the first Yemeni student, the poor kid, and the only scholarship student at the school. As we walked together to the principal's office, he tried to make light of the situation, but his gentle jokes only frustrated me more. I was ashamed to be in trouble for something that none of the Western kids would have done. I didn't know the word "gauche," but that was how I felt—like an unruly village child, all rough edges, an outsider looking in at a place I felt I didn't belong.

My mother came to pick me up, and she did not find any part of the scenario funny. "Do you know how hard I worked to get you into this school?" she asked, her fingers tightening around my wrist as we hurried out to the car. "You have to behave, or they're going to kick you out!"

The only reason I was at this school in the first place, learning English surrounded by the children of diplomats and dignitaries, was the kindness of my mother's boss. I had put both my future and her reputation on the line.

"You're the only scholarship student," she reminded me as she started our car's engine. "Don't you understand? We can't even *dream* of affording this place. Wait until your father hears about this."

In Arab culture, fathers are not the dads you see in Western sitcoms. The father is the patriarch, the protector of the family, who deserves respect and reverence. I didn't curl up next to my father on the couch or put my arm around his shoulder. We had a much more formal relationship, and in some ways, a more distant one too. I did feel deeply connected to him, but my mother—like many mothers—was far more involved in the day-to-day business of my life. When my father came home, I needed to be quiet. If he needed me to do something, he told my mother.

I was grounded for two weeks, said my father.

Later that night, I tiptoed out of the room I shared with my grandmother in our new house, stood in the hallway, and listened through my parents' bedroom door as they discussed the day's events. I felt sorry for what I had done and worried that I had caused trouble for my mother at work.

But then I heard my father's voice. "I am so proud of her," he said, laughing. "She stood up for herself and punched that boy right in the nose. That's my girl." I could hear the surprise in his voice.

Straining to hear more, I stood quietly in the darkness, fists clutched to my puffed-up chest, as I realized I was my father's daughter. For the first time in my life, I felt as if we understood each other.

My two-week punishment was intended to teach me to show proper respect to everyone, but I wasn't bothered much by it. Being grounded meant little to a kid who was hardly allowed out of the house anyway.

I felt different from the Western girls, with their straight hair, their much-coveted school bags, pencil cases, and stickers, their cool confidence, and their snacks that came from America. The more self-conscious I was about my differences, the more I feared rejection. The more I feared rejection, the more I wanted attention.

"Stand up for yourself," my father always told me. "They are *not* better than you." I not only stood up for myself, I forced my way in, in the play yard, in the middle of the baseball game—even when no one wanted me to play—and into the group of cool girls, no matter how many times they told me to go away. I chased a boy named Russell, my crush, around the schoolyard, even though I knew he didn't like me.

When I was challenged, reprimanded, or, even worse, ignored, a feeling of defensiveness crept in, and I grew even more determined to stand up for what I wanted. My sense of justice and fairness has always been both my strength and my weakness. *It is not fair to exclude me,* I thought, *so I won't let you.*

My grandmother covered for me sometimes when I got into trouble, out of allegiance less to me than to my father, whom she never wanted to upset. She wasn't shy about how much she hated my wild side. She tried to teach me proper Yemeni ways, like how to sit without spreading my legs, how to cover my head properly, what to say and what not to say. *You should be grateful, Alhamdulillah. You have to pray, Zahra. Ask God for forgiveness.*

I respected her, always, but I began to listen to her less and less. And that was much better than the way I behaved with my parents—especially my mother. "I don't care!" was my new favorite response to her as I slammed the bedroom door shut. "I *want* you to leave me alone."

I spent as much time as I could at the homes of my American friends, soaking up every possible drop of Western culture I could—an opportunity that was available to few Yemeni girls my age. I did not want to *be* Western, but I longed to have more—more adventure, more color, more flavor, and more of what seemed so readily available to my classmates.

The United States was a utopian society for kids growing up in Yemen in the late 1970s and early 1980s—a place where things we never thought could happen occurred. The land where desires became realities. America sold a dream to the rest of the world in a very powerful way—by catching the hearts and minds of youth around the world. It is a sharp contrast with today, as Yemen's young people, who are largely illiterate because of poverty, economic strife, war, and conflict, see only one thing: American bombs.

I did everything I could to appear more Western. I took scissors to the new pair of American jeans my mother had sent away for. I'd wanted cutoff shorts, so I yanked the threads at the bottoms to fray them appropriately.

"*Why*?" cried my mother.

"The other kids wear shorts to school, *Mom*," I said, using the name some of my friends used for their mothers. I thought it was cool then. Today, I love that my children call me Mama, the Arabic way; however, even they call my mother Mom.

My parents didn't like my behavior, they didn't like my language, and they really didn't like the attitude of superiority I was beginning to show toward some of our family members.

I complained about going to the area of town where most of the Harazi family lived, which was near Bab al-Yemen, the gate to Sana'a's Old City. The streets there smelled like raw sewage, probably because raw sewage had nowhere to go but down those streets. The family lived in apartments above little shops, sometimes ten flights up dark, centrally enclosed staircases with uneven steps.

Going back to our ancestral village of Haraz felt just as bad: the mountain roads were treacherous, the homes were crowded, and the only bathrooms were outhouses on stilts with holes cut into the floor. The children stared at me, and I refused to play with them. They were rough, and I couldn't hold my own. In time, I refused to go altogether.

In trying to fit in with the kids at school, I started rejecting everything that wasn't a part of the world I wanted to belong to. "Do you think you're above the rest of us?" my mother would ask sometimes. "Above your cousins? Above me and Baba?"

I exhausted my parents, I know. I was too young to understand that my mother was an outsider herself and was also struggling with identity while playing so many roles in our new life. To me she was simply a hindrance to what I wanted to do. But in addition to being my mother, she was a wife, sister-in-law, daughter, and so much more. She was a force to be reckoned with at work and a breadwinner at home; then, in her off hours, if there were any, she was my father's right hand, copyediting his long and complex government reports.

I wish I'd had as much pride in her then as I do now.

My Western immersion was working—I had lots of friends at the international school and felt that I belonged more and more each day. My parents began to fear that their daughter was turning into an entitled little brat rather than a good Muslim girl. They were afraid that if I did not find a way to fit in in Yemen, I would not be accepted and my life would be more difficult. The expats were not there to stay, but I was.

The summer before I turned ten, my mother took me on a vacation to Mombasa—a popular beach town on the coast of Kenya—to soften a blow I hadn't seen coming. I played in the sun all day; at night, I dreamed of telling my school friends about the coconuts we drank from, the sandcastles I'd built—all the fun I'd had. Recognizing how caged I was, my mother gave me a taste of freedom—of what life might be like if I were not constantly told what to do.

She didn't force me to sit quietly as she brushed through my crazy thick, curly hair; she didn't yell at me to stay out of the sun, and soon my skin was the same color as the Kenyan kids I was playing with.

That summer instilled in me the same lifelong love of travel that lived in my father's and grandfather's hearts. When I was away, I could feel free.

Our plane touched down in Sana'a, and my father met us at the airport. He took one look at us, and then, without a word to me, he turned to my mother. "What did you do with my daughter, and who is this African child you brought home with you?" he asked.

I looked at my mother with wide eyes. Was I in trouble? Was she? She closed her eyes. "Let her be a child, Anwar. Ask her how her vacation was. Give her a hug." My father stiffly obliged, and then he went to wait for us in the car. I didn't know what I had done, but I knew he was not happy.

A few minutes later, my mother and I ran into my school friend Kelli, who had spent the summer back home in the U.S. Pacific Northwest. While I was excitedly chattering to her about the beach and about school, which would start the next week, I overheard my mother say to Kelli's mother, "Zahra's moving to a local school this year."

Maybe she didn't think I'd hear, or maybe she did and figured it was as good a time as any for the bomb to drop. I wheeled around in shock, as Kelli's parents quickly ushered her away, smiling politely. I didn't even notice. "NO!" I cried.

"We are living in Yemen," my mother said, "but you have not been acting like a good girl. Your father is moving you to a different school, where maybe you will start to behave." My mother had planned to tell me this news in Mombasa, but instead she had decided to just let me enjoy my summer.

Not interested in giving me a break, she began to walk away with our luggage. I watched in disbelief, and then I started crying, throwing myself down on the dirty floor. Travelers stared at us as I screamed "You can't make me!"

Finally, my mother peeled me off the floor and dragged me to the car, where my father was waiting for us. For the next week, I was inconsolable.

CHAPTER FOUR

I landed in a world where the rules were hard and fast. All the Arabic schools in Yemen used textbooks sent by the Saudi government's ministry of education, masquerading as aid to the country. In reality they—and thus we, the students—were steeped in Wahhabism, an austere, ultra-conservative form of Islam that is about as distant from true Islam as you can get. The Saudi doctrine is extreme, unforgiving, and rigidly fundamentalist and, in my opinion, has no place in the modern world.

During class, I sat in a room with bare gray walls, shoulder to shoulder with my fellow students, all of us on a hard bench facing a single teacher at the front. There was no joking with the boys or playing together at recess. There were no sports, no gym classes, no music, no art. Instead, there were five different religion classes. This was a new, bewildering world, one that was as alien to me as I was to it.

We were encouraged to seek righteousness, but wrapped inside those lessons were small, hard kernels of fear and suspicion. Most of what we were taught amounted to avoiding temptation at all costs and shielding ourselves from the influence of Western infidels. You should not look directly at a man, should not show your wrists or a strand of hair. "Should not" after "should not": Sex is only for procreation, not for pleasure. You can't eat with a fork because the Prophet ate with his hand. But, of course, it had to be the right hand.

Unfortunately, fear—not life—seemed to be the theme of study.

All of that was in direct conflict with the Quran, the holy book for Muslims, which I was also required to learn. The Quran tells us that God "does not intend for you hardship." I read passage after passage about how we should be kind to strangers, how we are all God's children, how we never should hurt another living being, how war is to be fought in self-defense only, how women and children are to be protected at all costs.

How was it that what our textbook was teaching us was so different from what God was saying? It was the beginning of a lifelong conflict with religion.

Once again, I was the strange girl who didn't belong. Only this time, I wasn't too Eastern—I was too Western. I walked in on the first day wearing my American school miniskirt and stood out as if I were naked. The hallways seemed hushed, as if everyone was afraid of something. The girls and boys were separated, and every girl was wearing the hijab except me.

I thought my classmates would welcome me as the cool kid and want to know about my worldly adventures. Instead, they took the wind out of my sails in two seconds flat. Most either ignored me or looked at me with disapproval and scorn. I realized in a moment of shocking clarity that I was nothing here, and if I wanted to be accepted, it would be on their terms—not mine.

The one good thing about having attended the international school was the clear edge it gave me in English class. In everything else—math, geography, history, cultural studies, biology, physics, and chemistry—I was completely lost, for they were all taught in Arabic, a language I didn't yet know how to read or write. I spent almost half my time buried in the Arabic–English dictionary, trying to translate my textbooks.

When I tried to speak Arabic, everyone laughed, just the way I would laugh at my mother when she tried; I was rightly served a taste of my own medicine.

The culmination of each of my classes was a pass-fail final exam. If I didn't get 50 percent or above in a class, I would need to take the test again at the end of the summer. If I failed three classes, I'd need to repeat the year. These were high stakes for my father, who worried about my disobedience and stubbornness, as well as the fact that I did not have any brothers to protect me.

Math was my weakest subject and also the only one my father could help me with, since his Arabic was as bad as mine. A wrong answer meant a beating, and there were a lot of them. That was nothing new; it was part of the culture at school and at home—*not* disciplining your children was considered bad parenting. Sitting there at the table with my father, papers smudged from my tears, I saw the frustration in his eyes.

In my mind, each punishment only confirmed my fear that I was not smart. In his mind, we were still refugees living on borrowed time, in danger of losing everything with the slightest provocation.

"You have to do this right," he told me. It was the same message conveyed by every crack of my headmaster's stick at school, which I was also uncomfortably familiar with: *You will fit in.*

Though my parents themselves did not share the rigid beliefs taught at school, I was too much of a rebel to be trusted. Concerned that I would be labeled a "bad girl," they kept a tighter hold on me than many of my classmates' parents did. Every outing request had a hundred questions attached to it: How long will you be gone? Who is going to be there? Whose house is it at? In the end, the answer was usually no. School trips? No. Sleepovers? No. That feeling of restriction did not help me behave; it made me more desperate to be bad. I did not know then how that desire for freedom would become a central driving force in my entire life.

If my father was the provider for the family, my grandma was its life, as consistent in her love for us as she was in her habits. Since both of my parents were working, she was the one to greet me, every single day, when I came home from school. She made me an afternoon snack of porridge, thick with milk and immensely satisfying; *khameer*, dough cut into triangles, deep-fried and served with honey; or shrimp chips, deep-fried and puffed into delicious crunchy squares. My memories of my Uma never have the sound of her voice in them—just her kind eyes and gestures of love.

The help was not allowed to go into my grandmother's room; she considered it clean only when she did it herself. She was fastidious, and she cleaned, vacuumed, and did her own laundry until the day she died. She would change her sheets if they were so much as touched by a male, even if it was one of my uncles. If someone touched them again after she'd changed them, she would once more strip the bed and put on another clean set without saying a word to him about it.

Like most women of her generation, she was the queen of the family—the all-powerful matriarch—and also entirely dependent on my grandfather.

My grandfather was quiet and unassuming but had a strong personality. He had managed to keep the family together through the upheaval of leaving Uganda and resettling in Yemen, and his words had authority for all. Being retired, he found solace in taking me to and from school. "Bint' Anwar, bring me a glass of water," he would say to me, every single day, as soon as he walked in the front door. I would run and get him a glass, happily looking forward to the hug that I would get in return.

He loved soccer and would dress up and go to the games. He also gambled on soccer teams at the post office. He went to the market to get groceries for the family. And some evenings he went to the old souk to meet his family and friends. He read a lot, but we could see the sadness in his eyes; as happy as he was to be home, the loss of everything he had built in Uganda had devastated him. His dreams for his family were broken.

Three years after our return to Yemen, my grandfather planned to go to Haraz with his cousin for a visit. The day before he was meant to leave, he felt uneasy. My grandmother was surprised: he had made the trip many times. "I don't know why," he said. "I just don't want to go."

My superstitious grandmother did not like the look in his eyes. An hour before the cousin was supposed to arrive, she ushered him out of the house and told him to go on a long walk. Her heart was as uneasy as his was. She said she would tell his cousin that he was sleeping and not feeling well. But several hours later, just as he walked back down our street, his cousin pulled up.

"Sorry I am late, *Amu Rizq*. I got tied up in the shop and couldn't leave until now. Let's go."

My grandfather did not have the heart to disappoint his cousin now that he had arrived, so he went inside and told my worried grandmother it was fine. He would be okay.

A few hours later, on the narrow road that wound up the mountain to Haraz, they got sideswiped by another car that was going too fast. Their car ran into the side of the mountain, while the other car fell off it.

My grandfather's cousin escaped without a scratch. My grandfather also didn't have a scratch on him, but he hit his head on the dashboard.

Two weeks later, without waking up once, my grandfather died.

Bodies are not buried in coffins in Yemen. We believe we came from the earth and we should return to it. The dead are wrapped in a simple white cloth and buried without a headstone, just a small plaque on the ground. They are also brought to the house for the men to visit before burial.

I was a child, and no one paid attention when I walked into the living room with the men and saw my grandfather's body. I remember reaching out to touch his face. I was only five and didn't understand much of what was happening. I went back to the women's quarters and told my grandmother that my grandfather was funny. When she asked me why, I said, "He is smiling while he is sleeping. He must be having a good dream."

I was too young to understand the tears that ran down my grandmother's face and why she gripped my hand so tightly.

My grandmother's steeliness remained, but the reach of her personality diminished after my grandfather's death. It looked like she had physically shrunk, when in reality, only her authority had. Now, the role of matriarch belonged to my mother. My aunts were by now all living in London, and though fiercely independent, my full-of-life grandma was suddenly someone who'd had the life taken out of her.

After my grandfather died, she became my roommate, and so I would end each day to the soft sound of her falling asleep and the sight of her tiny chest moving up and down in the bed next to mine.

Like my parents, she was invested in my propriety—and my piety. She tried waking me up at dawn for prayers, but I would never get out of bed, and soon she gave up. I did not want to do anything that someone else told me I had to do. If I was forced to go to the mosque, I would pretend to pray instead of saying the words I knew how to say.

These days, I have been away from prayer for so long that I don't feel worthy of being heard. When my faith is shaken, I'll call my mother and ask her to pray for me. If there is one thing in this life I believe in, it is a God that answers my mother's prayers.

When I was just six years old, my mother took me back to India with her. We covered a lot of ground while we were there, trying to see as many relatives as we could. She would relax and let me roam. Knowing her trained eagle eye was at rest, I got into adventure after misadventure.

I loved *panipuri*—a crisp fried shell filled with tamarind chutney, potato, onion, and chickpeas and doused with flavored water—despite the fact that the vendors fished into their wheelbarrows with their filthy hands to hand it to me. Those street snacks, as well as swimming in the lake with the house boy (after my mother told me not to—and especially because she told me not to), regularly landed me in a hospital room, one time for three weeks, with every parasite known to man.

On one of our last mornings there, my mother took me for a walk and uncharacteristically stopped to buy *panipuri* on the street. It made me worry: I usually got into trouble when I bought *panipuri*, and now Mama was buying it for me?

"There is something we have to do, Zahra," my mother said, as she crouched down to talk to me. "Don't worry, it will be fine, and we will go for ice cream afterwards, okay?" We continued on, down an unfamiliar street and into a dark, cluttered room, where we met an old woman with a stained white sari and misshapen fingers. The woman drew the curtains and told me to lie down on the narrow bed in the corner, and I felt a fear beyond any I had ever known.

My mother always wanted to do the right thing. And the right thing, as all her neighbors and friends in India told her, was to have me circumcised. They discussed it over tea in my grandfather's flat, while I was in another room; they reassured my mother that the practice was good for women. Lessening the passions of a woman would lessen the problems she would have. I suppose they thought it would make me a better wife one day. Perhaps it would have. It was the right thing, they all agreed. It was tradition.

Female circumcision, or genital mutilation, is a cultural practice in parts of Africa and the Middle East that predates Islam and has nothing to do with the religion. In India, which has a large Muslim population, only my family's sect practices female circumcision. Many women from the community insist that this practice is egalitarian, as both men and women are circumcised. I would note that for men, the circumcision is done for health and hygiene, while for women, the operation is meant to curb sexual desire and independence by removing the clitoris—to tame them.

The arguments hardly matter, however; our women rarely argue. They accept any and every decree told to them. They do so because they believe, but more than that, because they want the best for their families. The threat of social boycott or excommunication for disobedience is so deep and so real that most women fear if they do not comply, then they and their children will be ostracized from the close-knit community. This fear has long prevented all women, from any faith really, from raising their voices against any oppressive practice.

It was, in this way, very simple. My mother was from this community. Circumcision was our custom. It did not cross her mind to say no; in fact, saying yes was one more thing that, in her mind, she could do to protect me.

"Mama, who is she?" I asked my mother. "What is she going to do?"

With tears in her eyes, my mother simply shook her head.

But I did not just say no; when the old lady tried to make me lie down, I fought her like a wildcat. "Help me, Mama!" I yelled, kicking. When the old woman tried to pin me down, I bit her fingers.

The old lady implored my mother for help, and for a moment my mother just stood there, frozen. "Where did you get this devil child from?" the old woman asked, backing away, glaring at my mother as I retreated to the corner of the bed. "I have never had so much trouble."

These comments, meant to make my mother feel embarrassed, instead filled her with a profound feeling of relief. She had never felt sure about her decision to have me circumcised; she knew what it meant and how it had changed her life. She didn't know if she wanted that for me. My mother walked over to me. "She is a stubborn child," she apologized, trying to pick me up. "She never listens to anyone. Let me take her now. I will bring her back and we can try tomorrow."

Later that night, as I slept, she phoned my father at home in Yemen and told him what had happened. My father said simply, "Leave my daughter alone."

I wonder if it was the distance that made him say that, or the fact that he could not stand any more harm coming to any of us. Whatever it was, I am forever grateful.

In those days, in that place, circumcision was a way for mothers to protect their daughters—like my grandmother protected my mother—and to ensure that they were a part of society, that they belonged, that they found good husbands, that they survived. The practice is barbaric and wrong, but it is hard to universally condemn people without understanding exactly what goes into such decisions.

As devout as my mother was, when the time came, she looked beyond religion to do the right thing for her daughter. I cannot even begin to recognize how different my life would be if my father had not intervened, or if my mother had made any other decision that day.

• • •

By 1982, we were living in my parents' dream house, a modern bungalow-style home built by the same people who had built the new Sheba Hotel. My mother had cleverly arranged to import materials for the house together with the hotel's materials, and to hire the hotel's Indian construction crew, so that we would have a home we could never otherwise have afforded.

We had come a long way since we had first arrived in Yemen, when we lived with all my uncles and aunts in a two-bedroom house. Now we had a beautiful home, and in the garden, a separate structure housed the domestic help and had room for men's gatherings.

As I settled in at the Arabic school, I began to feel the influence of religious customs. One morning I came to the breakfast table wearing a hijab and sat down defiantly. My mother looked at me, and then at my father, with sadness in her eyes. My father nodded at her and then at me. They understood why I was doing it.

From that day forward, I wore the hijab at school, feeling a bit less like an unwelcome intruder. My look evolved until it matched that of my conservative classmates. About a year later, I began wearing the abaya, the long black robe that goes from neck to floor. This had nothing to do with my inner spiritual life and everything to do with wanting to be accepted.

"I'm not going out with you," I told my mother one day, standing in the doorway of her room as we were getting ready to go to a party. "You need to dress properly."

My mother covered herself at certain events, as a sign of respect. But she also loved experimenting with fashion; the abaya she liked best was sheer, and as far as her newly devout daughter was concerned, not a proper abaya at all. It was fine, she insisted.

Her outfit revealed nothing untoward; she had a long-sleeved dark dress underneath. But that wasn't the point, in my mind.

"It embarrasses me, Mama," I said.

"Zahra, did one of your friends say something to you?"

"They don't need to," I said. "Please? Why can't you be more like the other mothers?" I knew I'd crossed a line, but I didn't stop. "And please watch your Arabic. Last time you asked Hana how her mother is, you said 'him' instead of 'her.'"

My mother turned her face away so I would not see the tears in her eyes. She knew my struggle to fit in and tried not to be hurt by my words. My friends' mothers covered up more than she did, they spoke differently than she did, they were more . . . Yemeni than she was.

She wanted to help me, but she couldn't. Not if she didn't want to lose herself too.

The universal law of adolescence is that I was going to be embarrassed by whatever my mother did. But in this case, she herself was desperate to fit in and do the right thing. She had been trying to find her place for far longer than I had.

Perhaps I knew that. Perhaps that's why I also turned away to stare out the window. I didn't want to see her face and her sadness that the one person in the world who was hers, whom she could fully be herself around, was ashamed of her.

CHAPTER FIVE

The Arabic school did not have the effect my parents desired. They were not so focused on whether I looked the part of the "good Muslim girl"; they wanted me to *be* one. I, on the other hand, had learned my lesson well at the American school and knew I needed to force my way in or I would stay in the corner of the classroom by myself.

I talked back to the teachers. I stood on the upstairs landing with a bucket of water balloons, waiting until a group of boys lined up below, and then tossed them down on their heads. I chewed on sunflower seeds, spitting the hulls on the classroom floor and driving my teachers mad. I rebelled in any and every way I could.

The punishment for each offense was ten strikes across my palms.

Our principal, a short, round Egyptian man with a white beard, always wore an off-white safari suit and carried a long plywood stick. "What is wrong with you?" he said, each time I was dragged to his office. "Why are you here this time?" His stick made a sickening sound as it whooshed through the air onto my outstretched hand. Eventually, he stopped asking why I had come; as soon as he saw me, he just reached for his stick.

I hated the punishments, but I loved how I was gaining grudging respect from my classmates. They waited for my next move in fascination, and I didn't disappoint.

What finally helped me break through to the popular girls at the Arabic school was my proficiency in English. A girl in my class asked about an assignment one day, and instead of giving her advice, I offered to do it for her. Her reaction shocked me: for the first time, someone in school looked at me with a tiny bit of admiration.

And that was when I realized I could change my standing in school. I started doing their homework, going as far as helping kids cheat on their English exams, sometimes writing the exam for them. The girls were delighted, and all of a sudden, I was part of a group of friends. The inner circle. The one I had fought—even changed the rules—to belong to.

I had thus learned the important lesson of being useful to others and being clear about what you can offer. Over the years I have turned this knowledge into a strength that helps me in business and in relationships. I am a connector, a problem-solver. I take charge and do what needs to be done. I don't worry about what others can do for me; I focus on what I can do for them.

I really believe in the power of helping others, the power of karma—what goes around comes around. When you lead with your heart, people will follow. It really can be that simple.

Plus, now I do it on the right side of the rules . . . most of the time.

I was envious that many of my new school friends walked home from school together, so one day I begged my driver, Abu Amin—a kindly old man with bottle-thick glasses who drove with his chest pressed up to the wheel—to let me walk home. "Just today. Don't tell my dad," I said, then turned around and ran off before he had much of a chance to respond. I walked all the way home with my friend Salwa, reveling in the freedom but not dallying for even one second.

But my haste did not matter in Yemen, a society not known for minding its own business. When I arrived home, my father was standing at the door, furious. People had called him at work to say they had seen me walking down the main road.

"Why do you do this? Why do you keep bringing shame and attention to this family?" he asked, glaring at me. "Why can't you be good?" I didn't have an answer.

The next morning a new driver was waiting for me, and on most days, he barely spared me a glance.

Any rebellion I could possibly have dreamed up at home was nothing compared with what I got into in Europe. From the time I was ten years old, my parents saved up all year so we could take an annual summer trip overseas. The plan was the same every year. We would start somewhere I had never been—Paris, Amsterdam, Athens, Rome—travel around, see the sights, go shopping, and then continue on to London to stay with my aunty Rukiya, who waited for me with cupboards full of the things I loved: Flake bars, strawberry milk, and cheese and onion crisps.

Every summer, I got to buy my clothes for the year in London. My father insisted that I think carefully about every item, make a list, and stick to a budget. My mother made me get practical things, like underwear and socks. I added ripped jeans, Madonna's lace headband with the big bow, and neon-colored leggings. I left my abaya and hijab in my hand luggage, and Yemen became something of a distant past as soon as we left the country.

I loved every moment we spent in Europe, although I often told my mother, who dragged me to every monument in the guidebook, that if I saw another church or another pile of rocks that used to be a building I would scream. I giggled with my friends when I brought home pictures of the naked statue of David, the same pictures that appeared in our textbooks with the offending parts blacked out, as nudity was not allowed in Yemen.

We spent the most time in England, with our family, most of whom lived there now. No matter how long we stayed, it was never enough. The green countryside, the busy London streets—it was like living in a movie. In many of the cities, girls who looked just a little older than I was were out walking around by themselves. Could I go to a café by myself? No. A concert? No. *That is their life, not ours,* I heard again and again. *You can see, but you can't touch.*

At school, I had learned to pray with prayer beads. You would never see my grandma without the beads in her hand—or my mother, for that matter. My repeated prayer became *Free-dom, free-dom, free-dom.* . . . It became a drumbeat in my head.

Abroad, I was more free to experiment, and I did. My first stop would be Hamleys toy shop, where I loaded up on all sorts of things I knew would entertain my school friends: disappearing ink, exploding pens, magic tricks, and the like. My favorite was the stink bombs, which I deployed with pure glee in high school when my hated religion teacher was in class. I did it once when my high school headmistress was in the room, and she thought it was him. I really believed she was going to take her cane to him.

A couple of those trips also included a stop at my friend Nadia's summer home, near Manchester. Our mothers had met at a ladies' luncheon in Yemen—two lone English speakers in a sea of Arabic—and our fathers had also become close friends.

Nadia and I spent years, in both Britain and Yemen, pushing every single limit we could. Stealing our parents' cars, driving them around the front yard, away from prying eyes, and then crashing them. We went to places we were not supposed to be. We bought long false nails and painted them red. When my dad saw mine, he marched me into the bathroom and watched while I tearfully ripped them off, one at a time. Another summer I bleached my hair blond and cut it in a mullet. My father dragged me to the closest hairdresser, who, thankfully, colored it back to its original black. (I didn't mind that punishment as much, as I looked pretty awful as a blonde.)

Later that year, back in Yemen, Nadia and I started stealing cigarettes, hiding them underneath my dresser, and sneaking puffs in the yard. We were grounded for weeks when we were caught. Only recently did I learn it was one of our neighbors who had told on us. His second-floor balcony was high enough to see over the sixteen-foot wall surrounding our house and shielding us—or so we had thought.

I had always wondered how my father knew.

Some of my parents' rules seemed unfair to me. They had told me stories about their own adventures—especially my father. For years I sat at his feet, listening to tales from the summer he was seventeen and hitchhiked forty-five hundred miles across Africa with three friends. Stories of tying himself to the tops of trees so he wouldn't get eaten by animals in his sleep. Stories of him and my mother breaking curfew and dancing into the night. My parents had been free to explore and experiment. I had every bit of the family's rebellious streak, but I lacked the freedom my elders had had.

I could not understand: How could there be one set of rules for them, one for my Western friends and cousins in England, and another one for me? My parents showed me the world and then told me it did not belong to me.

It seemed unjust.

When I argued, the answer was always the same: because you are a girl.

• • •

In Yemen, girls were not raised with the idea that we could be anything we wanted to be. Especially in those days, our choices were limited. During a time and in a place where women could not be seen eating in a restaurant—even with our families—it was rare to find women who worked. They were out there, but many were either women of the highest class, who had great connections, or foreign wives, like my mother.

My family saw the irony in this. When we had come to Yemen as refugees, her so-called low-class job stabilized my extended family, secured my first-class education, and enabled my father to build his own career.

Nobody told us girls to "Follow your dreams." They told us to behave, or to fix our hijab because our hair was showing. Few Yemeni girls plan on higher education, even during stable times; the girls whose first choice is university are the ones who haven't yet received a marriage proposal. In Yemen's tribal culture, the marriage of young girls is common; most get married before the age of fifteen. If you don't get married before nineteen, you are "on the shelf."

So on some days, I wanted to explore the world. Other days, my need to fit in got in the way, and all I wanted was to wear a white wedding dress and get married.

By the age of fifteen, I had given significant consideration to what does and does not make a good wife. And yet I had precious little exposure to men outside my family, let alone experience with them. Marriage talk was everywhere, but it was more like a G-rated soap opera—the intrigue of proposals, party planning, and dress buying—with a soundtrack of a thousand clucking mothers.

Yemeni boys and girls were together in the middle grades but then separated into different Arabic high schools. Sometimes the boys would wait outside our school gates after the final bell rang. They'd stand there, usually in groups, wanting to glimpse a crush, to lock eyes with a stranger, to drop a love note. I didn't have much of a chance to talk to them: I was typically heading home with our driver about five minutes after dismissal, long before I could make a lasting impression. Or so I thought.

"Hello?" I said once, then again, standing in our family's hallway, pressing the phone's round plastic receiver to my ear. After a minute of silence on the other end, a boy finally worked up the nerve to echo my greeting and introduce himself. His name was Sakr. One of my classmates had passed along my number. We probably spoke for a total of thirty seconds before I hung up, terrified that an adult might pick up in another room.

The next afternoon, the phone rang again. And the next. This little game went on for about six months, usually in those first few minutes after I had returned from school, before my parents got home from work. I would grab the receiver on the first ring and then hang up before my grandmother noticed I was missing; if she asked, I would claim it was a wrong number or a call for my father.

Then I came into class one morning and some of the girls were talking about a car accident that had happened the night before. A group of boys had been joyriding down the Sabeen Road.

One of the boys had died: Sakr.

Keeping my heartbreak about my innocent little "affair" to myself, I went home and sat next to the phone for hours, full of regret for something that never was. This was not a romance—I had never even met the boy—but in my limited world, it felt like the end of my life.

The extent of my sex education was "Never sleep in the same bed as a man," the advice my mother gave me the day I got my first period. It made absolutely no sense to me at the time. I was barely able to pass a man on the street. How and why would we get into the same bed? When some of the girls at school finally explained it to me, I did not believe them. After all the lessons about the taboos between men and women, all the talk about doing good deeds, they were telling me that *this* is where babies come from?

Moral and religious forces told us that remaining sexually pure until marriage was the right moral choice. We were taught that sexual urges were immoral, and that, if we didn't resist them, we would go to hell.

Our elders and teachers used intense shame as a weapon to make us fear our own bodies and needs, our desires, and our behaviors, and it would take decades to finally change the deeply entrenched ideas about love and connection that I knew were not right but that were a part of my belief system.

But even still, I had a sense of what I needed. *Free-dom*. The drum in my head kept on drumming.

CHAPTER SIX

My father's youngest brother, my uncle Hanif, is just four years older than I am. When we were kids, he was more like my annoying older brother, and our run-ins usually ended with bite marks and bruises. When we weren't fighting, he permitted me to tag along with him.

The arrangement worked well for each of us. No one really questioned Hanif's whereabouts if he was *taking care of Zahra*, and I was able to take in tiny sips of freedom because I had the protection of Hanif.

As sheltered as we were, we did find ways to explore. I especially loved going to the bazaars, open-air markets where very few local girls were allowed—mostly the foreign nationals or the girls who, like me, had foreign mothers.

The bazaars were something for the expat wives to do, a way to spend their time, give back, and be creative. The women sold the magical things they had made, with proceeds going to charity. If I did get a chance to go with Hanif, I would spend as much time as I could wandering through the rows of paintings, textiles, and handmade jewelry and buy whatever books I could get my hands on. That typically meant Harlequin romance novels, which I smuggled back home and hid from my father.

The summer I was fifteen, while my family was away in Europe, Hanif broke the rules and invited a friend over to our house. If they had stayed in the separate room for men, as they should have, my life would have been completely different.

My uncle's friend saw my picture on the wall and told Hanif he wanted to meet me, but my uncle worried that he would get in trouble for bringing a stranger into our family's private living quarters.

One Friday after we returned, Hanif and I decided to go check out the British bazaar. As usual, I obsessed over my outfit. That may be hard to believe, considering I was always covered in by-the-book black drapery. But fashion meant just as much to my friends and me as it did to any teenager. We just had different choices: a bit of lace on the wrists, or a subtle difference in the shape of a long sleeve, a flash of a jean-clad leg when we walked.

Since there was no school on Fridays, I could be much more daring. This was the eighties, and Michael Jackson was as hugely popular in Yemen as everywhere else. That day, I wore a red vinyl Michael Jackson jacket on top of my abaya. I am pretty sure it looked as ridiculous as it sounds, but in my mind, I was the pinnacle of fashion. I even put on my Madonna lace glove.

Hanif and I shopped around the bazaar as we usually did, trying to see everyone and everything, I was walking on a cloud of unexpected freedom when a handsome boy walked up; my uncle introduced us. He had big, beautiful eyes, with the longest-ever lashes, and after we talked for a little while, I could tell he was charming too. It was a little exciting to be talking to a boy without getting into trouble like I usually would.

He also seemed different from most of the Yemeni boys I knew. He had spent a good deal of his life outside of Yemen, which had led to his much more worldly personality. The son of well-known revolutionaries, he had been born in hiding and was smuggled across the border to Lebanon as a baby.

We became friends. Sometimes I would tag along with them, much to Hanif's annoyance and his friend's delight.

One day, when I was sixteen, Hanif told me that his friend had inquired whether he could ask for my hand in marriage. No, I said. I wanted to go away to university in England. It seemed too strange to even think about what might happen after that; it was too far into the future.

The possibility of going to university in London had always been the carrot at the end of my stick—making all the nos easier to handle because freedom was just around the corner.

After finishing breakfast one morning, I ran to the front door to speak with my father, who had his briefcase in hand. He was clearly in a rush. "Baba, before you go, can we talk about London?" I asked. "About school? I need to know what universities are near my aunties' houses."

"Zahra, girls in our family do not travel abroad alone," said my father, with a distracted nod in my direction as he walked out the door.

I have played this scene in my memory countless times. What I heard in my father's response was that he had never meant for me to go to university in the first place. He and I both knew how much I had struggled academically, and I was sure that was what was driving his decision.

I was filled with rage at the world, at society, at him. It did not matter how progressive my parents seemed, or how much of the world they showed me. When it came to my own life, I would be held to a different standard.

I began problem-solving. I did have options: I could apply to attend university in Sana'a, or I could get married. Okay, maybe not that many options.

My uncle Hanif's handsome friend was going to study in the United States, and if we married, I would be able to travel with him. It was a good match, and he was a good man. I told Hanif that I was ready—to tell his friend to come propose.

Most marriages in our culture are arranged by the families. A groom's female relatives, usually his mother, will suggest potential brides to him and his father, who decide based on family and class fit. I was hardly the perfect, subservient, obedient girl; no marriage of mine would ever be arranged that way.

My dreams of seeing America, which had begun during my earliest years at the international school, were starting to come into focus, and the idea filled me with a joyful giddiness I could hardly contain. If all went according to plan, then freedom would be on the horizon.

This talk of marriage came as a shock to my future husband's family, who had no idea who I was. He told them about my father, who had worked so closely with his uncle, Dr. Abdul-Karim, at the Central Planning Organization. There was some hesitation around the fact that my mother was Indian, and that my family was from a different sect of Islam than they were; as far as many people were concerned, we were not even considered to be Muslim. Would the family imam agree to marry us?

In the eyes of his family, I was a *mukhraja*—an "outsider." But he persisted, and in the end, the imam approved because of a misogynist technicality: a Muslim man can marry whomever he wants, from any religion, and have up to four wives at the same time. A woman does not have this right, nor the benefit of initiating or dissolving a marriage.

My future husband's parents sent a mutual acquaintance to talk to my father before making an official proposal. Aunty Asma worked with my father and was a good friend of our family. My father listened to the offer and, quite confused, began to say no. Before he got too far, Aunty Asma held up her hand and presented the possibility that I might actually be in agreement. My father stared at her, not understanding what she was saying.

By this time, I had already told my mother what was happening, in the hope she could persuade my father to agree. And all of a sudden, it was real.

"I don't know him very *well*," I said to my mother when she came to my room to tell me about Aunty Asma's visit, muttering something about Hanif and about the United States.

"Baba says you need to finish school before you get married," was my mother's reply.

That, to me, signaled approval. Indeed, my father was impressed by my potential groom's background, particularly his relationship to my father's much-loved former boss.

This proposal would bring my parents relief. A good match, a good family, a good boy—something every family wants for their daughter. Something they said they feared would never happen, given how much I misbehaved.

My mother kissed me goodnight and walked out of the room. "Tell Baba I say yes," I called after her.

Soon after, I heard my father and mother discussing my fate. I cracked my bedroom door open so I could listen.

My parents considered all angles. "We will never have a chance to really get to know a young man in this country," my father reminded my mother. "We have to trust that his family is good, and that means the boy is good." The boy's influence might be positive, my father rationalized. "At least she might stop getting into trouble," he said. "He might actually be the one to calm her down."

They eventually granted their permission on the condition that the engagement would last for the time it would take for me to get a degree at a university in Yemen.

The official proposal came soon after and my father quietly accepted. My mother laid out a high-necked white dress, with a lace bib and tiny pleats on the skirt, in preparation for the family's first visit.

When I pulled on the dress, the skirt fell only to my knees. When I expressed surprise, my mother sat me down and explained that they would need to see me as I am: "This is you. And don't cover your head, either. If they don't like that, then this won't work."

I nodded, trying to keep a smile to myself. Mama was finally being cool, and I was being given permission to be myself.

The first time I met my new fiancé's family, I struggled to understand what everyone was saying. His family's dialect was different from ours, as was their accent, and my Arabic wasn't so strong to begin with.

My future father-in-law made it easy on us, complimenting my mother and joking with my father. He reminded me of my grandfather—deeply connected to every part of the local community. My parents fell in love with him instantly.

We all sat around uncomfortably, making small talk, but when both fathers walked out to the garden, my heart jumped. A private talk between them would mean the engagement was official.

Around the world, weddings come with high costs. In India, the bride's family pays the groom's family a hefty sum—her dowry. In the Arab world, the groom's family pays the bride's family. Among the well-to-do in Sana'a, these were sizable transactions, with significant amounts of money and gold changing hands. But when my new father-in-law inquired about my price, my father's answer surprised everyone. "I don't sell daughters," he said. "I will instead buy a son."

My future father-in-law insisted: it was shameful to not pay a bride price. So my father asked for thirty thousand riyals, the price that had been set by the government to help people without means afford marriage. This was far less than was ever requested by any family of our station.

They understood the meaning behind my father's gesture— offering a token amount so it would not appear as if he were selling me—and were quite moved by it. Finally convinced that his son would be marrying well, my father-in-law accepted the terms, and the engagement was finalized.

Once my father received the thirty thousand riyals, he gave it to my mother to distribute among the family poor. Later that day, he came to me and pressed another thirty thousand riyals into my hand, telling me it belonged to me, not to him.

CHAPTER SEVEN

I went to London that June for our usual summer trip, only this time, I was shopping for an engagement dress: a gorgeous then, hideous today, pink satin and white lace mermaid dress, with a huge pink diamond-studded bow at the knees and lots of tulle underneath. Okay, well, maybe it was over the top even then!

I could picture myself making a grand entrance in it, while everyone I knew, dressed in their finest, would dance and cheer and whirl around me. My child's brain was thinking about the party instead of preparing for a commitment that most teenagers would be running from. This is what my seventeen-year-old life came down to, and I convinced my terrified soul that it needed to be quiet for a bit while I figured it all out.

Instead of an engagement, however, we had an *aqd*, a traditional marriage ceremony, because my future husband did not want to wait four years until I finished university to be married. After this ceremony, we would technically be husband and wife.

Typically, the *aqd* involves the bride's father and the groom; since the groom was in Oregon, his father served as a stand-in, talking with his son on the phone and relaying his answers. The men congregated in our men's room to chew *qat*. My aunties and my mother's friends sat together in our living room.

I sat with them in my magical pink dress, knowing little more than that at some point, my father-in-law and my father would shake hands, and then someone would put a handkerchief over them. I focused on my beautiful dress and the freedom it represented rather than the ties that were now binding me.

The father of my uncle Akil's wife walked into the living room and stood before me while I sat on the couch. "Do you agree to this union?" he asked in formal Arabic.

"What?" I asked—I hadn't heard what he said. He said, "Okay," and left the room. A minute or two later, I heard echoes of congratulations from the garden. I guess he thought I had said yes. I guess I had.

When my new husband came home later that summer, he could visit me without supervision. This infuriated my grandmother. "You're just in the next room!" I said, exasperated. "Plus, Uma, we're married!"

"You are not married until your wedding day," she insisted. "Until then, this is not proper."

We decided that now was the time to tell our parents we had no intention of waiting four years. We worked hard to sell my father on the idea that it would be better for me if we got married and I went to university in America.

I suppose I learned marketing long before I thought I had. My father, knowing this was what I wanted, reluctantly said yes.

Like the actual wedding itself, much of the wedding planning happened without my participation. My wardrobe was a happy exception. My mother and I flew to London for a second time that year, to buy my wedding trousseau, and went to Harrods for my wedding dress. After many years of making lists of necessities to buy on my European summer vacations, this was the ultimate indulgence. My parents let me buy whatever I wanted, and I felt like a princess as I glided around the famous department store's third floor in my magical wedding dress: a high neck, big puffed sleeves, and a fitted bodice that came to a point at the bottom over a skirt that puffed out before whooshing back in a long train. I put on such a show that a few tourists photographed me as I happily posed. As with my engagement dress, I cringe to see it in photos: it was the ultimate eighties abomination of a dress.

But that dress did have an exciting life. After my wedding, I gave it to a cousin to wear, who gave it to another cousin, who gave it to a friend, and so on. I saw my dress on distant friends and family in our village for many years, and it always made me happy when I walked into a wedding and saw what was becoming a very well-loved and well-used dress for many people who could not afford one.

For my trousseau, I bought silk dress after silk dress, with bow ties at the neck and shoulder pads—all of it more suitable for a forty-year-old. My mother tried to convince me to buy regular, Western-style clothes for our honeymoon, but I had a romantic image in my head of what a trousseau should look like and how a married woman should dress, and I would not be swayed. I also had no idea what the real world looked like, just visions from old movies. I even bought a pair of white gloves.

Our wedding was days long and had two thousand guests from around the world: India, Kenya, England. All of Sana'a's seamstresses stopped taking dress orders in the months prior; they were too busy with orders from the wedding guests, and others who weren't invited but decided they were coming anyway.

Besides our wedding gifts of gold there were also goats—lots of goats. In Yemen, when there is a death, a birth, or a marriage in the family, everybody shows up with food, which means goats. Imagine an invitation to a big party that says bring your own booze—BYOB. In Yemen, it's Bring Your Own Goat.

Everyone from our village wanted to contribute. My mother hired a crew of cooks, who slaughtered the goats in the Islamic way, cutting the large arteries in the neck and hanging the animals to drain the blood, which is considered impure. They set up a makeshift kitchen at the end of the yard because as men, they were not allowed in the main house with the women. For days, a river of red ran to our front door.

The henna party was a huge women's event in a big hall filled with bright lights, flowers flown in from London, and the most popular band in the country. My mother had supervised every single detail of the feast and had done it in her own way, hiring cooks from Aden. The spices were more Indian than Yemeni, both delicious and unexpected.

I came into the hall covered from head to toe; the women crowded around me, singing and dancing, and took me into another room to dress me in wedding finery. I had designed my green and gold dress, embroidered with 24-karat thread, and it had been made in Pakistan. Then I was presented with my parents' wedding gifts: a belt of gold coins stacked three on top of one another, heavy on my narrow hips, and a stunning emerald-and-pearl jewelry set.

Guests oohed and ahhed over me as they piled on even more jewelry. They placed gold bracelets on my wrists, draped necklaces over my neck, pushed rings onto my fingers. Soon I couldn't move. My mother did her best to keep track of who gave us what. My grandmother had a saying: "What belongs to others doesn't make it past the windowsill." In other words, we would need to repay the generosity of each gift giver.

We were one of the first Yemeni couples to marry at a Western hotel—Sana'a's relatively new Sheraton. The celebrations were separate: all the women—including my mother and aunties—were dressed in their finery and dancing at the Sheraton. The men feasted and chewed *qat* at the groom's house, while a singer entertained them. Typically, they do the *bara'a*, the traditional men's dance; the groom wears a turban and carries a big gold sword.

As these parties started, I sat in our family's living room with my eight flower girls. I had pink and purple eye makeup on—it was the eighties, after all. Sarah Ferguson had recently married Prince Andrew, and I had chosen exactly the same hairstyle as the new duchess of York—a huge head of curls that cascaded down from a wreath on my head. In addition to my god-awful hair and makeup choices, I had decided not to wear my glasses, which meant I could not see past a foot in front of my face.

"Did you not wear your abaya?" my new husband asked with frustration when he came to pick me up. It was too late now. I had not wanted to mess up my hair, I told him.

The drive from our house to the Sheraton usually took thirty minutes, but our procession jammed the roads for hours. His entire village, our entire village. Coworkers, friends, classmates, colleagues. Hundreds of cars slowly weaved their way up to the top of the hill, honking their horns every chance they got.

By the time our car passed through, people were lining the streets, wondering what was happening. When we pulled up at the hotel, we stepped into total chaos.

The Egyptian band my mother had hired was lined up near the entrance to greet us, beating huge drums and blowing into their bagpipes—sounds that many people in Yemen had never heard before.

When my groom helped me out of the car, a trumpet sounded, and the crowd cheered. I stood there in my Harrods dress and Pakistani jewelry, with my Yemeni husband, Indian mother, Ugandan father, and Western desires. In this way, I made an entrance that was a representation of everything I was—in fluidity and contradiction.

The crowd was so large we couldn't make our way inside quickly. But I could tell that hundreds of men were there. I heard some gasps and murmurs as I stepped out of the car, and I realized the disrespect I was showing to both our families. Usually, no one sees the bride arrive at her wedding; covered in black, she walks straight into the reception. I, on the other hand, stood outside in all my frothy white finery as the band played and the crowd continued to grow. And grow.

"We've already run out of food," my mother told me once we were finally ushered inside. Uninvited guests had shown up by the hundreds. She was mortified. All her friends had come fashionably late, which meant they were left with nothing to eat and not even a chair to sit on.

We caused such a ruckus at the hotel (at a time when hotel weddings weren't really a "thing") that ever since that day, wedding guests in Sana'a have had to show an invitation at the door to be allowed in.

We were not participants in our wedding as much as we were showpieces. We sat on a platform at the front of the room, like bride-and-groom cake toppers, while everyone danced below us. I felt like both a child at a pageant and a queen presiding over her subjects, as strangers continued to pour in, some standing on tables to get a glimpse above the crowd.

Since all I could see was noise and confusion and a mass of moving black blobs, the groom tried to fill me in on what he could. At one point his mother came over to scold us. "You are not supposed to know each other," she said. "Stop talking."

Chagrined, I fixed my gaze straight ahead, along with the frozen smile on my face. The closer I got to propriety, the farther away it felt.

• • •

Just before dawn, a smaller caravan of cars wound back down the hill, bound for Sana'a airport. With us were his whole family and my whole family, to see us off on our honeymoon in Morocco and Spain. From there we would travel on to start our life in the United States.

Unlike the rest of the travelers bound for Casablanca, we did not have to go through customs; instead, we waited in the VIP lounge and were driven right up to the airfield in that same sleek Mercedes. Our families gathered around us, and our luggage was loaded onto the plane.

As I stood next to my new husband in the early morning light, the adrenaline from so many days of revelry begin to wear off. In its place was exhaustion, and around the edges, a tingling sense of shock. Everything around me seemed unfamiliar.

My mother's eyes were red. My father, who had seemed puffed up and proud the night before, now looked thin and tired. While I'd been looking forward to leaving the country, I hadn't thought at all about the people I would be leaving behind.

At one point, while I was talking with one of my aunts, I saw my husband walk up to my father and touch his arm. I tried to listen; they were talking about my future.

"You know, even if it's just secretarial school," I heard my father say. "If she learns how to be a secretary. Her mother worked as a secretary . . . and did all right for herself."

He wanted to be sure I would get an education. I wondered at that. If my education was so important, why not let me go to London?

The realization that I did not know when I would next see my parents hit me with sudden force. In all the years I had spent trying to push them away, I had hardly given a thought to how important they were to me and how much I loved them. I saw now how much they had sacrificed for me—and how ungrateful I had been. I wanted to ask their forgiveness in that moment, but I had no idea where to start.

So instead we said quick and tearful goodbyes, and I walked toward the plane, my new husband beside me. We turned around and gave one quick wave before ducking inside.

"Who *are* you?" asked the flight attendant as she shut the door behind us. When we told her we were newlyweds and that we had married at the Sheraton the night before, she laughed. "We were there!" There were only about three airlines that serviced the city, and all the crew stayed at the Sheraton. "There was so much noise, we had to come down and see what was happening," she said. "It was you?"

Not long after takeoff, she came back to our row to tell us the pilot wanted to talk with us. This was long before you were not allowed in the cockpit. We ducked in, confused. The pilot turned around. "You see these black circles under my eyes?" he asked. "This is because of you!" He saw the wide-eyed look on my face and started laughing. "You kept us up all night."

"Sorry," I said, laughing myself.

"I have never seen anything like that. Your wedding was insane," he said.

The party is over, I thought, as my husband fell asleep next to me. My family was gone, and I was sitting next to a virtual stranger. My stomach turned as I noticed his scent, which I had first picked up on the night before. Not bad, just . . . different from anything that I knew.

We landed in Casablanca and were whisked away by yet another customs official. We had our own car and driver, compliments of the Yemeni embassy, as well as a tour guide in case we needed anything. Our escorts dropped us at the entrance to the hotel, and my husband checked us in, just as my father had always done—and would never do for me again. *This is what I wanted,* I reminded myself.

The car and driver came in handy, I'll admit, because the streets were *hot.* I wilted under those blousy silk dresses with the high necks and puffed sleeves. "I'm fine," I insisted, pushing my glasses back up my dripping face.

After a few days, we noticed we were drawing stares almost everywhere we went. We were confused by people's palpable suspicion and distaste, but then we realized: Morocco had long had a reputation for being a playground for Saudi and Emirati men. These so-called religious men, who were allowed to take more than one wife, justified their dalliances with Moroccan prostitutes by marrying them, for a short time, until they moved on to the next one.

When my husband asked a policeman for directions, he jeered, "Don't *you* know?" while looking right at me. "No, I don't," I said, very confused. Once he heard my Yemeni accent, he apologetically pointed us the right way.

At first, my husband and I fumbled through our conversations—we were newlyweds who had never been on a first date. At one point, he commented on my appetite and how much I ate. "Where does it all go?" he joked. I realized I preferred his tentative, polite behavior to what was looking like a growing sense of ease. Embarrassed, I tried to limit my food intake. Then I decided it was nobody's business how much I ate and that commenting on it was rude. And I told him so.

Our first fight was sparked by another offhand comment—this one about my clothes. It was so hot that we were constantly melting into puddles of sweat wherever we went—especially me, in the silk dresses I had come to loathe. But when he suggested that we go buy T-shirts and shorts, I was horrified. *Show my legs?* "No," I said. He told me I was married and with my husband and could do as I pleased. He sounded like a foreigner all of a sudden. What was he asking me to do?

"*I* told you that it was okay," he said again, more slowly.

I was having several realizations at once. One, my husband didn't feel bound by the same constraints as his parents. He was excited about introducing me to life in the United States. Two, he was telling me that I had his "permission"—something that was his to dole out, so far as convention was concerned. I could show my legs *and* be a good girl, he was saying, with little regard for the fact that what *I* wanted was to remain modest, as I had been taught.

"Listen, you've been very sheltered," he told me, on our last day in Morocco. "I want you to do what you want. I want to give you a year, you know, to explore. Go to school, go out with your friends. See what life is like, before, you know . . ." his voice trailed off to some kind of unknown inevitability. I thanked him, completely unaware of what life was going to look like, in that *freedom* year and beyond.

We landed in St. Louis, where we would stay for a few days before making the almost three-hour drive to the little town of Rolla, Missouri, where he had enrolled in school. My new husband had a little Mazda Miata sports car, which I had only ever seen on TV. Getting in and out of one, however, was not as effortless or cool as it looked on screen, nor was sitting so low to the ground in a world of two-ton Ford trucks.

We drove out of the St. Louis airport and onto the highway, and a sign for McDonald's turned my drowsy half-interest into laser focus. "Can we go get a Big Mac?" I asked. "Please?"

McDonald's was always the first meal I ate on our family summer holidays. It was a reminder of the life I had wanted to have. And so, at a McDonald's on North Tucker Boulevard, a Yemeni girl turned American housewife had a tiny taste of her new home.

CHAPTER EIGHT

The slogan of the city of Rolla, Missouri, is "in the middle of everywhere." It's true, geographically speaking: if you played a game of darts with North America, Rolla would be the bull's-eye. Many, many people make the obvious joke that it's more like "the middle of nowhere," but I loved my earliest days in classic small-town America.

The wide, paved streets were so different from Yemen's dirt roads and Europe's narrow lanes. The land's utter flatness was unique and fascinating too. In St. Louis, we had visited a huge American mall unlike anything I had ever seen, where, to my husband's relief, I had bought some more utilitarian American clothes that would serve me better. I wandered the streets of Rolla, went to the park and the movie theater, and generally just enjoyed being in public. The simple act of leaving my tiny little apartment, with my own key, and walking down the street was freedom.

Because our only income was my husband's scholarship, he kept us on a strict budget. Our apartment, like the rest of our lives in Missouri, was modest: a very brown, very drab two-bedroom apartment in student housing, with linoleum and cheap carpet on the floor. It was heaven.

All our essentials—from the furniture to the bedsheets to the picture frames—came from Walmart. And that was pure luxury.

I loved being able to pick my own furniture. On our shelves I arranged framed pictures of family members and little pieces of Yemen that I had brought with me.

Our social circle was mainly other Arab students at the university, most of whom were pursuing some kind of technical degree, and many of whom were, like us, on scholarship. There was a group from Syria, which was still a prosperous country then. Others were from Egypt or Kuwait. Like us, they were mostly students who had been lucky enough to win government scholarships to study in the United States. I wondered sometimes if they looked down on us: even in those days, Yemen was considered the poorest country in the Middle East.

That old "outsider" feeling crept back in slowly. Even among the Arabs, it was hard not to feel like the hillbilly cousin as a Yemeni, and I wasn't a "true" Arab anyway. I was a half-caste born in Africa, no matter what my passport said.

I was again stuck in between, too Western for our new friends, too Eastern for the Americans.

We all in some way were struggling to fit in and at the same time hold on to the life we knew. One of our new friends, a Kuwaiti woman, had all her family's food shipped from the Middle East. She talked about her amazing cheese for weeks while waiting for her shipment to come. But my eyes widened when she proudly showed us the case of blue tins of Kraft cheese that had just arrived. Did she not know the supermarket down the street had real cheese?

I was thrilled to be in the West, where men and women could sit at the table together and I could interact with others in a way I wasn't able to in Yemen. But our friends were from similar places, and a tin of Kraft cheese doesn't change its colors.

After dinner, the groups would separate the same way they did at home, and I would still be held at an arm's length from the men's conversation. I did not want to talk about diapers, babies, and fashion the way the other women did; I wanted to talk about business and politics. I went home and cried one day after a party where an Algerian woman had talked animatedly while she held her two-year-old, pausing every now and then to take a swig of milk from her child's baby bottle without even realizing what she was doing.

I got along well with many of the Syrian women, amazing cooks who were what we call "foodies" today. As we finished one meal they were already talking about the next one. I, on the other hand, was not as good in the kitchen. After the sixth week of eating curry, my husband finally asked tentatively, "Your mother told me you knew how to cook and you made dinner for the family every Friday?"

"Yes," I said innocently. "I made curry."

Unfortunately for both of us, society dictates that we are all supposed to be content in our roles even if they don't suit us. It would take time for me to perfect my new role as "wife." In the meantime, he tried to make good on the promise he had made to my father about my education.

Soon after we arrived, he overheard me telling one of our new friends that I had decided not to apply to the university for the upcoming semester. Later that night, he asked me why.

I brushed him off, but the reason was that my confidence was still shaky. American students seemed to know so much more than me, *and* they were so confident, and I was still trying to put together the pieces of my self-esteem.

He understood my reluctance, but he knew I needed to get out of the apartment—for his sake and my own. "How about the community college, like your dad wanted?" The next afternoon, he brought home a copy of the course catalog from Metro Business College for us to page through together. I settled on a six-month vocational program for business administration, but I was still intimidated by the thought of going by myself to register. I was completely convinced I wasn't good enough.

"I will come with you, but I am not going to speak for you," he told me. The next day, he drove me to the college and stood behind me while I filled out all the paperwork. When we left, two hours later, I had a little hop and skip in my step: I was enrolled in the Administrative Assistant program.

I started to relax and lean into my new life. I found the beginnings of a strength, boldness, and confidence I didn't know I had, a curiosity that I had long tamped down and learned not to access. This was the beginning of a lifetime of wanting to try things that made me shake with excitement and with fear. I started with driving school.

I borrowed a friend's car for my driver's test because our car was standard, which I couldn't drive. The driving examiner sat next to me and asked me to back up the car and get started. He seemed so stern, and I was nervous. I put my hand behind his headrest and turned to look behind me, as I had been taught. I checked my side mirror and my rearview mirror, took the car out of park, put it into reverse—or so I thought—and drove right into the fence in front of us.

My husband and the friend whose car I had just crashed were laughing so hysterically, they both fell into a bush. The examiner looked straight ahead, without expression. "Back up a couple feet and turn the car off," he said. I followed his instructions and then stopped, placing my hands in my lap and staring at them.

"Okay, then. I am going to pretend that never happened, and let's start again," he said with a straight face. To my complete delight, and my husband's utter shock, I passed my driving test.

• • •

"Typing school," as I called it, was a world away from my scowling high school headmistress and her army of suspicious teachers. I adored doing homework without the close companionship of my Arabic–English dictionary. Although I had dreaded accounting class, I did surprisingly well, and I carried the confidence I felt in the classroom back home with me at night.

My accounting teacher was a woman named Tina: beautiful and tall. I can still see her, wearing a gray plaid skirt and a white see-through shirt with a lacy red bra underneath. It was both elegant and suggestive. I was blown away by how effortlessly sexy a woman could look while still telegraphing her intelligence and control.

I had never aspired to be a sexy woman: women who tried to look sexy were exactly who you *didn't* want to be in Yemen. We were brought up to believe such women had no sense of dignity or respect for their families. I did not think I could be like Tina, but boy, did I want to. She was my new role model.

The first day of class, a woman named Peggy sat down next to me and immediately introduced herself. She was much older than I—in her mid-thirties—and was raising two kids. She was about as American as it got: a gum-chewing bottle blonde in stonewashed jeans. I was fascinated by her, and she was fascinated by me too: no one in her family had ever left Rolla. To her, Yemen might as well have been Mars.

Peggy was my introduction to a larger group of girlfriends, back in school with dreams of making more money or getting out of dead-end fast-food jobs. They told me about their lives, and I told them about mine, without hesitation. I was exotic to them, and they were interested in knowing more about "the other people." They asked a million questions. Suddenly, rather than fitting in, I was standing out—and it was glorious.

I started smoking again, knowing my father wasn't there to stop me. Neither could my new guardian—he had given me one year, hadn't he?

The only trouble with my newfound freedom was that there was nowhere to go. There was only one bar in town, which was where everyone spent most weekend nights. I was still a minor— just eighteen—and couldn't get in. I couldn't believe my bad luck. Finally, I was in a place without restrictions, and now I was too *young*? How was it that I was old enough to get married but not old enough to walk into a bar?

I was thrilled when my generous husband offered to buy tickets for a few of my new friends and me to see the next big band to come to town—Kansas. Peggy made sure I had the right outfit for my first rock concert: a pair of cutoff jean shorts—really faded, really frayed—and a pink belly T-shirt emblazoned with the logo of some band I'd never heard of. The first time I tried it on, I stared at my reflection in Peggy's full-length mirror and felt a wave of power; I couldn't have been further from the fight that my husband and I had in Morocco over my refusal to show my legs to men I didn't know.

Like my parents, I had learned to be a chameleon, and like my mother, especially, I was using my look as a way of communicating my worldview. When socializing with our Arab friends, I still wore long T-shirts and baggy jeans, or long, loose dresses like theirs. With my American friends, I could wear my beloved belly shirt and cutoffs. Oh my God, I loved that outfit. It was the ultimate freedom outfit. I did one last spin, nodded at my reflection, and followed Peggy out the door.

We danced the night away, and at the end of the show, the lead singer looked out at the crowd, thanking us as we all clapped and howled. "We're staying at the Howard Johnson's, if any of you ladies want to come over."

"Let's go!" shouted Leah, the wild child among us. She had long, dark hair, bright-red lipstick, and a cropped black leather jacket that she wore with her tight jeans. I followed them out to the parking lot. It was freezing out, and they were drunk; we broke into a run to the car, laughing as we got there. Never had I felt so carefree or so cool. "Sure, let's go," I said.

Since it was after hours, we needed either a room key or a code to get into the Howard Johnson's. After a couple of cigarettes and hopeful foreheads pressed up to the glass door, we started to punch in codes randomly. It took only seconds to discover that 1-2-3-4 worked.

We four girls walked through the hotel together, giggling, until we found the room. The door was open to the party inside. We made an awkward entrance, said some hellos, and then stood around with a bunch of other people. We tried to act natural, but before long they realized that we, or at least I, had come only to take pictures, and they kicked us out.

I didn't pick up on what the band was insinuating by inviting girls to check out their hotel room after hours, so I didn't entirely get what had happened, or why two of my friends stayed. But I did know enough not to say a word about it to my husband.

"I think that's enough," he said one day soon after. "You've had your time to explore. It's been more than a year."

He had given me a chance to have fun, and now it was time for me to toe the line. But what did he want me to do differently? He had already asked me to give up smoking, and I had, no questions asked. But other than that, I was not sure what I was doing wrong.

I had found a part-time job at a daycare in Rolla, which I loved: I got so excited about arts and crafts that I bought my own materials for crafts, which meant that each day, the kids went home with a new masterpiece. It was my first job, my first paycheck, and what seemed like my first taste of responsibility and adulthood. The kids were engaged and happy, the parents were thrilled, and we were all having enough fun that it did not seem to matter that I was doing most of the kids' work for them. The thrill of my first job lasted until one of my students, a mentally challenged child, bit me one day, drawing blood. I was absolutely fine, but when my husband got home and heard about it, he told me I was not allowed to go back.

I quit my job over the phone, without even a day's notice, after only a month of work. To this day, it is one of the most unprofessional things I have ever done.

"Not tonight" my husband would say if I told him I had plans to go out after dinner. If he did let me go, he would insist that I be home by a certain time. That restriction would stay in place for the rest of my marriage.

It was not precisely that he was conservative; he just did not know how to relax into our new life without completely losing me. Seeing me change so fast made his world feel more uncertain. He didn't know what to do, other than hold on tighter. But the more he tried to control me, the more I craved freedom. It would become a vicious circle for both of us.

About a year after our wedding, I returned to Yemen for one last party, a celebration called the *shikma*. This is a bridal shower, but held after the wedding so the bride can smoke *shisha*, a water pipe with fruit tobacco, and chew *qat*, things women are not allowed to do before marriage.

I had changed so much since I had been in America, but as I looked out at the walls of Sana'a's Old City through the window of my parents' beloved old Volvo, my married life felt like a dream. For the first time in longer than I could remember, I felt something other than claustrophobia. The entire city seemed refreshed, somehow. The multicolored stained-glass arches that framed nearly every home's windows seemed brighter. The smells of my city—frankincense, jasmine flowers, and hookah pipes—were sweeter, pulling me deep into old memories that I might otherwise have lost forever. *Sana'a is beautiful,* I thought. *She is proud, she is strong, she is me.*

It had taken leaving Yemen for me to truly understand how much I loved it.

I arrived with gifts for everyone I knew, all of whom dropped by. I hugged my grandmother tightly and told her how much I had missed her. Laughing, she headed right into the kitchen to get me a snack, as if I had never gone away.

As I settled into life back in my home country, I realized something: Now that I was married, my father didn't say as much about my comings and goings. If he ever questioned something, I told him I had my husband's permission; if my husband ever asked about the propriety of seeing this person or going out with that one, I told him my father was aware. All month long, I did as I pleased.

My friends hung on to my descriptions of America, just as I would have if the tables had been turned. I was surprised by my reaction to the lack of personal space in Yemen. I had become used to the American way, where a bit of distance was a sign of respect, and I liked it better.

When I had left Yemen, my girlfriends and I were still girls. Now that many of us were married, we could experience together the "real life" that had awaited us on the other side of marriage. We could chew *qat*, smoke hookah pipes, and wear makeup like all the other married women. I told my friends I would not be chewing *qat*; it was disgusting.

"Give it one year, Zahra," my friend Eman said. "Once you come back to Yemen, you will realize there is nothing else for us to do. Enjoy your American life while you can, because here, we are dying a slow death from boredom."

Sitting for hours every day, chewing *qat* and having the same conversations with the same people, seemed mind-numbing to me. My friends still had full awareness of themselves and their routines, but they were simply unable to change any of it. Women had a place in society, and you either conformed or you were left out. Slashing the days with *qat* was a way to tolerate the redundant and enraging ride that kept them in the passenger seat of their lives, a bumpy, nauseating, crowded ride about which they had little say; they didn't even have a good view. I empathized with them and understood why they did what they did, and yet, as someone who has always had an inability to sit still, I turned my nose up at the thought of doing the same.

While in Yemen, I wore the hijab, just as I had before I left. One of my friends asked if I also wore the hijab in America. When I told her no, she asked why, with curious eyes: "Is there a different God here that doesn't live there?" I was flooded with shame. *I need to do better,* I thought. When my husband drove up to meet me at the arrivals area of the St. Louis airport, I was out in front with my head covered.

"No," he said, as he loaded my bags into the trunk. He reminded me of the reason Muslim women covered themselves in the first place. The tradition comes from a long-ago time when women were considered property and traded as such. The hijab was a way to signal a woman's worth and remove her from being simply an object of lust. It showed she was someone to be respected.

"It is no longer necessary," he insisted, glancing up at the rearview mirror and then switching lanes. "The world has changed. Women are treated as they should be—especially here in America."

Did he not see the contradiction in ordering his respected, liberated wife to act differently than she wanted to? He didn't say anything further, so I figured I'd give *him* the chance to treat me with respect. "You can't tell me what to do," I said.

"Then you can go out by yourself. I won't go anywhere with you," he said. Which I did, for a few days, until I grew tired of being stared at. I wanted to feel like I belonged, not more out of place, so the hijab went back into my hand luggage, right next to my disappointment in myself, until the next trip back home.

CHAPTER NINE

About a month before my wedding, my father had discovered a strange growth on the ring finger of his left hand. He had chosen not to do anything about it just then, knowing how subpar the medical treatment was in Yemen, a country that spends only a fraction of its total budget on health care for its citizens. In Yemen, anybody who could make a sign was able to hang out a shingle and, with no education, practice medicine. So he waited for a business trip to India to have the growth removed in what should have been a simple procedure. Instead, the wound got infected, and the pain became a constant distraction. I told him he needed to see a doctor and have it examined, and he promised he would.

While on another business trip in Bonn, Germany, a few weeks later, my father walked into the lobby of his hotel and ran right into my mother. Her boss at the United Nations Development Programme had set up an appointment with an orthopedic surgeon he knew at the university clinic in Bonn, and she had flown all the way to Germany without telling my father to make sure he went.

He was frustrated by the fuss and reluctantly went for tests. The hospital kept him overnight for a biopsy, and the surgeon returned with the news that it was osteosarcoma—bone cancer. Three fingers and most of his palm would need to be removed.

"*Alhamdulillah*," said my father.

The surgeon was surprised to learn what the word meant. "Most people curse God when they hear news like this," he said. "They don't praise him."

Just as my grandmother had taught me the power of *Alhamdulillah*, she had also taught my father. Problems big or small are opportunities to prove yourself, to get stronger, and to live life to the fullest. I can hear her talking to my father in that moment. *Be grateful, Anwar: you have your wife, your daughter, and money to pay for your treatment, and the sun is shining.*

While my father focused on gratitude, my mother was so worried she called practically everyone she knew. Two hours later, the phone rang in her hotel room. It was my father's old boss, with the news that my father had been appointed to a post at Yemen's embassy in Bonn. He would be second in charge after the ambassador. My father couldn't possibly work, my mother said, reiterating the aggressive treatment schedule. She felt so much relief when she heard the terms of the contract. The implication was clear: there was no expectation that my father would put in an hour of work while in Bonn, and complete assurance that his checks would clear no matter what. He had served his country wholeheartedly, and now his country was returning the favor. My father, who had struggled with his decision to take his family back to Yemen for so many years, finally found peace with it.

They told me only that my father had been appointed to the embassy. As this was a dream of his, and a great career move, I was so happy for him. My parents stayed in Germany for over a year while my father had the surgery followed by thirteen rounds of chemotherapy. For each session, he was in the hospital for a week. At first, I knew nothing about his condition.

I didn't think much about the way his voice trailed off on the phone. He had always been a man of relatively few words. He did react with enthusiasm to the news of my success at Metro Business College, and to the idea that I might take a few classes at the university. I asked him what he thought I should study. Computer science, he told me: "That is the way of the future." My father, not knowing anything about computers, knew enough to see that writing on the wall.

One day, a couple of months after my parents moved to Germany, I came home to find my husband sitting at the table with a nervous look on his face.

"Surprise," he said, handing me an envelope with two round-trip tickets to Germany. I threw my arms around him and began dancing around with excitement. I raced to the phone to call my parents with the news.

My mother acted surprised but later told me about the New Year's Eve fireworks that would be near the basement apartment they were renting—in a beautiful part of town, near a lot of restaurants and shopping. Their landlords would be away on holiday and had generously offered to let us stay at their house.

I do not think I have ever been as happy as I was standing in front of their door, holding a bouquet of yellow flowers we had bought at the airport. When my mother answered, I wondered why she looked so tired. Then I looked past her and saw my father. My heart froze. He was so thin and pale. He had no hair, no eyelashes.

We come into the world believing our parents' presence will forever be a stable cornerstone in our lives. As if they were immortal and untouchable. This man had met the Pope and countless kings and heads of state. My father had always been larger than life to me, but now, I was terrified by the sight of him. "What is happening?" I asked. Looking down, I saw the tight bandage around his strangely shaped hand. His hand was mostly gone. I didn't know what cancer was, had never seen it, not in real life or in my limited access to television in Yemen.

I saw the concern in my husband's eyes, but the expression on his face was even. He knew. "You *knew* my father was sick?" My rage knew no bounds. I felt betrayed—by all of them. Why had they decided to let me find out this way?

"We didn't want you to worry," my mother said, which was little comfort to me.

"Do you think that's anyone else's decision to make?" I shouted. "You decided that you'd treat me like a two-year-old?" My husband echoed the argument that they were taking care of me, but I had never felt so isolated in my life. I started to cry.

"Zahra," my mother began.

"You had no right," I said. "I am his daughter. You had no right to keep this from me." But when I saw the exhaustion in her face, the fight went out of me. I realized the burden my mother had been carrying for so long—how hard it must have been for her to care for him by herself. As always, my mother sacrificed and the rest of us took. I reached out for her hand.

We stayed in Germany for three weeks, and our family rang in 1989 together from the stoop of the building. There were fireworks above us, and crowds of people from the typically quiet street greeted the future with noisemakers and bottles of beer and champagne. For one short moment, all was right with the world. It was enough to prompt me to make my own wishes, for a year filled with people, light, and happiness.

I felt such an incredible feeling of loss when we left the next morning. I hated being so far away from my parents, both physically and emotionally. I wanted to talk with them about the ways my husband and I had begun drifting apart: the more I was able to identify and articulate what I wanted, the more I learned it was not what he wanted.

I wanted to ask my mother if this was normal. What was the adjustment period until a marriage felt right? I had nothing to compare my feelings to. I didn't know what a more modern relationship should look like, or how happy I should expect to be.

My father took my hand as we were leaving and told me to get a good education. He was realizing I needed to have the ability to take care of myself, in case anything happened to him. He told me again that he'd heard computers were the future, and that he thought I really should study computers. He didn't know much else about it.

Maybe my sadness about leaving came from some sense of what my parents were still holding back from me—and what I would not find out until long after my father was in good health again. The fact was that the doctors had given him only six months to live. Everyone had conspired to arrange my visit because they thought it would be the last time I saw him.

Luckily, my father is a warrior.

"We'll be home soon," my mother assured me. It felt like cold comfort after she had refused my offer to stay. "Go back. Be with your husband. It's the right thing for both of you," she said.

I relented that day, but it was the start of a lifetime of pushing back if others attempted to have too big an influence on my life. I vowed that I would never again willingly let anyone make a decision for me. I would never again be in a position where someone else could withhold anything that would affect my life: not love, not money, and not time.

CHAPTER TEN

There was no son in our family to make my father proud; it was up to me. I began the computer science program at the University of Missouri–Rolla that winter only to realize how much I hated programming. Much of the work involved hours writing long strings of code; if I missed a single letter or space, the pages of code I'd labored over would not work. Computer science is all or nothing—zeroes or ones—and it lives and dies by the tiniest details, which, along with math, never were my strength.

My so-called adult life had not taken the shape I had imagined. I was struggling to learn programming, to learn calculus, and to learn how to manage my marriage. I began to wonder whether it might be time for us to start a family. I had long worried that I might have a hard time getting pregnant. My favorite aunt, Rukiya, could not have children, and my mother could not have any more babies after I was born.

Once my father's tribe discovered this, they had strongly suggested he take a second wife who could give him a son. My father had refused the idea, sacrificing a goat for forgiveness to the tribal council rather than following their decree. "This woman stood by me when I had nothing," he had said. "Do you think I will disrespect her when I have everything?"

But I hated being an only child, so I wanted to have many children—and I wanted to have them quickly. Now was as good a time as any to start.

Besides, a baby would also be a way out of computer programming classes. I didn't want to disappoint my father by changing my career course, didn't really know what I would do instead, and wanted to give him the son he never had. All good reasons to have a child, said my still-childish brain. Today, I wonder at that. We need to take a class and pass a test to get a driver's license, but there are no requirements to be a parent.

My husband and I tried, in those days, to take summer school classes in another university town so we could see more of the country. We spent our first summer in Kansas City. For our second, we went to Tyler, Texas, a small conservative town where the residents drove across the street to the next county for beer every Friday night. One Friday night in Tyler, new friends took us out to Main Street—to "a parade" that happened each week, they told us.

We stood there in complete shock as the KKK made their way across town with white hoods and burning crosses. The police stood around, and the town's African American residents went casually about their business. I could not understand how this wonderful place had people with hate in their hearts. America was full of such surprising contrasts for me. On one hand, it really was a place of welcome and success. On the other hand, something dark seemed to be simmering under its very bright star. I was confused. America didn't seem to be the land of the free after all, and even here, fitting in was not a given. Would I ever find a place where I belonged?

We were living in Tyler when I learned I was pregnant. My husband, surprisingly, was unsure about the news. He had wanted to graduate and find a job first. We hadn't had enough time to enjoy life, he said. We were still students and not yet set up in the way he wanted us to be. However, all I focused on was calling my parents, now back in Yemen, with the happy news. I was only nineteen, still trying to find my own way to adulthood, never mind motherhood. I was more excited for my parents than for myself.

My excitement about being pregnant dissolved the same way everything else seemed to at that time, and the first five months of my pregnancy were unbelievably difficult. I was so nauseated that I began retching as soon as I opened my eyes and did not stop until I closed them. I was losing weight, and the waves of sickness were so constant that I did not want to go anywhere or do anything. My husband tried to help, but he was so buried in his university classes and so unsure of what to do that any attempt from him only made me angry. He had a life outside of our bathroom, which seemed to be where I spent most of my time, with my head in the toilet bowl.

All his efforts backfired, like the time I threw up all over the dashboard and the front seat of the car when he tried to take me out for some fresh air.

In addition to nausea and dizziness, I also had gestational diabetes, which meant I needed to follow a very restricted diet. This left me only mildly irritable on my *good* days. I began attracting stares everywhere I went at school. While it was completely normal to have a first child at age nineteen in Yemen, I seemed to be the only pregnant student at the University of Missouri.

I felt hungry and exhausted, I had severe sciatica pain in my lower back, and if I had ever had any kind of filter, it was now completely gone. "I'm not getting into this goddamn car," I yelled at my husband, glaring at the Miata's low seat and holding my aching back. Two weeks later, he came home and showed me our brand-new silver Honda Civic, the replacement for his much-loved sports car. I was grateful, but only slightly—a seat that was a few more inches off the ground was still difficult to get into.

Very late in my pregnancy, we were at home making dinner when "America bombs Iraq" flashed on the screen. We looked on with horror as we watched the future of the Middle East change before our very eyes.

The American position was that they had warned Saddam Hussein and were preparing for war. We heard a different story from Yemen: the Kuwaitis were stealing Iraqi oil, and the Iraqis had been justified in invading Kuwait. Yemen sided with Iraq—the only Arab country besides Jordan to do that. That was the beginning of the end for my beautiful country. The Saudis retaliated, swiftly and harshly. They expelled the three million Yemenis who worked in Saudi Arabia, mostly in construction, cleaning, and other service jobs, and who sent home money to support their families. They returned to Yemen with no money and no job prospects—a devastating blow to our economy, which collapsed overnight.

We watched the destruction of Iraq on American TV, and then, on the phone, we heard about the heart-shattering destruction of our country in turn.

In the weeks that followed, we began to feel a kind of chill among our usually friendly neighbors. Hate crimes against Arabs drastically increased. Some Muslim students were attacked; so was a Sikh boy who was mistaken for a Muslim. The ignorance of racism is so revealing and easily evident. Hate doesn't care about the truth—it never has.

The situation was escalating, and quickly. Countries took sides, ground troops lined up, and Iraq started burning. My mother told me they could smell the smoke all the way in Yemen.

I was willing my baby not to come until my mother arrived to help, and I asked her to pray that my water would break about one second later. She was still in the air, almost to St. Louis, when I had a meeting with a professor to discuss the results of an exam. Before I reached his office, I took a bad fall on some ice near campus. The baby was fine; only my backside was bruised. And my ego.

As embarrassed as I was that students had rushed to help me, I was even more embarrassed by the effort it took them to get me back on my feet. The professor asked me when I was due, and when I said that day, he told me to go home: "This meeting is done."

A week after my mother arrived, the baby was still stubbornly not coming out, and I called my doctor. "I need to have this baby today, please," I said. I told him that my mother was only visiting for a month. She had to go back to work, I didn't know how to take care of a baby, I was only a child myself, and I needed her help. I pulled out all the stops—and a few tears—and a couple of hours later we were all in the hospital, my delivery induced and an epidural situated.

"This is a world away from where you were born," marveled my mother, as she looked around at the bright lights, the sterile equipment, and the drip of blessed medication flowing steadily into my veins.

An epidural is a magical gift to women. The doctors gave me a button to press whenever I felt the pain coming, and I kept pressing the button as insurance, to make sure the pain never came. With ease and speed, our tiny daughter, Amani, was born. She had gray eyes, fair skin, and blond hair.

My husband joked with the nurses: "Are you sure she is ours?"

My baby girl opened her eyes to three anxious adults watching over her. This moment was unforgettable. There is no time I would want to belong to as much as the one that made me a mother to this sweet face. I felt needed, wanted, and somehow more myself.

We named her Amani, which in Arabic means desires, aspirations, and wishes; in Swahili, it means harmony and peace.

Seeing my mother gingerly hold my daughter for the first time, I thought about how devastating the loss of my brother was to her—how overly careful she was with me. I now had a new perspective on my parents' fierce protectiveness and a new understanding of a parent's love for a child. I knew I would fight to the death before any harm would come to my baby girl.

My husband jumped into fatherhood with both feet. He even suggested not having any more children: he loved this child so much he didn't want to share the love with anyone else. Since he had to go back to school almost immediately, he envied the time that my mother, Amani, and I were spending together while he was in class. He fought for every moment he could get with his girl.

My mother and I weren't allowed to bathe her until he got home. He insisted that we would drown her if he was not around. *He* had to be the one to hold up his girl while my mother tried to wash her little body around his hands.

Eventually, my mother had to leave. I knew I would miss her, but more importantly, I was scared of being alone with Amani. Every time I breastfed her, she choked; milk seemed to come out of half a dozen different holes, and I was convinced I was going to kill her.

Amani's doting father was gone for five hours, driving my mother to the St. Louis airport. Anxious, I decided I would wait to feed Amani until he got back. My baby cried with hunger for two hours before I caved and fed her. She promptly choked, just as I was afraid she would, and after a moment of pure panic, I handled it in the same way my mother had: calmly patting her back until she took a deep breath again.

I happily realized we were going to be okay.

However, I was extremely overprotective. I still am. You would think that no other parents had children in this world. Our pediatrician, Dr. Brown, was on speed dial; I called him every single time Amani coughed, sneezed, hiccupped, cried, or even breathed a little funny. Meanwhile, her father was also placing his own late-night calls to the doctor; sometimes he didn't trust my relaying of a message and wanted to hear it from the doctor himself.

One morning, in a panic, I bundled Amani up and took her to Dr. Brown's office so he could see the terrible rash she had woken up with. Already familiar with our family's drama, the doctor took off all of Amani's clothes and handed her back to me with just a diaper on. "Please go home, and please put the rest of this stuff in a drawer," he said. "It is eighty-five degrees outside. She has heat rash." As he walked me out, he added, "There's no need to call me every five minutes; she will be fine." We agreed on a new plan: unless it was a real emergency, I would write down my questions and come to see him once a week.

Amani had colic, and like all colicky babies, she cried at the same time every day. She would start crying around six in the evening and wouldn't let up until midnight. By the end of each stretch, my nerves were shot. My husband started staying at school every night to study and didn't come home until after midnight; most of our neighbors, fellow students, followed the same routine.

"You see these dark circles?" my downstairs neighbor asked me at the mailbox one day.

"I know, I'm sorry." I shook my head apologetically. But I laughed to myself as I walked back up the stairs. I had come quite a long way since the sleep-deprived pilot had asked me the same question the morning after my wedding.

Right around Amani's six-month birthday, I realized I was pregnant again. My first feeling was panic—I was not ready for another baby. We had been talking about returning to Yemen. Since we had the privilege of going to school in the United States because of a scholarship from our country, my husband wanted to go home and pay his country back in service. The conversation changed a bit once I found out I was pregnant: we wanted our baby to have American citizenship like her sister. We thought it would improve her chances in life, so we would wait.

He accepted an internship in Dallas at a prominent oil company that had been working in Yemen since the early 1980s, and we loaded our Walmart furniture into a U-Haul. Juggling baby bags, my purse, a car seat, and a stroller—and, miraculously, Amani—I took a flight instead.

In Dallas, we found our first taste of prejudice, something we hadn't felt in Rolla. The majority of white people treated us like undocumented immigrants, and most immigrants didn't like us because we were not like them.

The sun was hot and unrelenting, the air was dry, and almost nothing about the place was as welcoming as Missouri had been. In addition, my body had not had time to recover from the last pregnancy, so the pounds were piling on.

Huge, thick black stretch marks snaked across my back and my thighs. The gestational diabetes came back with a vengeance, but this time I refused to diet, convinced that the blisters on Amani's thumbs from her sucking on them at birth were the result of the hunger I had put her through in utero.

I was exhausted, and I had a very colicky, very active nine-month-old who was already crawling, standing on furniture, trying to talk, and getting into a lot of trouble. She slipped out of her tied-tight stroller and disappeared into a shopping mall for ten heart-stopping minutes; she ate a live Texas-size cockroach.

She smiled, and my heart melted.

The truth is, I don't remember much but the bad from my year in Dallas, except for that smile.

When I was four months pregnant, I began to dilate; my new doctor ordered bed rest, and I developed a newfound love for other people's lives in the form of TV soap operas, introduced to me by Peggy. I bought her a plane ticket to come out to visit—her first time out of state and on a plane. Though we did a bit of sightseeing, at my insistence, we spent most of our time on the couch, watching television. Peggy was perfectly happy to not miss her beloved soap operas.

The Young and the Restless, *The Bold and the Beautiful*, *Guiding Light*, and *As the World Turns*. I lost myself in the fictional towns as she told me the storylines: the candlelight conversations and clandestine affairs, the births and marriages, funerals and divorces, crimes of passion. It was pure escapism, like the Harlequin romance novels I used to sneak out of the bazaars or the London bookshops all the way to my childhood bedroom, to read again and again.

Comparison to a life that was so made up and unreal makes your own seem so boring. I wanted to be free in the way these women were. Confident and funny. Capable and no-nonsense and wholly, effortlessly glamorous.

I often felt like the exact opposite of that. The freedom I found in driving my own car became complicated now that I lived in a vast city connected by massive highways I was too afraid to drive on. Before getting behind the wheel, I scrutinized maps, scribbling out turn-by-turn directions and often choosing the most circuitous route so I would not have to drive on a highway. At home, I fought a losing battle with red ants and an increasingly dirty house.

Long gone were the days of obsessively cleaning every inch of my world, as I had when Amani was first born.

We were still on a tight budget, since we were living off one salary and paying the Missouri hospital in monthly installments for the cost of Amani's birth. My doctor at the clinic told us we qualified for food stamps, and I filled out an application.

I will never forget standing, in those pre–debit card days, hot and sweaty and hugely pregnant, at the checkout of our local Piggly Wiggly, my grocery cart full of food and a screaming baby on my hip, handing over my driver's license so the cashier could verify my check.

The cashier looked at the food stamps, the big red MINOR stamped across my license, my pregnant stomach, and Amani with a look of such disdain that I resolved that from then on, I would pay for my groceries and leave the food stamps for those who really needed them.

I would rather have starved than have anyone look at me like that again.

My mother-in-law came to visit us, bringing her own baby— my daughter's uncle—with her. Her pregnancy had been a huge surprise to all of us, and we had learned about it only a few weeks before Wan was born. She had been too embarrassed to tell us that she was also pregnant. Her baby was only twenty days older than mine.

Sharing parenting adventures with my mother-in-law was a dynamic I hadn't expected. We had seen pictures of Wan—a big, beautiful boy with enormous eyes, the longest, thickest lashes, and puppy-dog cheeks—so we had tried to prepare her for the fact that Amani was a quarter of his size. I knew they would think we were not feeding her enough, or caring for her properly. Sure enough, right after she arrived, I overheard her as she talked to my father-in-law on the phone: "They weren't lying. Amani is the size of a *shusa*," using the word for "splinter" in Arabic.

As I got to know my mother-in-law outside of the drama of our wedding planning, I realized she was kind, wise, adventurous, and very smart—a wonderful woman for whom I have a world of respect. Though she never learned to read or write, she was used to navigating Sana'a's markets with ease. She brought that same confidence with her every other new place she went, inspiring me to be more adventurous and courageous. I always have wondered, had she had the opportunity, what amazing things would she have done with her life?

As my due date approached, I took Amani to the mall near our house to pick up a few things for the new baby. I was walking through the mall when a gorgeous woman passed. I don't know what it was about her that made me take notice, but I can still see her in my mind's eye, as if it were a scene in a film playing out in slow motion. She was tall and thin, with waist-length dark hair; she strode past me effortlessly, her long legs clad in a pair of perfectly tight black leather pants and high, high heels. She carried a single shopping bag with complete confidence.

Still thinking about her, I caught a glimpse of myself reflected in a store window. Makeup was a thing of the past, my glasses were smudged with baby handprints, and my hair was a frizzy mess. My maternity dress was a size 16. I was a prisoner in a body I didn't recognize, as though I had mistakenly wandered into the wrong dream. I kept walking toward Toys "R" Us, trying to ignore the tears that wanted to escape from behind my oversized glasses.

The uncomfortable wait for the baby to come became even more so, physically and especially emotionally. I was worried I would not love this new baby as much as I loved Amani. How could I possibly have the capacity? My heart was already full with a love for my child that seemed so complete and overwhelming. I tossed and turned, worried about this baby and what life for my child would be like.

All my worry vanished seconds after I saw my little Hanadi. She came four weeks early and weighed almost nine pounds. Giving birth to her consisted of a thirty-minute stint in the delivery room and a couple of almost painless pushes. I held her in my arms and learned that a mother's love for all her children has no bounds. Hanadi, whose name means beautiful, captivating scent, had the sweetest face and the thickest shock of black hair. She found a space in my heart that was as big as the one her sister held.

Unlike Amani's colicky first year, Hanadi was a happy baby who slept all day. The running joke in our family was that Amani, blond with gray eyes, looked like an angel, and Hanadi, with her cute chubby cheeks and sleepy smile, acted like one.

When Amani was born, her father had been a student with a flexible schedule; now he was working long hours, trying to prove himself. Exhausted from erratic sleep patterns, I was simply unable to reconcile the needs of two little babies and my own twenty-one-year-old needs. My defenses were up, always. Either he and I argued over every detail of our lives or he had nothing to say to me and we spent days at a time not talking to each other.

I had no desire to discuss my unhappiness with anyone, not even myself. My husband was my husband—there was no point in instigating a conversation with that as the only conclusion. The divide between us triggered waves of arguments, until we became two people who could not recognize each other.

We were good people; we just weren't good together.

Starved for companionship in Dallas, I had been thrilled when, one day while I was still pregnant, my childhood friend Salwa called our house. She had married and moved to Washington, D.C., with her new husband. Though our experiences were quite different, and we lived nowhere near each other in the United States, it felt like we were companions on a strange adventure. I was so happy to hear her voice.

"Salwa called today!" I told my husband, excitedly, when he got home from work. "After the baby comes, we're going to go visit her in Washington."

"We are not," he said, and informed me that I was not allowed to talk with her anymore. Other people saw Salwa as a "bad girl." Just one wrong move in Yemen gave girls a reputation they could never shake, even something as harmless as smiling at a boy. Salwa was bolder and braver than I was, taking risks and going after what she wanted in a society where freedom was harder and harder to find. I had always seen her as a badass. I was furious to hear in his voice the same judgmental obsession with reputation that I knew so well and fought so hard against.

But now I was too tired to fight. It was hard enough just to deal with the laundry. Salwa, and my indignation, dropped off my priority list.

This sounds like denial, and for a long time, it was. But filing my feelings and frustrations away was also a coping mechanism—I didn't realize it at the time, but this kind of compartmentalization was a saving grace.

Eventually, I needed to face reality. My mother had come to Dallas briefly for Hanadi's birth, and I missed her and her loving help. "I can't take care of the girls on my own anymore," I told my husband one night, not long after she left. "I want my mother, and I'm tired of fighting with you. We both need a break. I'm going home." He agreed with an evident relief that made me resent him more.

I prepared to leave, trying to anticipate what I would need back in Yemen. Hanadi was only forty days old; my mind kept coming back to the lack of adequate health care. The available medical supplies in Yemen were usually either expired or made in China and of questionable quality. The same brand of baby formula had a completely different ingredient list depending on whether it came from a shelf in Texas or in Yemen—even though it was manufactured in the same factory. We loaded what seemed like an entire pharmacy into suitcases. We bought a year's supply of diapers and baby formula and shipped those too.

The pediatrician gave me vaccine vials so I could keep the girls on schedule. I carried the tuberculosis vaccine in ice and stowed it in the airplane's refrigerator during the flight home.

On my final day in the United States, I went out for a long drive by myself. I didn't know when I would be behind the wheel of a car again. I was running away from my new life by going back to my old one. Yemen was calling, and I had to accept that along with its siren song was the sound of its shackles.

CHAPTER ELEVEN

Some things remained the same at home: my grandmother still served my favorite breakfast of fried liver with onions and tomatoes and *khubz*, the fire-roasted bread she made every day. She made me my favorite shrimp chips and *khameer*. Only now she was caring for two generations. She was smitten from the moment she laid eyes on Hanadi; my baby girl slept in her bed with her and was constantly by her side. I never asked why her connection with my younger daughter was so strong. Perhaps it was because my grandma felt useful, needed in a way she had not been in recent years. I was just grateful for it.

Amani had spent the first year and a half of her life in the relative comfort and ease of America, spoiled by my visiting in-laws as the first girl in the family. Hanadi did not have clean doctors' waiting rooms or air conditioning, but as I watched my grandma rock her, touching her soft head and singing, I understood that she had more.

Between my grandma, my mother, and Olivia, who had been my nanny and was now my children's, I had plenty of childcare for the girls and opportunities to leave the house, and so I did. Once again, no one told me what to do or asked where I was going. I was my husband's responsibility, and he was not here to monitor my behavior. I spent most of my days with my girlfriends, chewing *qat* and smoking.

I resisted at first: the act and the taste of *qat* seemed so repulsive to me, and during my time in the United States I had become much more health-conscious. I watched herders knock over garbage bins in order to feed the goats that we then ate and fed to our children. I knew that the chemicals sprayed on the *qat* trees were no longer even manufactured in the United States, let alone used there.

I sterilized everything and made my children brush their teeth with bottled water, not trusting anything that came out of the tap. Nothing seemed clean enough or good enough. Studies coming out of Jordan had found that cancer rates among Yemenis—especially throat, mouth, and stomach cancers—were much higher than average. And yet, in my mind, I had no choice but to give in when it came to *qat*.

Was I trying to fit in again, or was I looking for an escape? It didn't matter, because my friend Eman was both right and wrong. She was right in telling me I would succumb to peer pressure and a way out of the incredible boredom of life in Yemen for its women, and she was wrong that it would take me a year. It took exactly two months.

We sat indoors for hours, often with little or no ventilation because of the superstition that if you chew *qat* in a drafty room, you could get sick. The majority of women smoked: cigarettes, a *shisha*, or a *madaa*, a water pipe with tobacco. I started smoking again too. It seemed no worse than inhaling the secondhand smoke—and at least smoking kept my hands busy, if not my mind.

Chewing *qat* affects people differently. Many people feel happier; when I chewed, I became uncommunicative and quiet. I went home to my children reeking of smoke and not wanting to engage. When I spit the bundle of chewed-up leaves out of the back of my cheek at the end of the night, I'd gag, spilling the *qat* and most of my dinner into the toilet.

Throwing up usually made me feel better. And I did not mind that the baby weight was falling off much faster than might seem healthy.

My ability to come and go as I pleased lasted almost a year, until my husband's contract in Texas was up and he returned to Yemen.

At first, we moved in with his family, as is customary. Only, in our case, it was temporary. My father-in-law bought us a house in a newly developing suburb south of Sana'a, Al-Asbahi. The new house was remote and surrounded by mounds of dirt, with mountains in the background and no phone lines yet. This landscape was the norm in Yemen, a dry, dusty place where you might have to drill a thousand feet to find water.

The most distinctive feature of our mostly uninhabited new neighborhood was the presidential palace right across the street. An eight-lane paved road—one of the only well-maintained roads in the whole country—lay like a canyon between us.

Once we moved in, my husband would take our car to work and not come back until evening. I spent most of my time at home with the girls. And while we had lots of people in the house, I couldn't talk to the driver, the guard at the gate, or the gardeners because they were men. All of the kitchen and housekeeping help were Somali and didn't speak Arabic. I was so lonely and bored.

What we did have were some foreign television stations, courtesy of the big satellite dish on our roof. I spent my days in front of the TV. The girls and I would flip channels to whatever limited options we could find. Every afternoon we got Latin American soap operas that were absolutely not age-appropriate for my girls, but we watched them because the only other option was nothing at all.

The lack of control I felt was magnified by the political situation, which seemed more and more precarious. The unification of North and South Yemen had happened in 1990. There were high hopes at first, but none of the promises, pledges, and accords between the two sides—the former backed by Saudi Arabia; the latter, also known as the People's Democratic Republic of Yemen, by the Soviet Union—were honored, creating an unsteady balance of power.

The medical system had not improved in the time I had been away. I went to the local clinic thinking the doctor would chart my girls' growth the same way Amani's had been charted. I still had their medical booklets from the States, and I wanted to fill in the new growth details. But during the appointment, when I mentioned measuring Hanadi's head circumference, the way they did in America, the doctor said, "You want us to measure what?" When I insisted that the baby be weighed, the nurse walked away and returned much later with a filthy-looking scale she had finally found under a bed in the guardhouse.

I told them both I'd changed my mind, wrapped my girls up, and went home wondering how I was going to manage if anything actually went wrong. I didn't have to wait long to find out.

My mother arranged for the UN doctor to visit the house to give the girls the vaccines I'd brought over from Dallas, as Amani's tuberculosis vaccine was now due. My happiness that the vaccine could be administered in our home turned to terror that night when her arm swelled up with a lump the size of an egg. The site near the injection looked angry and red. Panicked, my mother made another phone call to the exclusive clinic the oil companies funded for their employees and got us an appointment there. I was not entitled to go to the clinic, as I was merely a Yemeni citizen, but my mother and her magical connections came through for me the same way they had my entire life.

Tuberculosis is a live vaccine, which means part of the virus is introduced into the body. Amani was just eighteen months old—and given her reaction, the doctors said the virus would move into her lungs and probably kill her. Dr. Veerman, the Dutch doctor at the clinic, asked me to hold Amani tight, and so I wrapped my arms around her little body. Before I knew what was happening, he sliced into the swollen red injection site with a sharp scalpel, cutting almost to the bone for about four inches down her tiny arm. My body flooded with panic as Amani's eyes rolled back in her head, her lips turned blue, and she slumped against me.

"What did you just do?" I screamed.

They had to get the pus out as soon as possible, he told me calmly, as he unwrapped a roll of gauze and pushed it into the wound. "Do you think I am crazy, to put her under anesthesia in this country?" he said. He didn't have a way to save her if anything went wrong, he explained. As Amani's shock started to wear off, extreme pain set in. I could barely hold her down as she writhed in agony, tears pouring down both our faces.

The next day, Dr. Veerman's face scared me as he pulled out the gauze. The wound filled up with pus again as fast as he pressed it out. My father-in-law quickly arranged for us to fly to Germany that night. There, Amani was put under and her wound cleaned; she was put on large amounts of antibiotics that were almost too much for her tiny body to take and an adult dosage of the anti-tuberculosis drug, which she had to take for six months until we traveled back for a checkup and my baby girl finally got a clean bill of health.

My grandmother often urged me to spend time with her, and I tried to visit as much as I could. Since we did not have a phone in our house, I could not call her, but I made a point to stop in to check on her when I could—usually when I was out running other errands. I felt a particular urgency the week my parents were in London for the wedding of one of my cousins, Sabiha.

"Binti, I need you to come and spend time with me," my grandmother said. "I'm not going to live forever." She had said that so many times that week, I was starting to worry.

"Don't say that, Uma—you will live forever," I said. "Tomorrow is Friday, and I will come and spend the whole day, I promise."

I left our house early the next morning. But when I arrived at my family's house, all my uncles' cars were outside. "She is not well," my uncle Mahmood told me. "The doctor is with her now." Uma's pacemaker, which had been installed in London on a medical trip years earlier, was giving out, the doctor said. "There is not much we can do. Sana'a is not equipped for that kind of surgery, and neither is her body."

In a panic, I realized I needed more time with my grandma than I was going to get.

A few hours later, my mother appeared. Unbeknownst to all of us, she had left London a week before Sabiha's wedding. After talking to my grandmother on the phone, she told my father that something was not right and she needed to go home. All the family in London, my father and uncles and aunts, were upset with her. But my mother's instincts and heart have always been right. It was as if she knew my grandmother needed her to come back. Together, we sat with my grandmother for hours that felt like seconds. At four o'clock, for the fifth time, my grandmother tried to sit up and look for Hanadi. "What time is it? Did you give Hanadi her milk?"

"Don't worry, Uma, she's fine. I just fed her. Don't worry about her now, just get better," I said.

"My time is up, Binti," she said. I tried to soothe her, but she continued. "Take care of yourself and your daughters, Zahra.

They need you." My grandmother had never said a word to me about how much I was neglecting my daughters . . . until now. Two hours after that, she was gone, and I realized I owed her and my daughters much more than I had been giving them.

As fortunate as I was, in health, in family, and in material wealth, the dark recesses of my mind had a strong grip. I was depressed, but there was not much to be done about it. Searching for psychological help in Sana'a was inconceivable. The city did not even have a dialysis machine, let alone a shrink. Depression and anxiety were not pathologies that existed or would be addressed. "What do you mean, depressed? Get over yourself, people are starving. Say *Alhamdulillah*" would be the response from just about anybody. I realized I needed to get out of the house and out of my own head.

A government or corporate job was not a possibility, so I asked my mother for help. She knew the headmistress of a local school run by the Pakistani embassy; they were looking for English-speaking teachers. The headmistress could see I spoke English better than most in the country, so she didn't care about my lack of a degree. She hired me to teach a second-grade class.

I loved working and the sense of purpose it gave me, even if the circumstances were not ideal. My classroom was chaotic, overcrowded, and under-resourced: I had sixty students and only thirty desks. I was responsible for all the subjects—math, science, gym, music, Arabic, English, religion—with no background in teaching. It was a challenge, but I welcomed it. That said, "Kids, go play outside" was my curriculum for gym, music, and art. I had not been allowed to participate in gym class myself, and I had zero musical ability and no art supplies. My hands were tied.

My job at the Pakistani school was my first real taste of answering to someone outside my family. I learned how to organize a lesson and build a teaching plan—and so much more. I learned how to remain aware and understanding of both the weak students and the strong learners. How to communicate with, manage, and win over parents, students, and school administrators. How to earn people's respect through diligence, results, and, most of all, leadership.

Ultimately, the work was not enough to temper my growing sense of frustration. Parents complained that I was not as strict with religion and Arabic as I should be. And not strict enough in general. I refused to employ corporal punishment the way the other teachers did. Lacking a big stick, I had little power. However, using fear is the weakest way to motivate someone to learn. I had learned that lesson well from the bleeding palms of my own childhood.

"I think I have to quit my job," I told my friend Carina toward the end of the school year. "I'm not good at it." Carina was a beautiful Scottish woman married to a Yemeni man. She was smart, sassy, and full of fun and life. "I don't know how to bring so many kids along with me, and I don't know how to leave them behind. It's a losing battle."

"You should teach at YALI. You might have a better chance with adults and with more resources," Carina said, using the acronym for the Yemen-America Language Institute, a foreign-aid initiative of the U.S. State Department to help Yemenis learn English. "Your English is perfect," she said, "and they pay really well, and in U.S. dollars." It was one thing to get hired to work in an elementary school, but teaching adults on behalf of the U.S. State Department? I knew I was not qualified in any way. Yet when Carina introduced me to John Kincannon, the program director, I spread a thick layer of confidence over my uncertainty and talked my way into a job offer.

When my busy husband heard the news, he hesitated. This was not working at the Pakistani school with second graders; this was working with adults—mostly men, some from the oil and gas industry. Yet two thousand dollars a month was a king's ransom in Yemen. My father and husband *together* did not make that much. He gave the job his blessing.

I could not contain my excitement when, finally, my first morning at work came and I walked into the YALI building. It was furnished by the American embassy and had shelf after shelf of American supplies to which I had not had access before. But the students at YALI were older—and much less respectful than second graders.

That first day set a pattern that was repeated every new session: men walked into the classroom, took one look at me, and walked right back out again. Part of being a man in my culture meant not taking instructions from a young Yemeni woman—"Yemeni" being the operative word. A foreign woman would have been treated better.

John Kincannon intervened. He told each student who requested a different teacher to stay in my class for three days; if the student still wanted another teacher, he would oblige. To my delight, in all my time teaching there, only one man left after the three-day period ended.

My time at YALI taught me very quickly that if you want respect, you need to be tough. In this case, instead of scaring my students into submission, I created a set of unbendable rules. If you show up late for class, even by one minute, then you miss that class. Don't bother knocking on the door, because it will only lead to your missing the next class. Likewise, if you take too long on the ten-minute break, even by one minute, you have to wait outside until after class to collect your belongings. No compromises.

I didn't let students raise their hands to answer a question; I called on them. I made them work in groups, men and women. No separation in my class.

The rules were not fun, but my class was the most fun my students had ever had—it was so incredibly rewarding to see the shyness melt away from the women and the men alike. To see respect growing in their eyes for each other and for me, their female teacher.

I also discovered a whole world of propriety—and pitfalls—for working women. If you smile, it is an invitation. If you tell a joke, it is an invitation. Simply being myself was an invitation.

In my class of mostly men, a few were particularly tough to deal with. One afternoon, an older student with intense brown eyes put a Coke on my desk after the break. I looked him in the eye and said, "Thank you, but I am not thirsty." I knew that accepting a gift, even one as small as that, would be opening the door for him to take another step. He left it on my desk, insisting that I take it, and then came back up to my desk at the end of the class, angry that I did not drink it.

Refusing his gift amounted to rejection, and Arab men do not handle rejection well. Insecurity plays a big part, and so does society. Women are raised to fulfill the needs and egos of men, and men are raised to expect that.

In addition to working all day at his engineering job, my husband decided to moonlight as a small business owner, opening a costume jewelry store inside one of the new malls in Sana'a. He asked for my help with the merchandising, and while I was not able to travel to the markets, as he could, I could choose from among the samples he brought back from India and Turkey. I also designed the store interior, picking the colors, displays, logo, design, and carpet. It was my first attempt at entrepreneurship and marketing—and it was an utter failure.

Once the newspaper came off our windows and the shop opened, I stayed completely behind the scenes. It was not appropriate for women like me to participate or even go to the shop. I never met our employees. But even from the shadows, I learned a lot about building a business.

Unlike most of the other stores, which were crammed with goods, ours was minimalistic and classy, with bright white walls and single pieces of jewelry draped on rich navy velvet stands. I had picked the kind of jewelry I would wear, simple and under-stated. And I chose young, hip designer brands that were on the pricy side.

This was my first lesson in understanding your target audience. The shopping in Yemen consisted of stores crowded with cheap products made in China, busy hubs of haggling over prices. We had a sign on the window that said "Prices are set. No bargaining allowed." People only came into our shop to laugh at how little product we had and how expensive it was. They wondered at the lack of color and the high prices. Most Yemeni women could not afford what we had to sell, and the middle class to which we were attempting to cater did not seem to exist in a country that was growing more economically polarized by the day.

After a few months without sales, we shuttered the store, and our friends, family, and I had boxes upon boxes of jewelry to wear for a very long time.

Soon after we closed our doors, I learned I was pregnant again. A wall immediately went up in my mind; I was unable to even consider the possibility of having another child. I was twenty-three years old. I was raising two little girls in a society that didn't want them to succeed. Medical services were scarce, and our medical scares and the lack of educational opportunities made us terrified of what our children's future would look like. We were still trying to establish a normal life in Sana'a, and there was a growing sense that political stability and possibly even safety were in the past.

I simply could not imagine having another child in this country at this time, in the current climate. In secret, I researched doctors who would help. I do not even remember making the appointment. I went to a clinic where nobody knew who I was. I gave them a false name, and they didn't check my ID—they never did, as the majority of patients they saw had none.

My only real recollections of the procedure are the small, smelly, dark room and the searing bolt of fear that struck me when I saw the examining table, dirty and alone in the corner of the room, looking just how I felt at that moment.

When it was over, I was consumed by searing guilt. I felt hot and angry one minute, ice cold the next. Night and day, I thought about the baby I had not wanted to bring into this world. A gift given and then thrown away.

I had made a decision for my family but was completely overwhelmed by what I had done. What if God punished me by taking away one of my girls? I choked with fear and regret as I held my girls tighter. People say you forget and that time will heal the ache, but they don't know what they are talking about. You don't forget—and time is not that forgiving.

My grandmother began making regular visits to my dreams. In reality, my neat-as-a-pin grandmother had never been seen without her scarf and matching veil; beneath that fabric was a long, perfect braid that no one but me, in our shared room at night, ever saw. My grandmother was kind and gentle, never raising her voice to anyone, yet in my dream, her hair was wild, her arms were crossed, and she looked at me without saying a word.

Her look of intense disappointment caused me to wake up in a cold sweat, my heart filled with grief. I was navigating the harsh reality that *Alhamdulillah* can be difficult.

No matter how grateful I was for the life I had, and I did have so very much to be grateful for, I was also capable of making decisions that slapped that gratitude in the face.

I came to fear those dreams, and for years after that, I always knew when they were going to come: every time I stepped outside of the imaginary lines society had drawn for me.

By 1994, the political turmoil that many had long feared was reality: high-level resignations, serious governmental gridlock, and an increase in violent incidents from both government forces in the north and southern separatists. Rumors began to swirl that there could be a ground war in Sana'a, which terrified both sides of our family. Soldiers on the street could very well mean looting or indiscriminate acts of terror that no amount of class or clout could deflect. Hiding at home would be no assurance of safety.

My worried husband brought home an Uzi submachine gun and a handgun and said he wanted me to learn how to use them. I shot one in the garden, and the kickback dislocated my shoulder. I never picked up a gun again, the idea of shooting at a human impossible to consider.

We decided we would take the girls and leave the country for a while, until we knew how the situation would escalate or until things settled. We booked tickets to spend a month in Cairo; our flight was scheduled for the afternoon of May 4, 1994.

On that morning, around five, we awoke to an unfamiliar rumbling that shook the entire house. We jumped out of bed, and my husband went up to the roof to see what was happening. About a second later, he was back downstairs. "It has started," he said. The sound of explosions and shattering glass filled our ears.

That morning, we discovered the true purpose of the large paved road between our house and the president's: it was built for tanks and warplanes. Our house was in the middle of a military base—and next to the president's emergency runway.

We were at war with the south.

We ran into the girls' bedroom, where both Amani and Hanadi were awake and crying. We grabbed armfuls of bedding and raced downstairs to hide underneath the staircase—as far away from the breaking windows as we could get. We tried to distract the kids by arranging their pillows and stuffed animals into a little fort and telling stories of good times. When that didn't work, I started to play "war" with the girls. Surprisingly, that was more effective, and Hanadi started to laugh at every explosion.

Hours later, the explosions stopped, and we found shells and shrapnel scattered across our flat roof and our garden like the aftermath of a metal snowstorm. We later learned that when the north and the south had drawn their battle lines, southern forces had quickly set their sights on the presidential palace—one of the northern nerve centers. They launched a Scud missile, which triggered air defense artillery that, apparently, had always been hidden in our neighborhood's rolling hills.

The airports were shut down to all Yemeni citizens, but members of the foreign community were being evacuated by their respective embassies. We got a call from the American embassy, giving me details of the evacuation for the girls and letting me know that as their mother, I was permitted to go with them.

We talked about what to do, and my husband said he was staying. He didn't want to leave his parents or his job, which was paying him four times his regular salary to stay. My parents were unable to leave the country as well, and we didn't know how long the conflict would last. We were worried that even with my husband's higher salary, which amounted to less than a thousand dollars a month, we could not afford a prolonged stay abroad for the girls and myself.

I decided we would stay together. I wonder today whether

my wiser, older self would make the same decision I made then, gambling with my daughters' lives.

We took the girls to my parents' house, which would certainly be safer than ours. Any further attacks seemed likely to be aimed at other government offices and officials—including my husband's family. The next day, the president declared a thirty-day state of emergency that he would later extend, as the war we had feared finally broke out in earnest. Southern separatists declared a new state, the Yemeni Democratic Republic, which launched a series of air and ground campaigns.

The United Nations called for a ceasefire, but northern troops continued their march south, capturing Ataq and closing in on Aden. Thousands were killed, many of them civilians. In the last days of the war, as many as two dozen—or more—people were killed every day, victims of the ground war that had thankfully spared our city.

Eventually the government forces overwhelmed Aden; the president granted amnesty to the rebels and exiled their leaders. I wish I could say that peace was restored when the state of emergency was lifted in July, but the government was fearful and sometimes forceful about dissent, and it maintained a strong grip on society. People were detained without explanation, and the government tried to control the media. The sense of fragile security that the fortunate among us had felt for decades never returned.

Still, during the months of war, our life often felt surprisingly normal. The men left the house for work each day as if nothing out of the ordinary was happening; on the way back, they stopped for groceries. It's hard to explain, but life during wartime is the same as it is during peace.

Strife surprisingly brings peace and contentment into sharp focus, because there is nothing you can do about the rest of your life. Each day is no different from the day before, and you forget about fear and focus on life.

I once again noticed the early symptoms of pregnancy. For a long time, until I had to admit the truth, I tried to ignore them. Finally, I went to the lab for a pregnancy test. I had not a single doubt in my mind that I would carry this baby to term; not only that, but I already loved the baby with all my heart.

Two days later, while we were visiting my in-laws, the phone rang. It was my mother. "Zahra, you are *pregnant*?" she asked, a catch in her voice.

"How on earth do you know that?" I asked.

"Gamila," my mother said. Her friend's daughter was a doctor at the lab where I took the test. Gamila had seen my name on a test tube, pulled my file, and told her mother the news. Her mother had called my mother. The Yemeni ladies' grapevine was alive and well, even in wartime, and privacy was never granted to anyone.

We learned we were having a boy during my six-month ultrasound. My doctor also told us the baby's head was too big and he would be intellectually disabled. These days, I hear, that doctor runs a corner grocery store in Canada, an occupation I imagine suits him much better than medicine.

At the time, believing I was expecting a child with special needs confirmed for me the wrong I had done. *I deserve this,* I thought, realizing how much I loved this new life growing inside me.

In my eighth month, I got very sick, with high fever, head-aches, extreme vomiting, and chills. The symptoms continually worsened, the fever spiking so high I was slipping in and out of consciousness. The doctor suspected malaria, and the bloodwork confirmed it. Not only was it malaria, but it was a deadly strain called *Plasmodium falciparum*. The medication I needed to take in the next twelve hours would be fatal for the baby but would save my life, said our new, seemingly more trustworthy doctor.

He asked my husband if he would like to authorize the administration of the dose.

Knowing the unreliability of medical services in Yemen, my husband requested they repeat the test immediately, just to make sure. An hour later, the second test came back negative. Looking more closely at the original results, the doctor admitted they had read someone else's sample by mistake.

Once again, we had wandered past the limits of Yemen's medical system—and found our way. In fact, I had severe pneumonia. I was pumped full of many doses of antibiotics, and my resilient, strong little warrior continued growing inside of me.

I knew I was one of the lucky few. With the shortage of physicians in Yemen, especially in the rural areas, most women in the country were not able to seek medical care even during childbirth. Our new doctor urged us to go to Sana'a's general hospital for the delivery. Knowing the horrors of the medical system in Yemen, we refused. After all we had been through, my husband was more comfortable with a small private hospital.

"You don't understand," the doctor told us. "There will be nothing there—no medication. Nothing. At Al-Thawra Hospital, we have it all, if we need it."

We still said no.

My parents, who had far more experience with hospitals in Yemen than I, urged me to go back to the United States or even England for the birth. That seemed too difficult; taking the girls would be expensive and leaving them behind was not an option. Again, I decided to stay.

Delivering both girls had been a breeze. *Women have babies here every day. What could possibly go wrong?*

My mother-in-law advised us to wait at home even after labor began, because we did not want to be in the hospital longer than we needed to be. "And don't get on the hospital bed until I get there," she added. "I boiled some sheets for you and wrapped them in plastic so they'll stay clean."

Boiled sheets? I laughed and told her she was being silly.

My contractions began the next day, and, worried by her instructions, we waited too long. By the time we arrived at the small hospital, I was in blinding pain. Rivers of agony gripped my body from chin to knees. The elevator was not working, and walking up the five flights of uneven stairs to the delivery room took me forty minutes.

I finally made it up those stairs and into a tiny room lit by a single bare lightbulb hanging from the ceiling. A gurney sat by itself in the middle of the narrow room. The floors were dirty, the walls were streaked, and the windows were bare, with a clear view of the apartments across the street. "There is no way I'm getting on that. You made a mistake," I told the doctor. "This must be the room reserved for the livestock." He looked at me with an exasperated sigh and what was to become the night's litany: "I told you to go to Al-Thawra Hospital."

The cleaning lady came over to the gurney; I refused her armful of sheets, which had stains and holes in them. She bristled when she heard that my mother-in-law was bringing clean sheets: "What do you mean? I washed these myself," she said indignantly. The doctor made her hang them over the windows.

Finally, my mother-in-law arrived with the much-needed clean sheets. The cleaning lady pulled a chair up next to my head as I lay down and began, in inquisitive Yemeni style, to ask questions about my husband and my family, hoping for an explanation as to why I was acting so particular. Did we have some high status about which she was unaware? She wanted to know where we lived, and how much money my husband made. She also told me that women who think too highly of themselves go to hell.

"Please get her out of here," I said to the doctor in English. As she was walking out of the room, in wandered a cat, pus oozing out of a damaged eye and clumps of fur missing. The cleaning lady told me not to worry about the hissing cat because they had a rat problem at the hospital, and he was a good cat that took care of them. My doctor quickly ushered her out of the room before I lunged at her.

I started vomiting repeatedly, heaving and shaking. They needed to give me something to stop me from losing *all* bodily fluids, but as predicted, the hospital had nothing. The doctor quickly wrote out a series of prescriptions and shoved them into the hands of my husband, who had already mapped out all the pharmacies within a short walking distance, knowing that finding everything he needed at one was a dream that was not going to come true.

I refused to let any family in the room, not my mother, not my mother-in-law, and not my husband. Unlike my first two deliveries in civilized American hospitals, this was the first time I was not in control of my body, and I couldn't bear the thought of anyone witnessing what I was going through. I screamed with pain while my poor terrified mother was paralyzed outside the door.

The Russian nurse, angry that we hadn't known enough to slip her a bribe when we arrived, was aggressive, slapping my thighs and telling me to be quiet. The pain was coming too hard and fast for me to do anything about her at the moment, but I filed the moment away for a future reckoning, which, when it came, saw her on the next plane out of the country.

My anxious husband returned from the pharmacy carrying an IV with anti-nausea medication that was supposed to help me but instead had the opposite effect, and my breathing slowed. I slipped into unconsciousness. I don't remember much about the next hour. They say I stopped breathing; later, we found out that my reaction was caused by expired medication, something nobody noticed in the commotion of the day. This was a common occurrence in a country that had little access to medication.

Two hours later, the electricity went out and we discovered the generator at the hospital was not working. The nurse lit a candle.

That single, lonely candle became my savior, one bright light for me to focus on for the rest of my labor. It soothed and comforted me as the pains racked my body, and after several mind-numbing hours, my boy, my beautiful son, Ahmed, was born. He was named after my father-in-law—a name decided long before his new parents were even married—and he could not have been more perfect.

As soon as he was born, he was handed to my mother-in-law, who immediately took him home, out of fear of infection. I did not get to hold him or even see him before she left. The doctor started sewing up the large tears in my body, every stitch feeling like a sword instead of a needle. Then I heard him say, "She is hemorrhaging. We need to open her up again."

"Absolutely not," I said to the doctor. "Feel free to do whatever you want but only after you put me to sleep." My son was safe, and I wanted medication *now*.

The doctor looked at me incredulously. "You might die."

I told him I didn't care. I was finished with this stupid country and its stupid medical system. I glared at the Russian nurse as I spoke.

"Get her husband," he said.

"That is not going to help you," I not so calmly told him. "Nobody is going to touch me until I say so."

Since it was two in the morning, the doctor wrote directions for my panicked husband to go to the house of the anesthesiologist, who had no phone. He got there as fast as he could, pounded on the door, and, when the doctor finally opened his door and claimed it was too late at night for him to go to the hospital, he offered him a thousand-dollar bribe.

The doctors finally administered the anesthesia and proceeded with surgery. In the meantime, unbeknownst to me, my son was rushed back to the hospital. The nurse hadn't tied his umbilical cord well in the darkness, and he too had started hemorrhaging as soon as they got home.

At the hospital, the infection my mother-in-law had worked so hard to avoid set in, and by morning, Ahmed's tiny little body was raging with fever.

When I finally opened my eyes, after more than forty hours, my family were by my side, fear etched into their relieved faces. I looked at them and told them my arm was hurting. "Your *arm* hurts?" asked my husband incredulously. We rolled up my sleeve—I was still in the same outfit I had been wearing when we arrived at the hospital—and discovered that my arm was black all the way from my fingertips to my shoulder.

It was deep vein thrombosis, a blood clot that had formed in my vein and blocked the blood flow in and out of my arm. With the stress of the previous two days and the unreliability of the hospital and its nurses, nobody had noticed.

The doctor cut off my watch and wedding ring from my swollen hand and wrist and put me on blood thinners and a multitude of antibiotics.

Finally they let me go home to my new son and my bewildered daughters. As soon as I saw the baby, the previous three days melted away—until the midwife and nurse started massaging my arm to loosen the clot. I swear, every single swipe felt like hours of childbirth all over again . . . three times a day . . . for the next month.

• • •

According to tradition, new mothers must observe a forty-day postpartum rest called the *walad*, where women come to sit together, laugh, and dance. It is meant to help with the baby blues and prevent postpartum depression. I always thought it was a beautiful tradition until I had to observe it.

The new mother lies on a throne-like bed in the living room, receiving visitors all day, surrounded by brass jugs of rosemary and wearing necklaces of red coral to ward off the evil eye. She is fed copious amounts of food prepared by the family, to make sure she has enough milk to "fatten up" her baby.

Every day, they made me chicken soup with vegetables—from a whole baby chicken—which I was required to eat. Also, I had to drink two raw eggs mixed with things I didn't bother to ask about, since I was already having trouble keeping it all down.

Women flooded our house, staying for hours past their welcome, bringing their water pipes and cigarettes. I had to sit still, decked out in finery, receiving the guests all day instead of spending time with my girls or getting to know my son. Then, at night, my husband would come home and get upset about the secondhand smoke his children were breathing. He had never succumbed to the allure of chewing *qat* or smoking cigarettes like I and the rest of our society had, preferring to keep his body clean and healthy.

After ten days of this madness, much to the mortification and shame of my mother and mother-in-law, I shut it down. "Forty days are done, according to my calculations," I said. "Let your friends know that tomorrow is the last day."

They scrambled to get invitations out and hire a singer and a Quran reciter. I was decked out in silver, coral, jasmine flowers, and bunches of rosemary. The house was soon packed with female family and friends, not only in the living room upstairs where I was, but also in the hallways and the living room downstairs.

My mother-in-law brought my son to me only when he needed feeding; she swaddled him to cover him up and also weighed him down with bunches of rosemary and talismans to keep evil spirits away. The birth of a boy was such a big deal that they did everything in their power to protect him. Incense burned along with the water pipes, and the air was thick with it all.

The day simply could not end fast enough. After everyone went home, I breathed a sigh of smoke-filled relief that my home and my life were once again mine, and that I could finally focus on my newborn son. For the next two months, my child's body was pumped with stronger and stronger doses of antibiotics that he just kept resisting. Thankfully, the antibiotics eventually did their job. I was finally able to relax a bit as I watched him recover, although I was still on high alert, sterilizing everything he came in contact with.

Each time my children were in danger, I felt a kind of shaky remove from my own life. There's no limit to what I would do to ensure their survival—even if it means sacrificing my own life.

How could we possibly protect our children in this country?

"What do you think about Canada?" said my husband one day, coming home and pushing immigration papers in front of me. Confused, I looked at him. This was the man who had insisted on coming home from the United States because he wanted to serve his country. I never believed he would be willing to leave, let alone initiate a move.

I didn't know much about Canada—only that it had some oil and some mountains and was unbelievably cold, and where it was located on a map. I thought more bears lived in Canada than people. Did they even have a summer? I am an absolute information hound, and Google is my best friend, but in those days in

Yemen, before personal computers and smartphones, I had hardly any information to go on.

The easiest way for us to immigrate was through the skilled worker application, and we hired a lawyer to help us, knowing the process could take months or even years. In order to immigrate to Canada as a skilled worker, you must pass a criminal background check, medical test, language test, financial viability tests, and level and location of education tests.

You get points for each, and if you reach an acceptable number of points, you eventually get your papers.

So we lined up more doctors' appointments than I care to count and took out a loan from my husband's family to pad our bank account for the financial means test; after we qualified, we returned it. The process happened shockingly fast—and we were approved in just three months.

We were moving to Canada.

I finally felt the weight in my lungs lift, as I breathed in a possible future for our children instead of simply concern for the next day.

My husband's family did not fully understand what we were doing or why. As far as they were concerned, we were leaving behind a perfectly good life. We had a beautiful, healthy family, a house, a job, a car. What else could we possibly be looking for?

CHAPTER TWELVE

Our family arrived in Canada in the summer of 1996, when Ahmed was only six months old and the girls five and four. Saying goodbye to Yemen was both easier and harder than the first time. Easier this time because our children's future without the move seemed so bleak. The hard part was that I now had a better sense of what we were leaving behind.

During the past four years, I'd had the chance to really get to know my mother, and I appreciated her so much more. I was no longer a kid rejecting the family that made me different; I was an adult embracing it.

The first few hours of immigrating to a new land brings a feeling of infinite wonder, like landing on another planet. The sounds, smells, energy, and colors are all overwhelming. There is so much novelty that no matter how hard you try to hold on to the person you thought you were, you can't. Though we landed in Calgary with no one to greet us, the officer who presented us with our Canadian residency papers upon arrival also gave the girls maple-syrup lollipops and little Canadian flags on wooden sticks.

Let me back up for a minute and tell you about music class in Yemeni schools: you learn to sing either a religious song or a patriotic one. So here we were on our first day in Canada, at the customs office, my little girls standing tall, clutching their candy in one hand and waving their new Canadian flags in the other while pledging their allegiance to Yemen.

When handed the flags, our girls started singing *"Biladi, Biladi, Biladi al-Yemen, laki hubi wa fuadi al-Yemen."* ("My homeland, my homeland, my homeland Yemen. You have my love and my heart, my homeland Yemen.") When the officer asked us what the girls were singing, we stifled our laughter and simply said they were happy to be here.

As my children settled into their new country, I hoped they would be able to embrace the new culture but also respect and preserve their own. That they did not feel those feelings of shame and insecurity that I had as a Ugandan in Yemen or a Yemeni Muslim in America.

No shipping containers of furniture were to follow; we wanted a clean start in our new home. We had ten suitcases because two per person was all the airline allowed; we had filled them with our most precious belongings and left everything else behind. Once we checked into a family-friendly motel by the airport and picked up a flyer that had rental listings, I began to feel relief. I had missed so many little things about the West—the grocery stores, the food, the cleanliness, getting behind the wheel of a car.

Drivers did not incessantly honk their horns here, things were orderly, people drove between the white lines instead of on top of them, and you stood in line instead of pushing your way to the front. Everything was new and exciting, yet old and familiar at the same time. I took so much pleasure in introducing my children to their new world, watching their little faces shine with wonder.

After a few days looking at different homes, we signed the lease on a promising-looking townhouse in a neighborhood called Abbeydale: reasonable rent, with two bedrooms upstairs.

We settled in quickly, with the cheap used furniture I thought would suffice until I had a better idea of what our lives were going to look like. I proudly displayed a lineup of ten ceramic houses, white with blue trim, that had been given to us during our KLM flights to Canada. The houses had alcohol in them, poured into the chimneys, which were sealed with wax. Alcohol was *haram*, forbidden, but the houses were divine. I drained the alcohol out and scrubbed them down.

Strangely, the thing I was most excited about was the fact that I didn't have a nanny, maids, a gardener, or a driver anymore. I felt free and in charge, queen of my home and my kitchen. I knew where things were because they had been put there by me. Even cleaning my own home was a joy, although I will admit that the shine wore off of that work pretty fast.

We did not have much money, and we were living off meager savings, but we were better off than most immigrants. We did not need government assistance, so we did not have to answer to anyone. We had enough to take the kids to the zoo or the mall without concern. We were adjusting more easily than other new immigrant families; I was grateful for our financial advantage, which made our experiences as newcomers less stressful.

I was also so grateful for my command of the English language and lack of an accent to hold me back. It took me years to realize the benefit and the privilege of those few childhood years I had spent at the American school.

The reality of Abbeydale was a little different from the picture of Canada I had in my head. We didn't realize that the majority of our new little pocket of the city lived in subsidized housing, and we were one of the few families that actually paid full rent. On our first night, we woke up in fright to the whole house shaking. We found out that the freight train ran through the backyard. The house shook several times during the day and night. And some drivers really enjoyed using their horns, especially at night.

We were surrounded by colorful characters. Some were great

neighbors who helped us immensely then and became friends over the years. But others bewildered us. We awoke one night to the sound of yelling and a body being smashed up against the other side of our bedroom wall. We listened, eyes wide, wondering if we should call the police, but being as new as we were in the country, that seemed scarier than what was going on next door.

Those fights were simply a part of our neighbors' daily life and soon became a part of ours; she was as big as he was and certainly seemed to be holding her own with him.

Sometimes they took their arguments outside, while their eight-year-old daughter watched with an expressionless face from the upstairs window. Cassie started to spend more time at my house than her own after I came home with the kids from school one day to find her sitting on her front steps wearing a T-shirt and no coat. Winter had already started, and it was below freezing outside.

I asked her why she was sitting outside, and she simply said, "My mother is mad. She locked me out for coming home late." I couldn't understand how Cassie could have been late, since I had just gotten home with the kids and I had a car. I invited her in for dinner, and it seemed that she rarely left after that.

My husband's days were filled with job research and phone interviews, mine with our home and the children. We enrolled Amani in first grade and Hanadi in a Montessori preschool. The girls had to adjust to being separated for the first time in their lives. They had done everything together before this: they had slept in the same room, played with the same toys and friends, learned in the same class. I even dressed them the same. It was harder for Hanadi than Amani, because Amani got to go to the big-girl school and she didn't.

Slowly, their individual personalities were taking shape. Amani, my fussy baby, had grown into a very agreeable child—a classic "oldest" and a total mama's girl. She spent her days with her nose in a book and was practical and helpful around the house.

Hanadi was the dreamer, talking to herself, playing with her Barbies, and constantly inventing new stories and scenarios. She lived in a magical world of her own creation, and from her stories, it sounded like it was glorious. Ahmed was my sweet little baby boy who simply smiled all day long.

The children were embracing Canadian culture and changing so fast right before my eyes. In contrast, I felt very unsure of myself, not confident in my ability to participate in this new society. I worried that I might say the wrong thing, do the wrong thing, that people might laugh at me. I felt as if I was being left behind.

On top of that, all the potential freedom in the world did not make up for the fact that we were trapped, literally, by the Canadian winter. The year we arrived, Calgary got the heaviest snowfall it had seen in twenty years—snow like we had never seen before, cold like we had never felt before. Getting the children in and out of snowsuits, and in and out of car seats, seemed to consume my entire day. Some days I did not have it in me to bring them home for lunch; I brought sandwiches and fed them in the hallway at school instead.

With no connections, my husband struggled to break into the job market. He was committed to finding a job, but in the oil and gas industry in Calgary, it seemed that getting a job required knowing someone, and we knew no one.

The uncertainty and rejection were hard on him. After all, as far as he was concerned, his role was to provide for his family. He was a smart, hardworking, capable man with a ton of experience, and the only thing holding him back was where he was from.

Eight long months after our arrival, my husband finally had a breakthrough and got his first job offer. But the job was based in

Lloydminster, a five-hour drive from our home in Calgary. The kids were settled in school, and there was no way we were going to uproot them again. The only way it could work was if he stayed in Lloyd for the work week, coming home late Friday night and leaving again on Sunday night.

He was really happy to be working, but he was exhausted all weekend from driving home after a long week with no break. And being at home all week alone with the kids exhausted me too.

Our support system might as well have been on another planet. Phone calls home were expensive; FaceTime had not yet been invented. To save money, we bought a calling card and called Yemen once a week. We were missing them. And then, thankfully, my in-laws came to visit with both of my husband's younger brothers.

When they arrived, the kids were excited to show their grand-parents their new home and all their toys. I had prepared a full table of food, Yemeni style, hoping to show them that our new life in Calgary was a good one. But they had been in the house for only five minutes when the freight train came.

My father-in-law looked up at me, reached for the coat he'd just removed, and walked out the front door. I followed him out to where he'd stopped, next to the passenger door of our car, and asked where he wanted to go.

"To a hotel," he said, and that was the end of the conversation.

Nothing we could say would help them understand how this tiny row house on the train tracks in this frigid part of the world, far from any help or family, was better than the life we had left behind.

They stayed in that hotel for three weeks, leaving the littlest boy with me.

One morning, after a really fun day at the zoo, the kids and I woke up feeling ill. I went to the grocery store as soon as I realized I was getting sick and somehow managed to buy enough food for the next week. I had no energy in my body, and the kids were cranky and restless. We all felt lethargic and feverish, and as the day went on, we started scratching our arms, hands, and faces. With no idea what was wrong, I called our new doctor's office to book an appointment.

"Chicken pox," said the nurse. "Stay home."

In Yemen, we had many dangerous diseases to contend with—malaria, typhoid, and cholera to name a few—but I had never heard of chicken pox. No one in our families had ever had it. Once the nurse explained the virus to me, I called my in-laws and told them to stay at the hotel and not come to visit. I told my husband to stay in Lloydminster. None of the adults could afford to contract it, and my husband had just finally found a job. Getting sick was not an option.

I was itchy, achy, weak, and exhausted, and yet I had four miserable little children to take care of. All of a sudden, my nanny and the maids did not seem like they would be an imposition on my freedom anymore.

Two days later, the mother of one of Amani's friends called to ask if she could bring her daughter over to get exposed to the virus. "Do they know how this feels? They *want* their kids to have it?" I told my husband over the phone. "People here are crazy."

The kids eventually got better, and so did I. My in-laws and the boys went home; my parents visited for a few weeks soon after. The kids immersed themselves in school, in dance and other classes, in playing with their friends. They had homework and field trips. My husband was busy and distracted at work; when he came home, he was tired and wanted a break.

In Yemen, I had family and friends to visit but was not allowed to go out when I pleased. In Calgary, I had all the freedom but nowhere to go.

We had been there almost a year, and I was bored out of my mind. I knew the patterns of the sunlight across the carpeting and what times the furnace turned on and off each day. Once again, I felt pushed close to the edge of sanity. Nothing was coming and nothing was going—or even moving—during the day. Just me, the walls, and the humming of the kitchen appliances.

One Saturday morning, while the girls were out with friends and Ahmed was napping, I told my husband I wanted to do something. "Something," I repeated, in response to his quizzical look. Take a class, volunteer. Anything. I appealed to his memory of being stuck at home for so many months and how mind-numbing it was. He reminded me of our financial reality, which did not include much room for childcare costs.

He did not mind spending time with the kids, he said, but shouldering most of the weekend childcare burden after a long work week and ten hours of commuting didn't seem fair to him either. I understood his point and suggested that maybe it was time for me to get a job.

"Who is going to hire you?" He was not trying to be unkind so much as pragmatic: it had been terribly difficult for him to find work in Canada, even with a degree in engineering from one of the best universities in the United States. I was not going to be able to teach in this country, where, unlike Yemen, they actually required teachers to have an education. He wanted me to eventually go back to university, so I could get a "real job."

Although I knew he meant no harm, his question unleashed an electric and increasingly familiar anger in me—dual feelings of rage and despair heating my skin until I wanted to jump out of it.

"I am going to the mall," I said. My husband, very well acquainted with the signs of my anger by now, did not even try to argue. An afternoon of retail therapy seemed like it would do the trick. Loaded with bags full of things for the house we could little afford and that would get returned the following day,

I wandered around the shopping center, trying not to dwell on what he had said.

Calgary's Northland Village Mall had typical small-town shops, soft rock radio on the loudspeaker, and thick scents of rose perfume and deep-fried corn oil. I walked the corridors of the mall until I noticed a sign in a window: "Help Wanted." I walked into the Danier Leather boutique in a trance. The beautiful woman behind the counter, with short bright-red hair, reminded me of Tina, my long-ago accounting teacher. *Nancy*, said her nametag. She was the store manager. "I would like to apply for the job," I told her.

Previous retail experience, *no*. Credit history, *no*. Degree, *no*.

"I'm not qualified for this, but I'll work really hard. All I need is a chance," I told her, prepared to bargain with her the way my mother bargained for a bushel of okra in Bab-al-Yemen.

As far as I was concerned, rejection was still an opportunity for negotiation.

However, it wasn't necessary. My earnestness turned out to be good enough for Nancy, who asked when I could start.

Like the rest of the staff, I would be expected to wear at least one leather article of clothing. "If you sell it, you must wear it," she said.

Islam forbids using the skins of animals, and I had never owned anything made of leather in my life, let alone the bomber jackets and trench coats that filled the racks at Danier. My newly adopted Canadian style was a standard uniform of baggy jeans, oversized flannel shirts, and running shoes.

"I will take the suede skirt," I told her, reaching into my purse and pulling a few twenties from my wallet. She counted back my change, and I rubbed the bottom of the skirt, feeling the thread of the hem, then the hide, between my fingers. Its musky smell was strange. But it felt more like cloth than like leather. That made it seem less offensive somehow.

I walked out of the store with the comforting weight of the skirt in my shopping bag and a feeling of joy in my heart.

I had a job.

When I returned home, my frustrated husband asked all the questions I hadn't thought to ask myself: "How is this all going to work? Who is going to take care of the kids?"

I told him I could work and still do everything in the house and look after the kids, but we both knew I was making a promise I could not keep. The timing of my shift, and the fact that we did not have family or household help, meant he would have to be home with the children. I reassured him that I would work just a few hours on the weekends, and that, if it became disruptive in any way, I would stop.

I was overly optimistic and simply wanted to get my way, and he gave in because he knew I wanted it so much.

My selling leather vests at the mall wouldn't make any real difference to our joint bank account. "It will not change anything for us," he said.

But the job changed everything for me. It was not about the money. It was about having something that was only mine and maintaining it for that reason alone. It is hard to describe the liberation I felt, simply getting dressed up, driving my car to the mall, and walking into my job. Unlike in Yemen, there was no fear that I would be bothered—no catcalls, no one trying to touch me inappropriately. I could wear what I wanted, and no one would think to criticize it. I grew to love my suede pencil skirt. Tight leather pants and a cute little brown suede vest soon followed.

We earned a 3 percent commission for every item we sold. When a customer walked in, my coworkers would race to the door, trying their hardest to make a sale. I hung back, watched, listened, and learned. That minimum-wage job gave me the first irresistible inkling of what was to become my career. I knew how to close a sale. Reading people was an art: you could motivate them and change their behavior. I got hooked on marketing in its simplest form.

I had, in trying to find someplace where I fit, found a hunger I could not shake.

Working retail became a psychological dance: Did this woman want me to compliment her? Did that man want me to leave him alone? Was it ever worthwhile to truthfully answer the question "Does this make me look fat?"

I realized all it really took was knowing how to listen and then knowing how to react. I saw my customers' insecurities and vanities, their hidden desires. I loved dressing the customers, watching what caught their eye and then navigating the decision-making process with them. I could guess what they wanted by what they already had and the way they behaved: in marketing, this kind of classification is known as psychographics, though it would be years before I learned that word.

I began to sell more and more, outearning my more aggressive counterparts and eventually taking home more commission than any staffer in town—even though I only worked weekends and some evenings. My confidence and competitive spirit grew with each sale.

Week after week, my husband challenged my decision to work. I understood that, for practical and logistical reasons, the kids needed me and he needed me, but I did not relent.

That changed one day, when one of my coworkers came in with a cold sore and my beloved job's fate was sealed. I have always had a phobia about cold sores; they are viral and once you have one, it comes back forever. *Cold sores forever* was all I could think, watching my coworker pick at her lip and then touch the cash register and the phone.

Never has there been such motivation to pursue higher education. And much to my family's relief, I quit my job.

My time at Danier had lasting benefits. After years of pregnancy, weight gain, and total avoidance, I had reacquainted myself with the mirror. My jeans were getting tighter, and the colors I wore were getting brighter. These changes were about more than looking good; they were about having the freedom to choose and experiment.

Like my mother before me, I could dress to prove to myself and the world that I wasn't an object to be hidden away.

The idea of choice was powerful for me. I had begun talking about it more and more with a new friend, a Yemeni woman who was even newer to Canada than I was. Ishraq had grown up in Cairo, which meant she was infinitely more cosmopolitan and fashionable than I was. She was a photographer and an artist, and also a newlywed—radiating happiness and beauty. But she really missed her friends, life, and career back in Egypt.

We became close and spent much of our time talking about the lives we were so sure we would one day live.

My husband was transferred to Calgary when his company was acquired by another, and one of the first things we did when the new job became official was buy a house. Or, rather, he bought a house and then showed it to me. I was too excited to get mad, and it was a great step up from our little row house.

Our new home was in a development where you could select the style and color of your house the way you might pick a sweater out of a catalog: Tudor, ranch, Santa Fe, colonial. Ours was a Santa Fe, thousands of miles stylistically from cold Calgary, salmon pink on the outside, with curved archways, columns, and the colorful tiles of the American Southwest.

It had previously been owned by a family from Hong Kong, who had sold us all their furniture, which was very ornate and oriental. The carpets were apple green, and the peach-colored drapes were poufy layers that looked like they had leaves etched in them. So here we were, a Yemeni family in a Santa Fe–style house with shiny gold Asian furniture and our Dutch ceramic houses.

My husband was supportive of the idea of my going back to school, starting with a few night classes; however, he did not approve of the path I chose: drawing classes. He had bigger aspirations for me and wanted me to think of a better, guaranteed career. Art classes seemed like a waste of our hard-earned money—and he asked me what on earth I was going to do with an art degree.

I was not thinking about a career or even really comprehending what "career" meant—the word seemed reserved for doctors, engineers, and lawyers. I pushed back. I wasn't ready for university, and these drawing classes were what I wanted to do. We came to a compromise. He'd let me take the classes if I did not "waste" our weekends; instead, I would take night classes, after the children went to bed.

In Yemen, drawing, painting, and sculpting were indulgences pursued by foreigners only, and my mother was one of them. Since I can remember, she would save up her money for our European trips, when she could buy her precious oil paints. Then, all year, she doled them out in tiny little amounts so she wouldn't run out before the next summer. She had no formal education in art, which meant the objects in her paintings were painted in completely different perspectives—the same building would have a bird's-eye view and a worm's-eye view. It was charming and uniquely her.

Her painting became famous in Yemen, and all money she

made from the sales of her work went directly to charity. When I was old enough, I painted alongside her. My mother had always told me how good an artist I was, taking my scribbles and hanging them on the walls of our house.

I needed only a few hours at the Alberta College of Art and Design to realize my mother had lied to me all those years ago. I was not only not a great artist, I was a terrible one.

Most of my classmates in the drawing class were eighteen-year-olds, full of piss and vinegar. Some had piercings, tattoos, and similar avant-garde ideas about style. They had more talent in their little fingers than I had seen in my life. They didn't know what to make of me, and I didn't know what to make of them.

But I admired their deep love—almost a reverence—for art and the process of making it, and I appreciated the way they made me feel young and carefree again. Evening classes were fun: going out at night was so taboo for women in Yemen that I felt sophisticated leaving the house after dinner and coming home at almost midnight. Every night felt like an adventure.

One of my first classes was figure drawing, which, of course, involved drawing a figure—a naked one. I felt shock as Santa Claus walked into the classroom and took off his clothes. He was big, with a large belly and a full white beard. I had never seen a live naked stranger before, and the blood rose to my face. I couldn't even look at him, let alone draw his private parts. "The whole body, Zahra, draw the whole body," my instructor would repeat all semester. "Yes, yes, I will get to it," I always responded, while focusing all my attention on drawing a giant kneecap or shoulder blade and not looking at anything else.

As I became more comfortable at art school, I also became more comfortable with the naked body—and with swear words, interactions with men, people from all walks of life, and a bohemian lifestyle that was worlds away from the home I went to every night. I was shedding layers of hang-ups and notions of right and wrong, though I stumbled every so often.

"Whoa, what is that smell?" I wrinkled my nose as a group of us walked into what was called the "graffiti stairwell." It was pot.

"Zahra," sighed my friend Mike, "you are so embarrassing."

The only way I could start a full-time program at ACAD was to find a good daycare for Ahmed. I felt tremendously guilty putting him in daycare at the tender age of two, especially when he got strep throat for three weeks after his second day, followed by two weeks of stomach flu after his first day back. It seemed that Canada was not as clean as I'd thought.

I stopped sterilizing everything Ahmed touched, as I had been doing since his birth in Yemen, in the hopes of building his immune system. Once our home life finally settled down and Ahmed stopped getting so sick, I applied to full-time studies.

Reviewing the course catalog, I understood why my husband was so skeptical about art school. The catalog included many fine arts—ceramics, drawing, printmaking, and fabrics—but nothing that seemingly led to a *job*. I knew I wasn't talented enough to make money from my art, so I talked to as many people as I could and learned that the degree most easily translated into a nine-to-five was graphic design.

I had no clue what "graphic design" even meant, but I researched what I needed to get accepted and tried to pull together a portfolio to submit. Other applicants had actual graphic design work in their books: logos, catalogs, magazines, advertising, and web design. I, on the other hand, had a few charcoal sketches. As the deadline approached, it seemed clear that if I simply submitted the selection of night-school drawings, as I was being asked to do, I would have no chance of getting in. So instead I called Eugene, the head of the School of Communication Design.

It was an unconscious move: I just knew that if I saw him face to face, I could try to convince him. And it was such a *Mom* move.

My mother forced her way into getting things done all the time. She drove down a one-way street almost every day, honking her horn and holding her hand up, because she couldn't be bothered to drive all the way around the block. Even the police officers eventually started waving her through.

She had taught me that you can talk your way into anything, or that if you can't, you should at least try. When I was young, she made every guest who came over for dinner help stock the shelves of the Mother Teresa home with everything from milk to toothpaste.

The never-back-down mentality I seemed to have inherited from my mother was now taking me to places where my insecurities didn't want to go.

I asked Eugene if we could set up a meeting so I could show him my portfolio, and he told me to submit it by the due date like everybody else. An in-person meeting was out of the question: they had four hundred applicants to consider. I told him I understood, and then I asked again if I could come see him . . . and again. Finally he relented. "You have ten minutes," he said. "Be here at eight."

I stood next to him, my cold hands clasped tightly, as he carefully paged through charcoal drawings that seemed to get progressively worse as I looked on. "Listen, I know this is . . . I know my book needs work," I said. "That is why I am here." I told him why I would be a good addition to the program, in terms of both perspective and discipline. I appealed to him as a parent, telling him about my kids. I told him how passionate I was about design. I told him it would make him look good to have someone like me in the program: I ticked all the diversity boxes.

I was convinced from the glint in his eye that I would be going back to school in my chosen program as I skipped out of the room eight minutes later.

• • •

I felt anxious for weeks after submitting the application, however. Restless. "Something is wrong with me," I told my husband one night, kicking off the bedsheets and getting up to toss and turn on the couch. A few days later, a test confirmed that I was pregnant.

I tried to be grateful, to see this unexpected news as a blessing: a growing family. I repeated *Alhamdulillah* in my head all day long for the next few weeks, trying to figure out how I was going to manage school, if I got accepted, and knowing I could not.

Then, one night in drawing class, I started bleeding. I immediately went to the hospital. Around 2 a.m., a young resident confirmed an early miscarriage. I had barely found out I was pregnant when I wasn't anymore.

When we finally got home at 4 a.m., I walked into the kitchen and saw a pile of mail on the table. At the top was a letter from ACAD. I opened it with shaky hands. It was my acceptance into the visual communication design program.

That night brought me an ending and a new beginning.

It Takes Awareness.

The thoughts, experiences, and abilities that make your identity unique are tougher to recognize than you may think.

The trouble is that none of us is objective. We tell ourselves a preferred version of a story so many times that it becomes the real version. Social nuances are lost in translation, and other people's perspectives of us are glossed over.

To get an accurate picture, you'll need to work toward a non-judgmental reflection of yourself. Your "shortcomings" may be your greatest chance to learn and grow.

How do you react to change, criticism, compliments, and pressure? How do you react to people? How do they react to you? Why do you behave the way you do?

Self-awareness is the cornerstone of emotional intelligence, according to psychologist and bestselling author Daniel Goleman. Goleman says, "The ability to monitor our emotions and thoughts from moment to moment is key to understanding ourselves better, being at peace with who we are and proactively managing our thoughts, emotions and behaviors."

The upside is a goldmine. Dr. Goleman notes that "self-aware people tend to act consciously rather than react passively, tend to be in good psychological health, and tend to have a positive outlook on life. They also have a greater depth of life experience and are more likely to be more compassionate."

Take control and you'll reap the rewards. A happier, healthier version of yourself is waiting to be honed.

Throughout the rest of this book you will find qualities that have helped me clarify my own sense of self. (To be honest, every time I decide to call this book done I think of another one to add!) Use these as a guide, but tailor your own list.

Be you . . . the improved version.

CHAPTER THIRTEEN

In art, as in life, the fundamentals are essential. That is why the first two years of ACAD's visual communication design program were spent on drawing, painting, and illustration—disciplines that were taught in intensive studios. My previous formal education had consisted of "Here is A, here is B, this is how you get there," with "this" most often being some form of memorization. Now, for the first time, I was being required to think creatively and solve problems. My classmates were extremely talented and had an ease about them. I was the "mature" student, with very little talent to show for my gray hairs.

On the first day of my illustration class, we went around the room, introducing ourselves. I was the last one to speak up. "I'm Zahra, and I guess I'm the oldest person here," I said. "I have three children." The other students laughed generously and raised their eyebrows with surprise.

"Three kids!" exclaimed our instructor, Tim. "You don't look like you're old enough." He was an incredible, celebrated artist, as well as a very attractive man—six foot four, with blue eyes, a beautiful smile, and blond hair. He also had a wicked sense of humor. "What are their names?"

"Amani, Hanadi, and Ahmed," I said, beaming with pride.

"Could you not have picked any easier names?" said Tim after he struggled to repeat the names properly.

"For who?" I laughed. "For you? They're pretty easy for me." He had the decency to look chagrined.

When I first started taking art classes, I also met Peter, a former oil worker with classic movie-star good looks. We spent a lot of time together at school and became fast friends.

One Friday, Peter and I were walking back to school after lunch. We passed a car parked on the street, and Peter pointed out the bumper sticker, an upside-down triangle with a rainbow running through it. "The universal gay symbol," he said.

I said "I know" very quickly, wanting to be cool.

Looking at my hesitant face, Peter said, "You know I'm gay, right?"

"Yes, of course!" I said. But the truth was, I had never before met anyone who was openly gay. I was taken aback, and felt a horrible feeling in the pit of my stomach. In Arabic school, we had been taught that homosexuality was a sin, and that the people who practiced it were going to hell. Like pretty much every other idea I had been taught at the time, I accepted it wholesale.

Peter and I walked the rest of the way back to campus and said a brief, breezy goodbye, but once I was home, I cycled through a range of emotions. At first, I felt betrayed—how could my new friend have kept a secret like that from me? Then I got angry because I had been taught that only bad people were homosexual. They were shunned and ostracized, and then they went to hell.

So what was wrong with Peter? Was he confused? Could he be cured? For most of the weekend, I stayed home and cried. How could I be friends with Peter anymore? I couldn't even imagine how I would feel when I saw him again.

And then suddenly my anger abated, like the air being sucked out of a balloon, and in its absence, a different set of questions arose. I questioned my faith. How could God have created Peter this way and then told him he had to reject who he was? I had always believed in a kind, merciful God, not the vengeful, angry God who wanted me to hate Peter. It seemed deeply wrong to hate anyone—isn't that what religion also taught us? Peter was good to the very center of his being, better than most of the pious men I knew who would point a finger at others and condemn.

My beliefs had long been changing, evolving, expanding. But for the first time, I made the decision to turn my back on what I had been taught. All I needed to believe was that Peter was my friend. I called him, told him the truth, and begged his forgiveness.

What Peter said to me broke my heart. He told me he knew I had lied to him about knowing he was gay. The lie, he said, had hurt him to his core. "Do you think I wanted to be this way? That I want to be shunned and treated like something to be kept away from?" he asked. He wished he wasn't, he said, only so he would never have to see the look he'd seen in my eyes in anyone else's again.

Peter and I remained close; he moved to Vancouver at the end of the school year, and I went out to visit him multiple times. He and his boyfriend thought my earnest obliviousness hilarious. One day they dropped me at the bank and waited outside, and then watched as I tried to get into the back seat of someone else's car. When I finally made it to theirs, he laughingly said, "Zahra, if you were a white girl, you would be blond."

We are so conditioned to believe what we are told—programmed to accept things at face value, especially if they are from a trusted source. We stop making up our own minds, asking questions, coming to our own conclusions. Believing in the things we want to believe in. We are afraid of being on the wrong side of what is socially accepted, even if it is right.

It Takes Inheritance.

People don't rise from nothing. We owe something to parentage and patronage. The people who stand before kings may look like they did it all by themselves. In fact, they are invariably the beneficiaries of hidden advantages, extraordinary opportunities and cultural legacies that allow them to learn and work hard and make sense of the world in ways that others cannot.

—Malcolm Gladwell, *Outliers: The Story of Success*

Our understanding of DNA has come a long way in the past decade. With a little bit of spit, you can learn your predisposition to a wide array of health conditions and how long you may expect to live.

But new research is telling us that genetics is more complex than that single vial of saliva. We may be more shaped by the genes we *don't* inherit than the ones we do. This twist of perspective has been coined "genetic nurture."

If a calf grows faster and stronger than the others, consider that it may be an average calf but its mother may have exceptional milk production.

If a child excels in school, consider that he may be an average child but his parents may be predisposed to academic excellence and push the child accordingly.

This was the conclusion reached by a geneticist named Augustine Kong when the first DNA-based studies of educational attainment came out in 2013. Children, after all, get their genes from their parents. It was possible, Dr. Kong reasoned, that genes could influence how far children got through school by influencing their parents' behavior rather than the actions of the children themselves.

For better or worse, this means we are all products of our backgrounds.

That is not to say there's no hope for those with less-than-great childhoods. In fact, they might have an advantage.

Consider that kids with genetically apathetic parents are forced to master self-sufficiency at an early age, forced to self-motivate, and forced to be more creative than their peers to make their way through life. Those kids are likely to become incredible adults, armed with innovation, hustle, and determination—gifts from their genetically ungifted moms and dads.

So if you're lucky enough to have had a great upbringing with genetically exceptional parents, revel in your bright memories and be thankful for the limitless opportunities they blessed you with.

And if your early life was with filled with struggle and a need for a maturity that defied your age, be grateful for that too. It gave you skills that can take you incredibly far.

CHAPTER FOURTEEN

I was working harder than I ever had before and, at the same time, trying to reconcile many different elements of my life— all of which were changing, quickly, and each of which needed attention. Balancing school with having three children at home meant I often had to work through the night just to stay current. And in turn that meant life at home became total chaos.

Our neighbors asked Amani one day about all the yelling coming from our house in the mornings. Amani told them it was me try- ing to get everyone ready on time. It took me an hour and twenty minutes to drive them to school and then myself to class every day.

For years, I had run a tight ship, setting strict ground rules about clutter. Aside from the walkout basement that belonged to the kids—and their toys—everything was perfect. The kids were allowed to bring only three toys out of the basement at a time. Shoes had to be put in the closet; jackets had to be hung up. The kids were responsible for cleaning up after dinner, and each of us made lunch for all one day a week. Friday was my day, and I copped out and gave them money so they could buy their own lunch instead.

"Hanadi, I just cleaned the house; can you take those toys and go down in the playroom?" I asked one Saturday afternoon when I heard her run up the stairs with her friend while I was getting dinner ready. As they walked away, I heard her friend ask, "Do you always do what your mother says?"

I shut off the tap and stood to listen to what my feisty child might say. Hanadi had middle-child syndrome, and probably for good reason. Amani could do no wrong and Ahmed, the baby, got away with everything. So Hanadi had to fight for attention any way she could. She was a firecracker—absolutely incapable of understanding the word "no," or of holding her tongue.

Hanadi thought about it for a full thirty seconds and then said, "Yes. Let's go downstairs."

Maybe she was listening after all.

But now, between my school and their school and all the driving back and forth to dance and hockey, I just gave up on order and cleanliness. I no longer had the time to get out my bucket of toothbrushes and swab the baseboards. When my friend Ishraq, who had a wicked sense of humor, gave Ahmed a toy drum set as a gift, I did not yell at them to keep down the racket or fuss when it became a landing pad for dress-up clothes, other toys, and dust. And I did not concern myself with fine dining so much as with bulk meals—casseroles, lasagna, and big pots of soup—that were meant to last all week.

To this day, we all hate leftovers.

On top of all this, our family had taken on a new responsibility: raising my husband's little brother. Wan had grown into an adorable, shy seven-year-old with big brown eyes and a hesitant smile. He was less than three weeks older than Amani, and he and I had always had a special relationship. During my in-laws' visit to see the new house over the Christmas holidays, I had attempted to help him with his English. I gave him a pen and asked him to write me a three-page story about a blue unicorn. Two hours later, after working very hard at it, he came back with a three-page-long sentence, with no punctuation and no beginning or ending. I realized we had some serious work ahead of us.

As my in-laws' Calgary visit drew to a close, I made them an offer: "Why don't you leave him here for six months, until the summer, and we'll enroll him in school and improve his English?" That would put him far ahead of everyone else when he returned to Yemen. They agreed because they saw the opportunity for him. They loved their son very much, and I was so happy that they trusted me with him.

We had an amazing six months of swim lessons, ski lessons, skateboarding, and a brand-new bike that he loved. When the summer came, he refused to leave. He locked himself in his room and said, "I don't want to go back." With his parents' blessing, I went to court to be appointed his legal guardian. The look on the judge's face when he found out I was applying to become the legal guardian of my young brother-in-law was priceless. "This is one I have never seen before," he said with a grin.

In the months and years that followed, full of doctor's appointments and parent-teacher meetings, he became like my own child—only I was extra careful about everything having to do with him. If one of my kids screwed up, they were mine, and I would be the one blaming myself. But my in-laws had entrusted their child to my care.

I was so worried about his future that, as strict and demanding as I was with my three, Wan had it much, much worse.

Life was a house of cards: one gust of wind—a kid's sudden illness or school drama—and I lost my ability to remain upright. However, my going back to school turned out to be one of the best things to happen to my kids. They learned independence, self-reliance, and hard work.

Let me rephrase that. They were forced to learn independence, self-reliance, and hard work . . . and they didn't think it was one of the best things to happen to them at all.

When the demands of school increased, entire days passed by in which I hurried them along to get chores done without asking them how their day was. And just as I was cutting corners at home, I was cutting corners at school to accommodate household duties and the kids' activities.

I told several of my first-year illustration teachers that I wasn't going to be an artist and that their classes didn't matter. I was going to "blow them off" because I had no intention of becoming an illustrator, I said, with a load of sweetness and honey in my voice. They didn't buy it. However, they still shook their heads, laughed at my audacity, and cut me a lot of slack as I raced off to pick up the kids at hockey or dance. Or at least most of them did.

Tim did everything but give me a break; however, he did it with a whole lot of charm. One day during class, as he walked by all our work on the wall, he sneezed loudly. "Excuse me," he said, looking at me with a grin and a raised eyebrow. "I'm allergic to really bad art."

In my second year, one of the first assignments in drawing class involved drawing a human skeleton. Without a good grasp of what the instructor wanted or much time to worry about it, I found a sketch of a skeleton that I liked. He looked like he was dancing. I enlarged it, printed it, copied it exactly—seven ribs on one side and eleven on the other—and handed it in.

At the presentation, when I saw my classmates' anatomically correct submissions, which they had actually drawn themselves, I realized I might have to talk my way out of this situation.

"Tracing Hallmark cards might have earned you a pat on the head and a gold star from your mother," said Karl, our instructor, with a dry edge to his voice, "but in art school, it gets you an F."

"But he has character," I said, and reminded him that nothing in the assignment said anything about an anatomically correct skeleton.

My grade remained an F.

Experiences like that helped me learn the most basic lessons of marketing: how to convince your audience that your hastily drawn, put-zero-effort-into-it homework is "art." In other words, the art of bullshit. I got very good at it, and by the end of my fourth year, I got away with turning in a crumpled-up ball of white paper for a final project when I ran out of time to do anything else. I waxed poetic about how it symbolized the great abysses of the winter sky in the depths of a depressed mind. I got an A−.

Art school was probably the best and worst education for a sheltered girl from Yemen. One morning, there was a naked girl in the cafeteria, wearing a backpack, buttering her bread as if it were nothing out of the ordinary. We were used to a very casual environment—paint-splattered T-shirts, charcoal-coated hands, and occasionally some ripped clothing—but this was something new. She had decided to be her own art project. She continued to walk around naked all day, but according to her prof, her body was not a work of art.

She got an F on her assignment too.

I was in line at the bookstore one day when I noticed that the woman in front of me was in my illustration class. I introduced myself and learned that her name was Louise. The casual chat we shared while waiting to buy our supplies cemented a friendship that has lasted through a lifetime of change. Louise and I were complete opposites in many ways, starting with our looks: she is a six-foot-tall blond beauty with emerald-green eyes. Our styles were just as different: I was all about deep color and the intricacies of ornate design; she loved Danish minimalism. I loved to cook rich, bold, experimental meals. She survived on open-face sandwiches. She was laid-back and calm, and I was (and still am) several bundles of mad energy.

And then there was Jon. Young and oh so talented, Jon was a farm boy from Saskatchewan who called me "Mom" in a very sarcastic voice every time I tried to mother him—which happened a lot. My kids still call him Uncle Jon.

Louise, Jon, and I, along with our friend Mike, created an inner circle of students who hung out together all the time, often at Vicious Circle, a bar with saggy couches and dusty chandeliers, or the Ship and Anchor, a popular hangout on 17th Avenue where, on sunny days, we would sit at picnic tables on the patio listening to live music.

Louise's typical response to me then—and now—was a wry smile and an exasperated shake of the head. When we met, I was getting up to things she had done in her teen years; she seesawed between being my partner in crime and the grown-up, with arms crossed, telling me no.

Louise is the only person in my life who knows absolutely everything about me, good and bad. I've always been able to tell her anything: insecurities, worries about my children, concerns about my marriage. We've talked about life and love and loss and everything in between. She still has a photo of me, taken at four in the morning, while we were working on a project for school; in it, I'm wearing oversized red velour pajamas, ginormous glasses, and rollers in my hair. Every time I get too full of myself, she threatens to post it where people can see it.

Everyone needs a good ego-disciplining friend like my tall, beautiful friend Louise.

When I could not stay at school for long hours or pull all-nighters in the studio, as many of our classmates could, Louise would come to our house to work and keep me company into the wee hours of the morning, drinking tea and eating biscuits.

My kids still call her Auntie Louise—she tells them not to call her that anymore but secretly loves that they do. She is less fond of my nickname for her: Weezy.

During one particularly grueling stretch of work when she was spending most of her time at my house, she said, "You know, your kids can't walk by without your reaching out to hug or kiss them or to tell them how good, smart, or beautiful they are. You have so much confidence and love for them. It's clear why they have so much confidence and love for themselves."

I was surprised because the thing is, I was pretty closed. I didn't like to share feelings or even talk about them. I was not comfortable with compliments, flowery language, or too many words. And I didn't love to be overly touched or fawned over.

But kids are different. They are special, vulnerable little beings whose future is shaped by how loved and cared for they feel. Their confidence is cemented by how many times we praise them for their efforts. My children are my entire world, and I will pull out all the stops to make sure they have the best chances in life. My unconscious efforts with them became more deliberate as I understood better what they needed from me and from the world.

However, in our house, the person that speaks the loudest is also the one that gets heard, and I have no problem taking my children's knees out from under them when they get rude or disrespectful or arrogant.

At first, Louise and me working together meant each of us was working on her own project in the same room; eventually, we were truly collaborating. As we'd lose focus or interest, we would switch computers to work on each other's project. We did amazing work together. We made each other better—most of the time. I was obsessive-compulsive and tightly wound, and Louise was patient and relaxed. I needed order and she needed chaos. It was a friendship made in a very frustrating heaven.

As you can imagine, art school had quite a drinking culture. By this point in my life, I was a world away from Arabic school and yet unable to let go of everything as I knew it. I didn't drink, which sometimes felt awkward. *Why don't I drink alcohol?* I asked myself. I was starting to have so many internal conflicts relating to religion—not my belief in God, which never wavered, but the ideas of what is right and what is wrong. So much is up for interpretation and questioning in any religion, and I had a hard time getting past my feelings of guilt and the decades of voices in my head.

Then came the Calgary Stampede, an annual ten-day, citywide bash that is a combination of circus, carnival, rock concert, and rodeo—a cowboy Mardi Gras. The event is an institution in the city; however, I did not learn about the corporate drinking culture around Stampede until the summer before my last year of school, when I worked as an intern for a downtown oil company. We had a huge party for Stampede, and I invited Louise to come with me. That event was just one of many that happened every day during the drinking fest otherwise known as the Stampede. All seemed to have an infinite amount of alcohol flowing from the taps.

When Louise and I walked in, we got an arm's-length strip of drink tickets. I turned to her, feeling mischief turn up the corners of my mouth. It was the perfect night for me to drink for the first time.

Louise sighed. "Oh, boy."

I started with a margarita, took a sip, and spit it out. "Yuck, what is this?"

Louise told me it was an acquired taste.

"Why on earth would anyone want to acquire this taste?" I replied, wrinkling my nose.

I ordered a martini next, and that too got handed to Louise. That's how the night progressed. I wet my lips with vile-tasting drinks and then passed them on to my loyal, accommodating friend.

I went home sober and disappointed. My sidekick, however, could not remember the end of the night or most of the following day. Louise, as would become the norm in the next few years, took a bullet—or ten—for me that night.

It Takes Perspective.

When an old farmer's stallion wins a prize, his neighbor stops by to congratulate him, but the old farmer says, "Who knows what is good and what is bad?"

The next day his valuable horse is stolen. His neighbor comes to console him, but the old man replies, "Who knows what is good and what is bad?"

A few days later the horse escapes its captors and joins a herd of wild mares, leading them back to the farm. The neighbor is happy for the farmer, but the farmer says, "Who knows what is good and what is bad?"

The following day, while trying to break in one of the mares, the farmer's son is thrown and breaks his leg. The neighbor calls in with concern and is told again, "Who knows what is good and what is bad?"

The following week the army passes by, forcibly conscripting soldiers for the war, but they do not take the farmer's son because he cannot walk. The neighbor thinks, *Who knows what is good and what is bad?*

This story is over two thousand years old, and it is one of my favorites.

It's also a favorite of David Allan, editorial director of CNN Health and Wellness, who writes a column called *The Wisdom Project* about applying to one's life the wisdom and philosophy found everywhere, from ancient texts to pop culture.

He observes that we use the good-or-bad dichotomy to categorize nearly everything in our lives—events, people, food, decisions, even world history. But the lesson of the story is that there is actually no such thing as good or bad. It's a false distinction and a trap that only causes psychic pain. Good things are constantly being born out of the seemingly bad, and vice versa. Often, it seems, it's just a matter of time until an event or decision from one category leads directly to one in the other.

When my dad got cancer for the first time, he was only forty-four years old. His reaction when the doctor gave him the news—"*Alhamdulillah*," or "Thank God"—may seem strange, but my dad intended to wait and see what happened with this horse.

Being grateful instead of angry changes your perspective. Instead of dwelling on "Why me?" you find the part of yourself that says, "I can handle this. Let's see where it goes."

How you see things is entirely in your control. Paint your world the color you like best.

Who knows what is good and what is bad?

CHAPTER FIFTEEN

My final years of art school had less to do with drawing and illustration and everything to do with human behavior—identifying a target audience and determining the best way to sell to them.

This is something I knew about instinctively and applied in my own life. The image I presented to the world was just as much a creation as what was on my canvas or in my sketchbook. Some aspects of my new persona fit into the idea I'd always had of who I was; others I was just discovering.

In order to succeed in art school, and get a proper job afterwards, I needed to act knowledgeable, sophisticated, and confident. Especially since I was convinced I wasn't any of these things. I had such huge gaps in my knowledge of popular culture. Growing up and living in Yemen, I had missed out on years of movies, music, and shows. I didn't know who Darth Vader was or that the Macarena was a dance.

But all of a sudden, I was not so far behind the class, and some of our classmates began consulting with Louise and me about their projects before turning them in. I was a pretty decent designer, but I was an even better creative director.

I tried to be as strategic as possible, and to ask questions that would help others take a similar approach. I put a huge amount of research into each project, incorporating any relevant cultural or historical context, as well as the business case, for any design or decision.

I now had a constructive way to channel my energy—namely, into my portfolio. I wanted a book that would illustrate my flexibility and my depth, and the fact that I could make choices that others didn't helped a great deal. Louise and I designed a magazine about urban development. I built a brand for an allergen-free bakery (in 1999, long before "gluten-free" was cool and I was diagnosed as celiac) and called it Rasa, the Sanskrit word for "clean slate." I created a catalog for a clothing store and an ad campaign for an oil and gas company.

Yes, you read that right: I knew that my market, Calgary, was an oil town and that I needed to appeal to the people who were going to hire me.

By the time I handed in an assignment, I could answer any question and defend any design decision, from using lowercase fonts to appear friendlier to incorporating minimalist white pages to appear more cultured. We were used to criticism in class—to hearing things like "It's not working" or "I don't see it." The teachers were tough on us; however, thanks to age, experience, and the thick skin that comes along with those two things, I was able to take most of that commentary and find solutions so I didn't hear it again.

Once I had developed more comfort and more confidence in my style, I stopped seeking out the opinions of my instructors. I was learning that presentation itself is also an art. If I showed them what I was working on, then I lost the opportunity to wow them.

I have learned, in art and in life, that you need to set your stage. Don't give anyone anything until you are ready, so their focus and attention remain on you—and so you can surprise and delight them. I learned to read the room, manage my audience, and lead them down the path I wanted them to follow. But I wasn't able to do that until I had confidence in my product—until I believed my work was good. Really good.

One of my favorite quotes is "If you show a client only what they are asking for, someone else will show them what they never believed possible." I was in the business of marketing, and I was getting better at hiding what I didn't know.

"You know, you've barely talked with us all semester," said one of my professors, Rik. "You really missed your opportunity to get good feedback." I told him I was doing fine and did not need any help. He was not impressed. As far as he was concerned, my arrogant attitude had little to back it up.

Weeks later, Louise and I presented our work to him. I fully expected him to find something, anything, wrong with our work, if only to simply put us in our place. After we finished the presentation, there was a pause, and then Rik nodded his head and gave a very rare "Well done." We were ecstatic . . . and learning what it took to impress.

Marketing is not just about selling a product—or yourself and your talent—it is about building trust. Rik never asked me about what I was working on again; instead, he anticipated the presentation, and I relished the response.

Toward the end of my time at ACAD, I began to spend time with my typography professor, Rita—a great designer and an especially gifted typographer who was only a few years older than I was. She was known to be standoffish with students, so I appreciated that she treated me less like a student and more like a peer.

Rita asked if I would be interested in modeling for a photo shoot she was arranging near Banff, and I jumped at the chance. It was a great opportunity for me to learn about the field outside the classroom, and it was a great personal opportunity too: my first road trip for "work" and to the most beautiful place I could ever imagine. When she told me to bring my husband, I asked if I could bring Louise instead.

Louise and I had an incredibly fun, all-expenses-paid trip to Emerald Lake Resort. Being in front of the camera was a new experience for me; I was the center of attention, something I wasn't used to, but it felt really good.

Before long, my friendship with Rita turned into a job offer: she was building a new agency with a well-known advertising exec, and she wanted me to join them.

"Working for Rita? She's difficult; you won't stay," said one of my teachers. Everyone who knew her reminded me of how tough she was—and how hard to work with. I waved off their concern: I would give it at least a year, learn everything I could, and then, if I needed to, I would move on. She was so incredibly talented; I knew it would be worth it.

I was so proud not only to be working for someone as respected as she was but also to be the first student in our class to get hired. It was not typical to find a job before the portfolio show—the culmination of the four years, where graduating students got to show off our work and people from the industry came to collect our business cards.

The night before the show, the phone rang after the kids were asleep. It was Ishraq. "Look, I know you're busy—I didn't want to tell you this, and it's not a big deal, don't worry," she said. "I have breast cancer, and my surgery is tomorrow."

Standing very still, I did not know what to say to her. I stammered a promise to visit right after my portfolio show and her surgery and then hung up, feeling numb. The next day I walked into her hospital room while she was struggling to pull her long, thick, beautiful hair into a ponytail.

"Can you help me put my hair up?" she asked with a smile. "I'm going to shave it tomorrow. It's going to fall out in a few weeks anyway."

That was when my tears came. I first struggled to hide them, and then struggled to stop. She laughed, calling me a silly goose: "What are you crying about?" She informed me that she was the one who was supposed to be crying, and since she wasn't, I needed to stop.

The strength of that woman was amazing. Her dedication to life, her spirit of peace, and her capacity to handle adversity were also tied up in her belief in *Alhamdulillah*.

It made me so sad to realize that only one of us was on the road to achieving the dreams we'd talked about in those long-ago days when she was a pretty bride and I was a weary mother.

ACAD gave me amazing tools, but working with Rita taught me design. She *was* tough, as advertised—a blunt instrument, though also exceptionally detail-oriented. Her business partner, Dan, was well-dressed, well-connected, and picky as hell. For a while, it was just the three of us in a small room tucked in a basement behind a larger agency's storage room. That sounds unglamorous, but it was a stunningly designed space you would never expect, hung with incredible art.

Dan was a perfectionist and also a bit of a bully. Midway through my first day of work, I stood up and put on my coat. Dan, without raising his head, asked if I was going to lunch, using a tone that implied I should be working instead. When I said yes, he asked me to run across the street and grab him a sandwich from the Danish deli. I looked at him for just a minute to see if he was serious. When I realized he was, I laughed and walked out the door.

I returned exactly one hour later and picked up my work again, without saying a word. It was the best thing I could have done because, from that day on, I got a grudging respect and everyone else got the bullying.

I was learning not just design but also conflict management. Every day, some sort of argument would erupt between Rita and Dan, two very volatile personalities, and turn into flat-out warfare. I learned to duck my head and stay out of their way until the storm blew past.

In my transition from Rita's friend to her employee, I realized how much my well-being depended on how she was feeling. If she was angry, a spark that could ignite in an instant, she would turn to me, eyes flashing, and the quality of my day would deteriorate quickly. However, although Rita had her bad moments, she had a lot of good moments too. I have a great respect for her talent and was grateful for the opportunity.

The first client I got to work for was a small storage company for oil and gas clients; our brief was to illustrate how the company helped clients get from point A to point B, so Rita and I created an elaborate pop-up element. The book folded in complicated and fun ways; we made it interactive for the viewer in order to convey how the company would go not only in a straight line but in every direction until they found the right path.

We illustrated the ways they were flexible and fun. It was a brilliantly simple solution to a complicated problem, and the book, my first real design job, won multiple international design awards.

It was such a glorious feeling to create an idea, see it come to life and solve a client's problem, and then get recognized for your effort. We went on to win many more awards that first year of my career.

I loved every aspect of working with clients—from meeting them for the first time to showing them the potential solutions to the problems they had shared with us. And inspiration for those solutions could come from very surprising places.

One evening the kids came into my home office to see what I was doing. I showed them a project I was struggling with. I had to design a campaign for a hair loss clinic. Amani quickly came up with an idea that was so brilliant I built an entire campaign around it. One ad showed a chimp who was bending over and looking back at the camera, the only nonhairy part of his body being his bum. It simply said, "Bald spot?" It's still one of my favorite campaigns.

After the ads ran, the clinic was booked in advance for four solid months—something that had never happened to them before. Nurses told us many people called simply to say it was a great ad, though one man cheekily called just to ask if the ad meant we were calling him a "monkey's ass."

The strategy behind the campaign was appealing to the actual target audience, which, surprisingly, was not the balding men themselves but their female partners. They were the ones who called the clinic with questions or to schedule an appointment. The ones who pushed their men past being intimidated or daunted. Our goal for the campaign was to create an approach that was fun and lighthearted.

Things were starting to really click for me. The more I understood good design and how to market it, the more confident I became. I loved how I could make ordinary things stand out as something unique, desired, even coveted. And I saw how powerful brands are. They give us identity: we can become an outlaw with a Harley, a creative thinker with a Mac, or an athlete with Nikes. They give us status: all you need to do is flash your red Louboutin soles and you stand a little taller. And they give us a sense of belonging.

Branding is the ultimate art of persuasion, and I loved everything about it. I loved dictating what was cool and convincing people to buy what I wanted them to buy, eat what I wanted them to eat, and go where I wanted them to go. An incredible high went with that power.

The more we won awards, and the more our name got out, the more I realized that what I really liked about my work was the strategy, idea creation, and problem-solving. It was as heady as a whiff of Arabian incense.

One day, when Rita and I were discussing a pitch we had the next morning, she said, "I'm not worried. You will flirt and win them over." Taken aback, I asked her what she meant.

"I don't mean in a sexual way," she said. "You attract people— men and women. It's part of your being so honest and open and curious. It's that smile, your innocence, and your talent."

I do have a wide-openness, a genuine curiosity and desire to understand other people's lives, their thoughts, and why they do the things they do. I am fascinated by human behavior and so interested in the stories that others have to tell.

The flip side is that people are drawn to me because I show an interest in them, because I am engaged and excited. Because I speak with passion. And because I am interested in them, people want to help me if they can.

While Rita may not have meant "flirting" in a sexual sense, she was teaching me that in Canada I was not free from the judgments and double standards that were a part of life in Yemen. They just looked completely different. Women were just as used here as anywhere else. Dan once pulled me into a project for a men's clothing store at the very last minute, insisting that I deliver a proposal to the client's office. "I'll pick you up and drive you over," he said. "I want you to meet the client. Give the proposal to him—not to anyone else." I agreed, wondering why he didn't just take it himself. I was busy and this errand would mean staying late again. "Asshole," I muttered as I got in the car. I dropped off the proposal and assured Dan that I'd handed it directly to the client.

The next day, I was on my way to see a different client—this time with Rita, and this time as part of the team pitching a major account. It was an important meeting, and I had dressed carefully, in wide-leg pants, a silk blouse, and heels. While we were out, I asked Rita what had been going on with Dan the day before.

The client had seen me at the office, she said, and he thought I was beautiful. Dan was being strategic about winning the pitch, which is why he dangled me in front of the client. When we got back to the office later that afternoon, I passed Dan in the hallway. He commented on my outfit and said: "Why didn't you wear *that* yesterday?"

"I didn't know I was going to be on display," I told him calmly. "Next time, tell me, so I can put on my fuck-me boots." He laughed out loud. That was the thing about Dan: he pushed as hard as he could to get what he wanted, but he knew the limits. When he reached them, he was graceful about backing off.

As put off as I was, it was another valuable lesson: there are a lot of people with talent, but what gets you the job is the relationship.

I was learning to dress with style and flair, to be trendy and cutting-edge in a way that was expected of a creative director. While still very conservative, I was starting to play with my ever-changing style again. When you are a creative, the clients expect you to be out there, so you can get away with a lot. They really don't want to see you in a button-down suit, looking just like them. They were looking for extraordinary talent, and we had to look the part. I was a work in progress: pushing the envelope at times and retreating at others. I started to experiment, to find a look that was uniquely my own.

I had brought my first paycheck to a boutique called Primitive and spent it all on a two-thousand-dollar suit made of stretchy black netting over heavy dark-purple taffeta, with a wraparound belt and a tight knee-length skirt. It was more money than I had ever spent on an article of clothing, or even an entire wardrobe. As soon as I got home, I felt sick about the cost, and it hung in my closet for months before I was able to wear it. The suit was a symbol to me. Polished, stylish, and sexy . . . a suit for the woman I didn't yet believe I was.

As I approached the end of my first year with Rita and Dan, I felt proud of what I had accomplished. Working for them had given me prestige, my first international awards, and a great education. Yet I felt a growing hunger, realizing more and more every day that a first job is only that, and that life is a series of opportunities to move up and move on. I needed to start networking in earnest, and quite frankly, I needed more people than just those two around me.

Each day, when I walked in and out of the office building, I passed one of Calgary's top creative directors, who was usually out on the sidewalk smoking. Trevor worked for the larger agency in the building, one of our rivals; I would smile at him as I walked by, and he would smile back. There had never been any reason to have a conversation with him.

One day, I mustered the courage to introduce myself. "I'm a designer who works downstairs, and I would love to show you my portfolio some time."

"How about noon tomorrow?" Trevor said with a smile.

I sat across from him the next day, describing the thought process that went into each project in my book. While I was talking, his demeanor changed, and he looked more serious and thoughtful.

"Listen, we're not hiring right now," he said finally. "But this is really good stuff. I'd be happy to send out some emails on your behalf." When I got back to my desk after lunch, I had seven new emails in my inbox, six of which were addressed to top creative directors in the city and cc'd to me. They all said the same thing: "I just met with Zahra Al-harazi. She has a brilliant design portfolio, one of the best I have ever seen. You really should meet her."

The last one was different, addressed only to me. And it was a gracious apology. Trevor had always thought I was pretty, he wrote, and that's why he had met with me. "I agreed to meet you for the wrong reason, and I didn't think I'd see much in your book, but I was blown away. My apologies for my behavior."

I was touched by his honesty and surprised by it. In my excitement to get an audience with him, I hadn't noticed anything. I was naive and innocent, and I didn't know enough to recognize the signs of his interest. I was open and friendly with everyone and didn't know how to be any other way. Sometimes a smile is simply just that, a smile.

One of the introductions that Trevor made was to Glenn, the creative director and a partner at an esteemed agency with offices in Calgary and across North America. He listened intently as I walked him through my work. "You have one of the best portfolios I have seen," he said finally. "But I would never hire you."

He then taught me a valuable lesson about knowing your audience.

"You showed up at our offices in a pencil skirt and heels," said Glenn. His agency worked for agricultural clients and owned their own farm, where the employees all worked for a couple of weeks every year; they all wore jeans every day. They even had a pig trough in their office where they threw in all their awards. They are very proud of who they are—and if I had just done some basic research, I would have known all that. Glenn then proceeded to tell me that, since I did not seem to know what the hell I was doing, I needed a good mentor. Him.

His offer made a remarkable difference in my life. He remains one of my favorite sounding boards, the person I rely on when I need to talk something out. He lets me work through the problem, listens, and then tells me to put on my big-girl pants and get going.

One of the most important pieces of advice Glenn has ever given me is that one person will never be able to give you everything you need. You need different people to feed the different parts of you. Thanks to him, I now have mentors who will advise, mentors who will kick me in the ass when I need it, and mentors who will simply listen. I have friends who will do the same. I have cultivated a wide network of the greatest of champions. I have often reached out to people, asking for mentorship, training, advice, and connection. I have never heard a single no. I was a nobody immigrant from nowhere, and not one single no.

Every email, every phone call, turned into someone I learned something from.

The offer I accepted wasn't from any of Trevor's contacts but from Larry, an advertising exec who had recently bought a design firm he planned to remake into an ad agency. With a seventy-person team and an extensive client list, it felt like the big leagues. Larry knew that his greatest challenge would be the staff and their loyalty to him, as he was making huge changes at the firm.

He was rough around the edges and, in some ways, that quintessential 1960s *Mad Men* ad guy: passionate, crass, smart, and driven.

When I got into the office on my first day, I learned he had hired me without consulting the head of the design department, who was understandably not happy. For months, I got the cold shoulder, significant client projects were taken out of my hands, and I was not invited to the Monday morning staff meeting. After a few months of awkwardness, I decided I could do without this kind of disregard. If I wasn't able to do good work or have fun, what was the point of being there and not home with my kids?

I checked back on some of the previous job offers and learned that a couple were still available. I walked into Larry's office, resignation letter in hand. He tore it up and said, "Give me three months." By July, I was the head of the design department and Larry's trusted advisor—although I think sometimes I was a bug in his ear and sometimes a thorn in his side.

My new sense of confidence and my ability to engage and work hard got me far in my new role and allowed me to win over the team. I was there around the clock when we had big deadlines and even when we didn't. I not only worked on perfecting the design department but also got involved everywhere. I lent a helping hand wherever I could. I smiled at everyone and learned the names of their dogs and their children's birthdays—both clients and the team.

It brought me much success and helped build a great team with great relationships that are still valid, still meaningful, and still some of the best I ever made.

I designed the company's brand, earning Larry's eternal love for showing him his baby in print for the first time. As I grew more accustomed to the practice of design, I focused on the art of business. I learned to engage clients, become their friend and advisor, and in turn make them my biggest fans. I was having the time of my life and soon became a permanent member of the new-business team. That meant a great deal coming from Larry, an ad guy who used to tell my design team that "designers are a dime a dozen." But he always said it with an endearing twinkle in his eye, and even though you knew he meant it, you were able to forgive him.

It Takes Resilience.

The *New Yorker*'s Maria Konnikova wrote an article in 2016 titled "How People Learn to Become Resilient." She concludes, "Resilience presents a challenge for psychologists. Whether you can be said to have it or not largely depends not on any particular psychological test but on the way your life unfolds. If you are lucky enough to never experience any sort of adversity, we won't know how resilient you are. It's only when you're faced with obstacles, stress, and other environmental threats that resilience, or the lack of it, emerges: Do you succumb or do you surmount?"

Human beings are prone to worry. We can take a minor thing and replay it over and over until it loses all context and scale. But, says Konnikova, that's a self-fulfilling prophecy. "Frame adversity as a challenge, and you become more flexible and able to deal with it, move on, learn from it, and grow. Focus on it, frame it as a threat, and a potentially traumatic event becomes an enduring problem; you become more inflexible, and more likely to be negatively affected."

That's good news. It means resilience is a learned skill and not something we either have or don't. If you want it, resilience is yours to enjoy. You just have to take a small step outside your comfort zone. Just one step. Every single day.

Adversity is inevitable in life, but self-pity is not. Apathy is not. Certainly, defeat is not.

When you make conscious efforts to frame your situations with positivity, they become sources of strength instead of chains.

CHAPTER SIXTEEN

Inevitably, as the demands of my career increased, my time spent with family decreased. In some ways, this was a natural progression. My husband and I were each busy with our careers. The kids were ever busier with their own lives, their friends, and their many activities. As every second became priceless, the almost three hours a day I spent commuting to the kids' school, downtown to the office, and back became untenable.

I tried to encourage my husband to spend time with my new colleagues and the design community. But he told me that he was perfectly happy to stay home while I went out—he said he didn't like my weird artsy friends.

We were building two distinctly different lives that just happened to meet up in the same house at night. His friends became his friends, and mine became mine. Coworkers would joke that I had secretly killed my husband and buried him in the backyard, and no one would ever know because they had never met him.

I tried all the time to pull the kids closer. I was strict, always worried about what could happen to them. I came by it honestly: my parents had put me in a glass bubble, and now I was putting my children in one. I worried about what they would do and what others would do to them. The rules were endless. *Eat all your food, especially at someone else's home. Thank them for the great food, even if it isn't. Be nice to your sister. Don't wear this, don't wear that. Don't make noise, your baba is home. Go do your homework. No, you can't go out.*

I was trying to shape them into perfect human beings, forgetting that they were already perfect human beings. The expectations my parents had placed on me, and that I had railed against, didn't have to be inherited by my children. I was trying to make them live in a culture that was no longer theirs, and I didn't know how to let go of the rigid rules I was breaking for myself.

One day, when my girls were about nine and eight years old, we were at a school concert and saw one of the girls' friends roll her eyes and be rude to her mother. Amani turned to her sister and said, in a stage whisper meant for me, "What do you think Mama would do if we talked to her like that?"

Hanadi looked at me and laughed. "Skin us alive and string us up by our toes," she said.

They were only partly joking.

Wan got the brunt of it. He was extremely good-looking and shy at the same time. He was also an incredibly hard worker—someone who gave it his all, all the time. He worked very hard in school and tried so hard to be good. It was never enough for me. The possibility of Wan's failure became my personal fear. I wore him like a badge of honor and wanted him to be the shining example of my stellar child-rearing.

There were moments when I wondered whether we had made a mistake in thinking we could raise Wan in a way that was right for him. My in-laws had the pleasure of spoiling him when they saw him, and my husband, his older brother, was hands-off: his view from the beginning was that children belong with their parents and this was a mistake. I was the one who had to dish out the punishments and make the rules.

My children had the comfort of knowing I was their mother and not going anywhere. But Wan worried about having to go back to Yemen. He also didn't have the advantage of the years of Canadian schooling the other kids had. The more I expected, the harder he worked. Unfortunately, I often neglected to notice or praise him for it.

Sometimes we pat ourselves on the back for doing what we think is the right thing, when the reality is quite different. I loved Wan like my own son, but I don't think I did right by him; I don't think any of us did. I wish I could do it all again, differently this time.

For years, my parents had been talking about retiring in Canada; another wave of violence in Yemen suddenly brought that goal into sharp focus. It was a true turning point.

My husband and I had finally received our citizenship at a ceremony four years earlier, without much fuss. We'd shown up in casual clothes, without the kids, who weren't required to attend. We had already felt Canadian for so long that the oath-taking ceremony seemed like simply a formality, and to be honest, we didn't quite understand the significance of what was about to happen.

We'd arrived to find a hundred people dressed in their finest, most of whom had brought their family and friends. They all carried flowers and flags and were so happy. We looked at each other in shock and slinked out as soon as we could, under the disapproving stare of the swearing-in judge.

Now, as we applied to sponsor my parents' immigration, we could not deny the value of our decision.

By the time we got through the process, after several rounds of paperwork and a fair amount of waiting, they were more than ready to move. Especially my father, who had grown tired of fighting the good fight in a corrupt working environment that didn't value honesty. It was time for them to go.

We are each taught what to believe, and many of us feel invested in those perceived truths. *We are from Yemen; we belong in Yemen,* my father had said so many times, and yet, eventually, his experiences showed him otherwise.

Shortly after they arrived in Canada, and fifteen years after his first dance with cancer, my father was diagnosed with cancer again. This time in his stomach. My parents worried it would affect their chances of citizenship; instead, within a week, he was in the Tom Baker Cancer Centre for surgery and some of the best care in the country. The fact that they were being treated no differently from any other Canadian after being here for only a few months filled them with gratitude and wonder.

My mother now volunteers at Tom Baker regularly, sitting with cancer patients, holding their hands, doing Reiki healing on them when they need some comfort.

Unlike my husband and me, who had arrived with tiny children and hearts full of optimism, for my parents, packing up and starting over in Canada was at best bittersweet. My mother was delighted to have her entire family back together, but she struggled with leaving Yemen even more than my father did. She had worked so hard, for so many years, to build a life there.

Once again, my mother shipped herself a container filled with her life's most important treasures. This time, they were in perfect condition when she was ready for them on the other side.

In her container was a box for me. When she gave it to me, she told me it was things I'd left behind in my room, and she wasn't sure if I still wanted them. I opened the box to find all the gifts my father had brought me over the years from his business trips to exotic places. A mink hat from Russia, a Pink Floyd CD from the United States, a string of pearls from Japan, a Chanel purse from France.

While I used to think that he was out of touch, now that I looked down on my new-old treasures, I understood that he was ahead of his time.

My parents found a house in Calgary that my mother decorated with great care. In their basement she installed a full Yemeni diwan, a living room with floor cushions that looks like the Roche Dubois Mah Jong sofa dressed by Missoni Home—expensive and cutting-edge design to the rest of the world and common seating in Yemen. She proudly shows it off to anyone who comes to visit.

Once again, I could sit on my parents' diwan. But now I was a Canadian citizen with a leather skirt in my closet, and I counted among my closest friends people who were gay, people who were of all religions, or of none. And I had, by this point, consumed copious amounts of alcohol.

My beliefs about right and wrong had shifted as I better understood the breadth of my choices, and I could more deeply own both the benefits and consequences of making them.

It Takes Joy.

Every violent roller-coaster ride has a peak. Each terrifying low has a high. In that moment lives deep fulfillment and contentment. Joy in the morning sun and joy in the evening stars. You, at your best, breathing in your own wonderful life.

And then repeat.

It Takes Belief.

It will all be okay in the end. If it's not okay, it's not the end.
—Unknown

It Takes Having an Opinion.

We must always take sides. Neutrality helps the oppressor, never the victim. Silence encourages the tormentor, never the tormented. Sometimes we must interfere.
—Elie Wiesel

CHAPTER SEVENTEEN

As I built my department at the agency, I got to live out the old joke that graphic design is advertising's poor cousin. The attention, the mystique, and the resources went to the advertisers; they were the ones who sold the big ideas and won the hearts and minds. The ad team—mostly guys—were the cool kids who came in late, drank too much, and worked however, and whenever, they wanted. They were seen as the visionaries, while the design team were simply charged with delivering on that vision.

Patrick, the creative director and my boss, was a celebrated ad guy from Toronto who had worked on some pretty big accounts in his time. Initially, he didn't seem to have much appreciation for the experience I brought to the table. Art directors see designers as a pair of hands to put on paper the ideas they come up with. We were much more than that, and I wanted a chance to use our skills and show the world what design can do.

Since Patrick didn't look to me for such wisdom, I sometimes vented in Larry's office, pissed off that I didn't have control over projects. Larry liked me—indulged me, even. But he too was an ad guy. "Zahra, do what Patrick tells you to do." I felt like I was back in Yemen, and I rebelled here too and went ahead, around, and sideways to do it my way.

Eventually I gained Patrick's respect at work and outside of it, and we became good friends. In fact, we spent a lot of time together. Until one day Larry pulled me aside. "You know," he said, "the optics aren't so good with you and your boss."

To say I was shocked was an understatement. Every day, I was learning something new about this adopted country of mine. I had come from a closed Eastern society where I got into trouble talking to a boy outside school grounds. Now I was being told that in this modern Western society, men and women could not be friends?

"Seriously, Larry?" I asked.

He held up his hands to cut off the conversation. "I am just saying your relationship is being noticed," he said. I told him I would not change my behavior. I did not come to Canada to worry about what a few closed-minded people would say.

No matter where I went, women's interactions with the opposite sex were being monitored, judged, and condemned.

As I gained more respect at work, I also gained the responsibility of leading client jobs. One of the new clients that came to us was an investment company just for women. I spent one afternoon listening to their plan to target recently divorced and widowed women by connecting them with a team of women who were not only savvy investors but also a shoulder to cry on.

That was enough for me. I went into Larry's office and said, "I am not the right person to work on this project."

I didn't understand the need for it—or like it. "I am a woman," I told him. "I have friends and many shoulders to cry on. When I go to an investment firm, it is for good, solid investment advice. If I wanted a good cry session, I would go home and watch *The English Patient*. I can't work on this, Larry; it's everything I've been running from."

I grew up in a culture where an absence of citizenship rights for women, combined with crushing poverty, created a society in which women are the property of men. The World Economic Forum's annual Gender Gap Report ranks Yemen as one of the worst countries for women to live. There, I had to sit in a separate room, away from the men; it was taboo to even have one see me without my headscarf on.

After having been banished to the women's corner for most of my life, being made to work on a "for women" product like this was infuriating. The fact is that female investors beat the returns earned by male investors on both an absolute and risk-adjusted basis. They're just as interested in superior investment results and tend to go a step further, looking for funds that act as a shock absorber during market downturns and companies that deliver positive social and economic benefits to the community.

But I was finding that this wide-open, full-of-justice-and-equality society, which I so firmly believed in, was not open and accessible to all. Women were treated better than they were in Yemen, but not by the huge margin I had expected. In both places they were given very similar pats on the head and platitudes.

To Larry's credit, he let me off the hook that time.

Since I was the head of the design department, I was also a people manager, responsible for the careers of my employees. However, the rules of engagement at the firm were tricky: just as Larry had hired me without consulting my boss, he hired a new designer without consulting me.

The person he hired had little talent and much arrogance and was difficult to work with. He eventually dug a deep enough hole for himself that even Larry wanted him gone. I was out to dinner with Larry and the head of account services when the two cornered me, telling me I had been right in my assessment. And then Larry said, "So we're in agreement. You'll have to fire him."

Wait, what? "You hired him. I told you he wasn't right for the team—you fire him," I countered.

Larry smirked. "You don't have what it takes to be the boss if you can't fire someone," he said. He was trying to teach me a leadership lesson; I believe he thought I was made of better stuff than I actually was. I had no intention of ever being responsible for taking away anyone's livelihood. Although I could tell Larry was disappointed, I resisted, believing this was not my ax to wield.

I had seen too much poverty, fought too many battles, to take on that burden. I would learn, in time, that true success depends on your ability to recognize what is right for the team and your willingness to step up and do what needs to be done for the good of the company. But at that moment, I was not going to be responsible for the loss of someone else's livelihood.

It would be some time before I could face the toughest stuff head-on, without automatically looking around for an escape hatch. Okay, that is a lie; I have never come to terms with that responsibility, no matter how needed it is.

In the end, Larry did the firing.

It Takes Hunger.

Listen closely to the fire in your belly. It burns with the knowledge of your unrealized potential.

What is it you want so badly that it almost hurts to think about? *Fight for it.*

It Takes Chutzpah.

There is an island that is disputed territory between Canada and Denmark. The militaries of both countries periodically visit to remove the other nation's flag and leave either a bottle of Danish schnapps or Canadian whisky.

CHAPTER EIGHTEEN

I kept my children sheltered as long as I possibly could, far beyond what I should have. I couldn't help myself. I knew better, but it was a big, bad, scary world out there.

Amani was probably the last girl in her class to be allowed to walk down the street to a friend's house alone. The first time I finally let her do it, after weeks of begging from her, she was already twelve—and I followed her in the car. I didn't think she saw me, but she did and was mad. She asked me if I trusted her. "Of course I do," I said. I told her she was my baby girl; I had always trusted her. It was other people I didn't trust.

She continued to walk to her friend's house, with me following her and her pretending to not notice, and we didn't talk about it again until a couple of weeks later when, late one night, Amani came into my room and threw herself into my arms, crying, "I am so sorry, Mama." I finally calmed her down and found out what was going on.

Ever the bookworm, she had been reading a book called *The Lovely Bones* that she got from a friend—a terrifying and captivating novel about a teenage girl who is brutally raped and murdered by her neighbor on her way home from a friend's house. The story is told from the dead girl's perspective from heaven as she watches her family fall apart.

She was so terrified of the book that she asked me to keep it for a few days because she didn't want to finish it just yet. Thankfully, for my own sanity, she continued to ask me for a ride to her friend's house for a little while longer.

Growing up, Amani was quiet, serious, and very smart. She was my little helper, my right hand—the one who watched out for everyone else. My little girl was practical and responsible, and I took that for granted.

Hanadi was the opposite: a Tasmanian devil on wheels. When Hanadi is around, the rest of us duck and get out of her way, then clean up the mess after she is gone. Like her sister, she was also an honor roll student. But she lived on a cloud, coming down to earth only when she chose to, usually with a story we had never heard before.

Amani thinks about something ten times, and Hanadi jumps in with both feet without a care in the world.

Once, on a trip to Europe, the girls each got five hundred euros to spend however they wanted. Amani spent her money wisely on sale items, buying a pair of Puma runners and a tiny Gucci purse that she still has, and put the remaining money in her savings account. Hanadi bought two suitcases of . . . stuff.

The one time they were a united front was when it came to my fashion choices. I will never forget standing in front of them in the very short cowboy-style denim skirt I had bought with Stampede in mind. Each of them shot it down, point-blank, in her own characteristic way.

"You are absolutely not leaving the house like that," Hanadi said.

"That is completely inappropriate mom-wear. Nope," added Amani, shaking her head.

Reluctantly agreeing with them, I sadly put the skirt back in the bag and put it in my car to return.

And then there was Ahmed, the long-awaited boy. His grandparents spoiled him terribly, and so did all his teachers—it was easy to do. With those big brown eyes and shy smile, he was the cutest thing. He was allowed to do everything the girls were not, like sleepovers and overnight school trips. I tried to give the girls more leeway, but their dad was still tied to the ways of the old country, where the standards for girls were different than they were for boys.

These exceptions did not serve my son well, and by the time he was in second grade, it seemed I was getting a daily call from the principal or vice-principal. Ahmed was playing with some of the naughtier older kids and getting into trouble, and his grades were starting to dip. It was exasperating trying to deal with a boy who was adopting the patriarchal ways of a society that was not his or mine.

The last straw was when his teacher and I caught him in a lie. Ahmed had told me he had no homework, and he had told his teacher he had forgotten it at home. I was so angry I grounded him for a month.

We were not always consistent about following through on the kids' punishments, but this time I stuck to it, making him sit at the kitchen table every night after dinner for two hours, doing homework and studying, without television, phone, or PlayStation privileges.

It had unintended but wonderful consequences: Ahmed had nothing to do but study, so he did. Then he aced a few papers and exams and realized he actually *was* smart. The praise he got from everyone didn't hurt, either. It made me realize that if you tell a child he is a bad kid over and over, he will start to believe it. From that day on, Ahmed found his academic stride and was also nominated as athlete of the year several times.

As the kids entered high school, I did everything I could to encourage them to spend time at home—that way, I could monitor them, meet their friends, and know they were safe. They had license to invite their friends over whenever they wanted. I would pay for pizza or make dinner; they could have the run of the walk-out basement and the big-screen TV.

Our house became a kids' hangout. The kids all went to the same school, and their friends' siblings did too. They all spent the afternoons together, and on most nights, I would need to count heads to know how many were staying for dinner or sleeping over.

That level of oversight became even more important to me once their dad began spending more time away on business. One day he came home with the news that his company was looking for some of its North American employees to work in Yemen. These were well-paying, sought-after expat positions.

I encouraged him to go for it. It was an opportunity to be closer to his family, who missed him dearly, and a way for us to make the distance between our two worlds seem a little smaller. And the money was so good.

At least that was how I framed it. He was concerned about leaving the kids and me for such long stretches of time, but I insisted. Just for a little while, I said, trying to persuade him to go. The job abroad had great perks: time off, frequent flyer miles. It was a way to get back to—and give back to—Yemen and potentially create an opportunity for the kids to get to know where they were from. But the truth was that in addition to all that, my heart was tired of being reminded daily that our marriage was in trouble.

I piled on all the good reasons until there was nothing left but "We need some time apart." By this point, we had evolved into strangers living under the same roof. I told myself he was not interested in what I was doing. Looking back now, what seemed like ambivalence on his part may also have been a defense mechanism. Why would anyone fight to be with someone when he felt resisted?

I felt guilty for being a catalyst in his leaving. After all, we had practically grown up together, we had kids together, we had lived several lifetimes together. I appreciated and respected that, in most traditional ways, he was a good husband and a great father. I had a lot of respect for the man he was, but did I love him the way I was supposed to love my husband? I wasn't sure.

While I carried guilt over his leaving, I knew him well enough to know he was also looking for an escape. I wasn't the wife he wanted me to be, he missed home, and he needed a break too.

It Takes Confidence.

Think of confidence as a living thing. A child of yours. You grow it by taking care of it. Feed your confidence daily, and it will get bigger bit by bit.

It's hungry for strategies that make it feel better: Get a great haircut, learn how to do your makeup well, and wear clothes that fit you properly (get things tailored!). Discover new skills, and then hone them after you acquire them. Exercise—study after study will tell you that people who work out lead happier lives. Read *everything*.

Become the most interesting person in the room.

You can feed your confidence endlessly, trust me. It will come back for more. It will never be full. It's a little bit greedy.

And when you run out of strategies, fake it. That works too.

Lift your head up, look the world in the eye, and act as though your jelly nerves are made of steel. Slow your breathing, lean back, loosen your jaw, smile, and listen actively.

I met Andrea a few years ago when we both attended a leadership conference in Washington, D.C. There were only six women at the conference, so I suggested to the organizers that we share rooms so we could get to know each other. Andrea put her hand up first and was my roommate.

When we met, I realized how shy she was and how beautiful she was inside. As we were getting ready, I told her I had spent a lot of time standing behind makeup artists and getting models ready for photo shoots and had learned a lot and *loved* doing makeup . . . did she want me to do hers for dinner?

Her eyes lit up and she said yes! . . . if I could make her look like me. I laughed and told her about my false eyelashes and my years of contouring training. That night she stood a little taller and smiled a little bigger, and she looked gorgeous.

I got this message from her a year later:

Good morning, Zahra. I am wrapping up my last day of committee meetings for Entrepreneurs' Organization in Vancouver and wanted to take a moment to thank you for the influence, wisdom and friendship you shared with me at LA14. I am so glad we were roomies! I am a different person because of you today than I was a year ago. New makeup, new eyelashes, new attention to how I dress and why. I have an increased level of confidence because I saw you blending your talent, intelligence and beauty and owning them all together. I am grateful for your friendship and wanted you to know you impacted my life in positive ways. Have a wonderful holiday weekend with your girls. I look forward to the next time our paths cross.

It made me cry. And it made all the times that I've been told I am bossy, too strong, or aggressive worth it. People don't need you to patronize them; they need you to use your talents to make theirs better.

CHAPTER NINETEEN

One day I got a call from Alison, a talented creative director I had met during my bid to leave my first job. She was one of the six that Trevor had introduced me to after identifying Alison as "a person Zahra should know." I had turned her down in favor of the job with Larry, but now, more than three years later, she was hoping we could meet for lunch.

Alison had built both a successful company and the lifestyle she wanted to live. During our first Trevor-arranged meeting, we had hit it off immediately. I was excited to see her again and to hear what she had been up to. Business was booming, said Alison, but her priorities were shifting. She had just gone through treatment for breast cancer. "I don't want to do this forever," she said. She wanted a business partner who would eventually buy her out. Was I interested?

"Yes, yes, yes!" I said. I was thrilled with the idea of having something of my own.

I knew I was not well served by managing my creativity in six-hour chunks and billing for it that way—I believed this took away from the final product, whether I was a designer or a lawyer or a cleaning service. I no longer wanted to be "on the clock." I wanted to be the decision-maker, directing my drive and enthusiasm into building something of my own. I believed in my heart there was a better way to treat clients, to treat employees, and to treat design, and I was champing at the bit for the chance to try it my way.

With Alison, I could have all that. She sat across the table from me, representing an established company with satisfied clients and real earnings. We decided to continue the conversation, and during our third meeting, Alison introduced me to her friend Tammy, another sole proprietor with whom she worked quite often. Tammy was successful, was well connected, and had a great laugh. That was all I thought I needed to know.

Tammy and Alison shared some clients, mostly local oil and gas companies. Theirs was a great partnership, Alison said, but it needed the energy, skills, and contacts I would bring to the table. Alison suggested that the three of us join forces.

I didn't know much about business, or anything at all about starting a business other than that long-ago failed jewelry store attempt in Yemen, but it all sounded great to me. Alison and Tammy co-owned a building in a hip part of town called Inglewood. We would share our offices with Connie, a well-known interior designer who had designed the magnificent space.

Alison and I shared similar ambitions for the kind of team we'd build and the ways we'd diversify our client base, experiment with new mediums, and provide new experiences on the page and online. At the time, in 2006, the design industry was evolving so quickly into digital that it was tough to tell a trend from a paradigm shift. But we both agreed that if we were strategic, we could stay ahead of both.

"We won't even have to start from zero," I told my husband, who was supportive of the idea. I was thrilled that he said yes, but I didn't like that I needed permission. However, my battle for independence had turned a corner; I no longer bristled at every perceived slight.

I am the first to admit how naive I was. Caught up in the excitement of owning my own business, I moved full steam ahead, not knowing that a partnership is like a marriage, and that unless you are compatible—unless you have the same goals in life and in work, the same vision for the company—it ultimately will not work. I liked both of my partners very much, but I did not do any deep research into their personalities, backgrounds, or previous working relationships, or more importantly, their ultimate goal for the company. I did not think to inquire about their values or their vision, nor did I ask about how we would handle conflict.

Now I understand that every relationship—be it with a partner in work or in life, or even a best friend—evolves over time. No matter how much optimism and energy you have going in, it means little if you have not laid the right groundwork. Establishing a good partnership relies less on lawyers and accountants and more on asking the right questions—and sitting still until you understand the answers.

I was in the midst of the conversations with Alison when, one day, Larry made a comment that had a particularly awkward landing. "I simply don't see this company without Zahra," he said. "Your energy makes this company what it is. Thank you." He said this as we stood with Patrick and Louise, our head of account services, on a train platform, headed back to the office after a meeting.

It felt as if he knew I was leaving, and when I made a very non-committal response about how important we all were, I could see I had confirmed his suspicion.

Two weeks later, I gave him my notice.

I always liked Larry, even when he would call me into his office to rant and throw things against the wall. He was rough and tough on the outside and a big teddy bear on the inside. In many ways we were kindred spirits who understood each other. I don't have a filter between my brain and my mouth, and neither did Larry.

I have a huge appreciation and respect for people who are honest and straightforward—with whom what you see is what you get.

My resignation letter offered a month's notice, but Larry tore it up and refused it.

I had made up my mind, I told him; I needed to explore this path. After trying hard to persuade me first that our start-up should move into their offices, then that I should take a year off and see if I wanted to come back, he gave up, and for the next month, he barely spoke to me.

The day before my last at the office, I said hello to him in the hall—he gave me a look and walked away. He didn't even come to my going-away party, instead sending Patrick and the rest of the company to the bar along with the company credit card.

After I left, I did not hear from Larry for eight months. I was deep into the new business when, very early one morning, his name flashed on my cellphone while I was still half-asleep. His voice echoed a bit as he told me he was driving in to work at their brand-new office and how sad it made him feel that I was not going to be there when he arrived. Then he hung up and I never heard from him again.

That was a classic Larry move, to try not to show too much emotion. No wonder we had gotten along so well.

It Takes Magnetism.

A person who has good thoughts cannot ever be ugly. You can have a wonky nose and a crooked mouth and a double chin and stick-out teeth, but if you have good thoughts they will shine out of your face like sunbeams and you will always look lovely. —Roald Dahl, *The Twits*

You need to be beautiful to thrive in this world. But let me explain.

Ugly is something deep inside of a person. It finds things wrong with every situation. It complains endlessly. It certainly doesn't tip well.

You can't ever please ugly, because it's determined to be that way. And that's all fine and good if you never leave your living room, but the world is home to billions of people who don't have time for ugly.

That leaves ugly feeling isolated, misunderstood, and alone, making it uglier.

On the other hand, a positive force attracts "luck." Like a magnet, someone who is beautiful inside will breeze through the world, finding helping hands at every turn. Their days are filled with old friends and new opportunities.

Because they are kind, they invite kindness. Because their smile is infectious, people smile at them.

They live their lives through a lens of respect and gratitude, honing new skills, embracing knowledge, and seizing each day, even the cold, cloudy, rainy ones.

Yes, good things just seem to fall into place for beautiful people. They even get to live longer, according to a 2016 study from the Harvard T.H. Chan School of Public Health.

The study found that women who were optimistic had a significantly reduced risk of dying from several major causes of death—

including cancer, heart disease, stroke, respiratory disease, and infection—over an eight-year period compared with women who were pessimists.

Which is good news for you, beautiful reader, and great news for everyone you know.

It Takes Patience.

First they ignore you. Then they laugh at you. Then they fight you. Then you win. —Unknown

CHAPTER TWENTY

We named our company Foundry. We all loved the timeless quality of the name: a foundry is where you take something incredibly solid, like metal, and turn it into something else that is useful, lasting, and needed. A place of hard work, sweat, strength, and rolled-up sleeves.

We dealt in the abstract—in marketing and communications—but what we created was also concrete. Because of our diverse experience and influences, we were able to walk in the shoes of just about anyone and be as pragmatic, creative, or impactful as our clients wanted.

Until this point in my career, I had been a designer and a salesperson. Now I had the luxury of spending time shaping strategy. This was what excited me most, so I slowly stopped designing and moved into business development. It was a whole new world: I didn't, at this point, even know how to read a balance sheet, let alone understand terms like "liability" or "equity."

Foundry was able to establish and maintain a reputation for pushing the envelope effectively and responsibly. We became known for stellar design, for understanding our clients and their customers, and for clear, solid strategy.

We had been in business for about two months when the marketing agency for the province's tourism industry put out a request for proposal (RFP). It seemed like every agency in the country was responding, and we were so small, and new, that it felt like too much of a long shot to even consider.

Tammy said no, the project was too much work . . . which is exactly why I wanted to land it. I have never liked the word "no." To me it's more of a motivator than any word of encouragement could be.

This was the start of our battle of differing opinions.

We went over the RFP questions endlessly, writing, refining, changing, and changing again. We had our first company portraits taken and scrambled to finish our website. And we tried to find the most unique solution possible, eventually deciding to hand-bind an oversized book on watercolor paper.

As with many proposals, there was a very strict deadline for submission. We had to deliver it by four on a Friday afternoon, at which point it would be time-stamped to verify that it had come in on time.

The afternoon the proposal was due, last-minute glitches took us down to the wire, and as I jumped into the driver's seat of my car, I heard a rip and looked down in horror. I had torn my pants all the way from the crotch to mid-thigh, leaving flesh and underwear in plain sight.

However, there was no time to do anything but drive, and so I did.

Then I remembered that short denim skirt I had planned on returning months ago. I had just fifteen minutes to deliver the proposal, so I grabbed the skirt from the back seat and wiggled out of my pants and into the skirt, making further progress every time I hit a red light.

I prayed I would not run into any of our competitors or, more importantly, the client, and that I could just leave the package quietly with the receptionist. I cautiously walked in, handed in the package, breathed a sigh of relief while turning to leave—and walked right into the client himself.

I mumbled a vague "Thanks for the opportunity" and raced out, hoping he hadn't looked down.

Shockingly, our effort won us the business—the client, Don, told us our proposal stood head and shoulders above the rest. But to Alison, he jokingly said, "It could also have been the mile-high legs she showed up with."

When I took off the skirt that day, it went back into my closet, where it hung untouched for many years, until Hanadi was in college and officially claimed it for herself, maintaining that its style was more suited for "her generation."

That tourism account led to many inquiries, which led to many pitches and many wins. With each of these wins came money and momentum. When we could, we freed up time to work with pro bono clients—a practice that enabled us to flex our creative muscles even more and give back to our community. Our work also led to recognition in the form of design awards. Each framed certificate that we hung on our wall represented credibility—and visibility.

As we grew, we were able to recruit a larger staff. We looked for team members whose visions were worthy of our clients' investments. They included one of our best designers, Jake, who recruited us instead of the other way around. A recent art school graduate based in Toronto, Jake had sent a couple of email inquiries that I did not have the time to look at or respond to. Then he sent one more email, with a subject line that immediately caught my attention: "Hey, you stole my website design."

I immediately clicked through to find a website that was (a) nothing like Foundry's and (b) brilliant. I invited Jake to come for an interview and hired him as quickly as possible.

We had so many stories like Jake's—people who came from everywhere wanting to work with us. Bright, young, talented. Crystal, Kylie, Emmanuel, Sarah, Macy . . . some of them former coworkers, some simply young talent and people I respected greatly. Louise, Laura, Susan, Nicolle . . . an amazing team the clients learned to rely on and loved working with. Victoria, Kira, Jen, Norm, Jon . . . each one becoming a part of my family.

In Foundry's first year, we brought in more than $1 million in sales; in the next, *Profit* magazine heralded us a Canadian women-owned business to watch. The year after that, Tammy and I carefully submitted our company's financials in the hopes we'd hit the magazine's Profit 100 list of fastest-growing companies. We did.

The most important message, for me, was not that we were succeeding. And it was not that we were talented. It was that we had built relationships and trust with clients we liked and respected.

Our clients had to feel their needs were being met. Early on, we had all agreed that the most important service we could provide to any client was to listen to them.

Whenever we made a presentation, we showed at least two concepts. The first one was always exactly what the client had asked for, to make clear that we were listening. For the second concept, we pushed as hard as we could in the direction we thought was best for their target audience and for the brand.

Nine and three-quarter times out of ten, the client went with the bold version, which was usually out of their comfort zone.

One of our favorite clients was a tiny little gas company whose chief financial officer, Sadiq, is also one of my favorite people. For starters, when he laughs, you can see his tonsils and hear him in the next room. He is one of the savviest businessmen in town—everything that man has ever touched has turned to gold.

But you would never know that by interacting with him. Sadiq is down to earth and humble; he was especially proud of his cheap office space and beat-up office furniture, letting everyone know that the company was not going to spend investors' money on silly things like fancy offices.

The most fulfilling part of our work with him was the fact that we were more than just hired guns—we were friends, confidantes, colleagues. We had wanted a seat at the boardroom table, and Sadiq gave it to us.

One day, as we were discussing their latest annual report, Sadiq said to me, "You know how you give me two options every year? And I always pick the one you want? This year, just give me one. Put your heart and soul into it."

That is what I loved about this man: the trust he always put in us, all the way back to the days when he waited patiently for my noncompetition agreement with Larry's company to end.

He raised the bar for us, and we wanted more than anything to make him proud. We won many, many awards as a result of our work with Sadiq. And though he put less stock in design-industry accolades, he loved that they meant so much to us.

A particular kind of empowerment comes with the trust of people you care about. All of a sudden, the bar is set so much higher, and there is no limit to the amount of good work you can do.

Another client we loved working with was Vince, a well-known entrepreneur and Grey Cup winner, who approached us for help with his company's brand. Vince is one of the most enlightened leaders I have ever met. Understanding intuitively how business and marketing go hand in hand, he made lightning-fast connections between his company, its offering, and its evolving business plan. He was a pleasure to work with—and a challenge.

During a work session one day, as we were trying to define the new company's values, he turned to me and asked, "What are yours?"

"Ours?" I replied, surprised.

Foundry had put a lot of thought into our name, but we had never identified our values. What is that old joke about the shoemaker's kids again?

Soon after that meeting, we convened the team to get clarity on exactly what we brought to the table. That was the moment when we turned from an above-average design shop into an industry leader.

It was a grueling process. We started with everyone throwing out words we thought expressed our values: experience, pride, performance, integrity, honesty, excellence. I played Vanna White and wrote everything down on big Post-It notes stuck on the wall, which soon filled with inspiration, achievement, and ambition.

As I wrote, I got more frustrated: the words were right, but I didn't understand why they didn't resonate and felt so wrong.

We took a break, leaving the notes up in our boardroom for a few days, and then it hit me. Those qualities were givens. They were mandatory, set in stone.

They were non-negotiable.

If we didn't have passion, diversity, innovation, quality, respect, and teamwork, then we should all just go home.

How could we make our values mean something?

I became obsessed. Everything we wrote down had to be essential. I realized that how you run your business also has to be how you want to live your life. For a business owner, the two are inseparable. How can you find passion in what you do if it doesn't fit your personal value system? The same goes for employees: How can you thrive in a company that doesn't fit your principles and ethical code?

You can't.

After weeks of work, we finally settled on five core values, which were less about what we promised to do and more about how we promised to act.

We didn't memorize them and put them up on our walls as was expected; we knew them in our hearts and we lived them every single day.

Keep good company—We are collaborators and we surround ourselves with those who are reliable, responsive, and dependable, people who are honest, respectful, loyal, and tolerant. People who are fearless, make confident decisions, and leverage opportunities. People who demand responsibility and want to be challenged. People who stand behind their work and who make emotional connections and solve problems.

Our loyalty to suppliers benefits them, and us, and pays a variety of dividends. I was fiercely loyal to Cleaver, a very popular restaurant in Calgary. I could call them on a Saturday night, tell them I would be there in thirty minutes with four people, and walk past the lineup at the door, right to my table.

Be curious—Experiment, push the boundaries, look around a corner, turn something upside down and see if it sticks . . . or if it breaks. That is the only way we can see where our successes and mistakes take us. Allow yourself the fun of a failure—experience it, revel in it, and take away something that you wouldn't have known otherwise. Curiosity did indeed kill the cat. But then again, it had nine lives—and learned something every time.

We can't expect to do something groundbreaking if we don't take a chance, step out on a limb while knowing it might break, and that if it does, we will still be okay. Nothing good in my life came of being afraid.

Never tolerate "okay" anything—Everything begins with the work. We can never afford to accept anything less than the best (not just our best, but THE best). Good work is the difference between an expense and an investment. Good work removes disparity and turns nonusers into users, and users into loyalists. Good work resonates, stirs emotion, and provokes a response. It always brings the viewer to their knees.

The only reason we won design awards is because we did good work. The only reason we won new clients, despite our lack of a sales team, was because we did good work.

Never allow yourself to be less than completely proud of what you put into this world. That doesn't mean you will win all the time. Design is subjective and so is style. I am, after all, the person who wore a Michael Jackson jacket and had a blond mullet.

Leave something behind—Creating a positive impact through our work is a constant ambition for us. Whether the project allows us to shift minds, touch depths, support our community, or simply embrace a good cause, we strive to leave something behind. Realizing that we have an influence on how our world is shaped is a huge responsibility. We give our time, our money, and our hearts in the hopes that we will leave our world a little brighter than we found it.

We started by giving $250,000 of free marketing to nonprofits and upped it every year. It was a complete win-win situation: we were happy because we were making a difference, and the nonprofits were ecstatic to have work they couldn't otherwise afford. Our clients rewarded us with more work, and the industry gave us recognition, new clients, and awards.

Laugh!

I am pretty sure I don't need to explain this one.

It Takes Courage.

The unknown is a vast canyon where everything you've ever wanted lives and waits for you.

Try to map every detail before taking a leap and you'll fail. At worst, it will make you risk-averse, and risk is a terrible thing to miss out on. Risk is life. Adrenaline-pumping, free-falling, finger-crossing life.

At seventeen, I married a man I barely knew and didn't know if I loved. It was a decision that has led to everything amazing in my current life. I wanted to leave Yemen, I wanted a family, I wanted adventure and opportunity, and with one terrifying leap into the canyon of mystery I got it all. And no, it wasn't horrible.

Consider parenthood: Would anybody really get into it if we truly understood before we started how hard it is? Blissful ignorance is a gift that leads to remarkable things.

And when crazy stuff happens, even better. You now have a great story to tell and experience to grow from.

Last week it was sunny and warm, and I sat at my office window and made myself appreciate it all. The haze of heat rising from the sand. The plastic plants in the boulevards. Bachelorette parties walking in happy herds. And me, healthy and young, able to do anything I wanted.

One day that will seem to come too soon, I will give anything to be back in this moment, full of possibility, breathing in the world instead of worrying about my white hair and the options that disappear with age.

I try to live the life I think the eighty-year-old me would want. I owe her some decent memories for lending me this able body and mind.

So do you.

On your path to the life you want, try not to forget that it is in progress now. Appreciation and gratitude will make you rich when you are old.

Yes, I take a peek before I leap, but then I jump with both feet, not knowing where I will land.

What you don't know won't kill you. Probably.

CHAPTER TWENTY-ONE

One of our clients, Kelly, suggested that one of us join Entre-preneurs' Organization. "It's the single best thing you can do," she told us over lunch.

Entrepreneurs' Organization (EO) is an invitation-only global network of business owners, with 170 chapters in more than fifty countries. We realized that joining EO would be great exposure for Foundry, offering introductions to entrepreneurs across indus-tries, not only in Calgary but also globally.

Kelly explained that the heart of the EO experience was the forum, a closed group of eight to ten people who meet monthly in order to challenge, support, and grow with each other. The meet-ings are completely confidential, and the members do not even tell their spouses about the discussions.

The way she described it was intriguing: forums were about business, but also about family life and personal growth. Rather than the 95 percent of feelings you'd share with an acquaintance you met on the street, you would share the 5 percent you feel you can't tell anyone else about.

To add to it all, they had a set of core values that felt so aligned with mine: *trust and respect, cool, make a mark, boldly go!* and my per-sonal favorite, *thirst for learning.*

Both Tammy and Alison had recently turned fifty, which was the EO's upper age limit for new members, so I was the only one able to join.

I was super excited.

I needed peers, people to teach me. Branding and design were creative pursuits, and sometimes insular. I wanted people to talk business with—a community.

I signed up for my first event: a dinner for new members at a local country club. I arrived alone, walking into a room where it seemed everybody knew everybody else. People stared, and surprisingly, almost immediately came over to talk to me. There were very few women in EO and I was fresh blood, especially for the forums that wanted a female member.

In typical EO style, people not only introduced themselves but boldly shared big pieces of their stories and themselves. Conversations became deep and personal very quickly.

I wondered if I had stumbled upon the best group in the world or the worst.

In time, that deeply personal connection and trust, along with high energy that hits the roof, complete and total enthusiasm, and a willingness to try anything and talk to anyone, became my whole world.

Every single person I met was engaged and driven, excited and curious. They all wanted to change the world and completely believed they could do it. Their energy was electrifying.

Up until this point, I had thought I was so different from everyone around me. I was always trying to calm myself down and fit into the group. Now, for the first time in my life, I was surrounded by people who felt exactly like me. I fit in, easily and willingly.

By the end of the night, I was sold—and had been approached by members of six different groups to join their forum.

During the next several weeks, I started the interview process with the forums. I scrutinized their paperwork, which included a forum constitution, as well as the mission and values that guided each group. Many of the groups contained only men—mostly by circumstance, not by choice. I wanted to be in a forum with another woman in it, both to temper the "maleness" of a group I would be traveling with and to put my husband's mind at ease. That tipped the scales in favor of a group that included Shashi, a fantastic female entrepreneur who owned a very successful chain of boutiques in town. We immediately had a great rapport—even by phone—and as I got to know her, I grew to have a tremendous amount of respect for Shashi. The forum group was called Vectra, and they prioritized family, fitness, and adventure.

Shashi invited me to sit in on part of their next meeting and have a formal interview afterward. I met a few other members of the forum and heard more about their most recent retreat in Arizona, which had included a skydiving trip. One of the members asked if I would do an activity like that with the group. Without pausing, I said no, keeping to myself that I am very afraid of heights.

The members were surprised by my response. The forum was all about unity, never giving up or being afraid, with a heavy side of all for one and one for all.

I wasn't having any of it. I would not go on a trip that forced me to do anything I didn't want to do. I had left that behind years ago.

They informed me that if the majority agreed, then I would have to do it. I said no, I wouldn't, and that I had several other forums waiting to talk to me. They looked at each other and asked me to leave the room while they decided.

After what seemed like an hour later, but really was ten minutes, they called me back in and gave me the green light to join Vectra.

They told me they admired my spunk. Later I would learn that they also saw what I'd thought were my well-hidden demons and wanted to know how they could help.

While part of me wondered what kind of cult I was joining, my experience at Foundry had taught me there are times when research and comparison shopping are essential, and then there are times when you need to seize an opportunity before it passes you by. So I became the newest member of Vectra.

Still, I started to worry. Inside this closed circle of total strangers, what would I *say*? When it came to business, I was the straightest of straight shooters—a bulldozer, as Alison once so eloquently put it. But not with my personal life, which was private.

I decided I would share what I wanted with them, get what I wanted out of the experience, and not worry too much about the rest. Nobody shares everything, right?

Wrong. In EO, you share everything.

The first retreat I went on with my forum group was a five-day, forty-seven-mile hike on Vancouver Island. The West Coast Trail is breathtakingly beautiful, following in the footsteps of the Indigenous peoples of the area. It is also a challenging hike that requires careful preparation and planning. I had never been camping in my life—never slept in a tent, let alone carried one inside a forty-pound backpack. We trained rigorously for two months, and I was pretty irritated. "What's wrong with sitting by a pool?" I asked repeatedly.

In the end, the experience was challenging and fun. And exhausting. Not five minutes into the hike, I fell while trying to take a photo and had to endure the rest of the trip with swollen, bruised knees.

Part of the hike was on the beach, and when the tide came in, we had to climb a ladder to walk on the ridge until the water retreated. If you've never hiked for hours on sand with a forty-pound backpack, I have just one suggestion: don't.

I survived on camaraderie, competition, and my forum mate Tim's magical backpack that held a boom box, a football, and bottles of booze.

When the tide came in and we had to scramble up the equivalent of several stories to higher ground, I tried to good-soldier it, but eventually my fear of heights got the better of me. It was the same familiar, terrible tingling in my body that had followed me around since I was a kid.

Through research, I've discovered that this has everything to do with my nervous system. It is a fight-or-flight response to a stressful situation. The line between fear and arousal blurs into a type of tingling in your privates that is not like the one you want.

But I don't like the word "fear"—I don't want to say no. For that reason, I had spent most of my life trying, in both small and outsized ways, to chip away at this most profound dread, from climbing down a mountain for water with my grandmother in Haraz to zip-lining in Costa Rica.

Now I was near the back of the pack and trying to pull myself up another ladder. I stopped for a minute and closed my eyes as everything—the exhaustion, the fear, the frustration—washed over me. I opened my eyes and felt my gaze pulled downward, my hands gripping more tightly as I began to panic.

"Hey, Zahra!" I heard Tim yell from below. "Those pants don't make your ass look good!"

I hightailed it up as fast as I could, and my laugh finally escaped when I got to the top. *Thank you, Tim, I owe you one.*

That trip was a great lesson in my own competitive nature. I learned very quickly that I could not stand to be at the back of the group, but I also did not need to be the first. I was happier letting someone else get the glory while pushing myself toward my own personal best.

Vectra was becoming more and more important to me—it was an outlet that was both supportive and invigorating, a series of one unique opportunity after another.

Life at the office was also not without conflict or mistakes, on all our parts. Both Alison and I were creative directors. Someone, at some point, must have given the good advice of "Never go into business with someone who has the same job as you." But at that stage in my career, I hadn't received it.

The overlap had been obvious to us from the beginning, and Alison had a suggested fix: "I'll creative-direct some clients, and you'll creative-direct others." In an ideal world, we would cross-pollinate, take a step back if a relationship became contentious, and, in some cases, work together on an especially demanding client. In reality, it confused the team because most days they didn't know who to talk to.

In addition, cracks started to appear in our partnership early on. Alison and Tammy were longtime friends, and they had styles that worked well together. They had each other's backs, intense mutual loyalty, and much more experience than I did. I, on the other hand, practiced a much more in-your-face form of problem-solving, one I called proactive and they called aggressive.

My partners saw value in putting our heads down and continuing to work on a project until we were finished, even as it began to go sideways. In contrast, I didn't really understand the "debrief" concept, or the point of "Let's talk about it afterward."

I come from a place where there is no such thing as personal space. Arab women will get in your face, stand an inch away, and then ask you how much money you make or whether your husband is good in bed. Sometimes, when I got too wrapped up in something at work, I forgot that we *do not* live in a world where everyone speaks out, freely discusses the problem at hand, and comes to a mutual agreement.

I wanted to climb aboard a high-speed rocket ship and win new business at the speed of light. I had no limits—not in my actions and not in my speech. Instead of diving right in, my partners wanted to think about it first . . . and go home on time.

When making important decisions about the company, Alison, Tammy, and I often found ourselves at an impasse. They were in retirement mode, while I wasn't. I constantly pushed to examine and change their long-held beliefs and practices; in my mind, not making a decision carried just as many consequences as making the wrong decision.

Still, they were the ruling majority.

There were times when each of us was right, and others when each of us was wrong. At the end of the day, we simply had different styles of working and little desire between the three of us to compromise. The more we tried to understand each other's points of view, the more we bumped heads. It became clear we needed outside help.

One day, Alison took me aside after a particularly hard meeting. She urged me not to respond, but simply to listen. We each took a deep breath, and she told me she had been worried about how we three were getting along. She thought we should take the Enneagram personality test to give us insight into how each of us operated—and what motivated us—to find out how we could work together better.

I knew I had to do some soul searching. After years of struggling to find a voice to call my own, I now had it turned up to full volume. Reluctantly, I agreed to give the test a try.

"Fine," I told her. "Let's get this over with."

The Enneagram test is based on a framework of nine different personality types. According to the literature, everyone has a little bit of all nine types, but a dominant type determines our behavior and our defense mechanisms.

To me it smacked of self-help drivel and what I called *kumbaya shit*.

When the results came back, they pegged Alison as a Nine: a peacemaker. Laid back, creative, supportive, and optimistic, Nines sometimes seek to avoid conflict. Their weakness is complacency, stemming from a desire to minimize upset and simplify problems.

Tammy was a One: a reformer. Ones are principled idealists, but their self-control can lead them into being critical and perfectionistic.

I was a Seven: an enthusiast—spontaneous and versatile but also liable to become scattered and distracted. According to the Enneagram Institute, my basic motivations as a Seven are freedom, happiness, and being occupied by worthwhile experiences. A Seven's bold pursuit of the good things in life is expressed in curiosity, optimism, and a sense of adventure, which can be contagious. However, one person's spontaneity is another person's impulsiveness.

Sevens can be anxious about making the wrong choice and missing out. To cope, they try to occupy their minds and keep themselves busy, constantly searching for more stimulation.

This kumbaya stuff was right—and it had me pegged.

I was a communications expert who needed to learn how to communicate . . . and bring others along. Meanwhile, Tammy needed to learn to accept opinions that differed from her own, and Alison needed to speak up.

We discussed our differences with a mediator, who told us all, in turn, that we needed to find better ways to deal with each other and with ourselves.

For a while, we were all in agreement that Foundry would stay in the building that Alison and Tammy owned. We agreed that rent increases would top out annually at $1 a square foot. But a few months into our partnership, that forecast changed. My two partners told me they had miscalculated. Significantly. They needed to bring in a lot more rental income in order to pay the mortgage.

That brought on mediator meeting number two, and more conflict. I wanted a certain degree of visibility in the business. And that was hard to come by. Tammy saw no use in new ideas of how to do business—why change what had worked in the past? She had always done things this way. I reminded her that we were not a sole proprietorship anymore.

She and I both dug in our heels and built walls instead of bridges.

Now that I look back, I see how we could have handled so many situations differently. How we could have done a better job of listening to each other. I learned that sheer willpower can build a company, but it takes patience, process, and people to keep it thriving.

It Takes Niceness.

The other day I was at the gym and overheard a conversation between two women about a mutual friend. They kept putting her down—her clothes, her looks, her hair, her job—but then adding "But she is so nice" in the most grating, irritating way.

Since when did being nice mean that you weren't up to par?

I am nice. I like to be called nice, I like to act nice. I like to do nice things for others. In fact, if I weren't nice, I'd have no power at all. Respect is born from how you treat people. When you're nice, you get niceness in return. Listen when others talk. Remember names. Don't take your bad days out on the people who work for you. Be nice.

Fear is not the same thing as respect. It's an empty sort of power that doesn't come with any loyalty. You may get to lead, but you're not really in charge.

According to a study published in the *Harvard Business Review* by leadership development consultancy Zenger/Folkman, the best leaders are a hybrid of "driver" and "enhancer." Drivers demand excellence, while enhancers are more like role models that treat employees like actual people.

The study found that 68 percent of those led by a boss who was both a driver and enhancer scored in the top 10 percent on "overall satisfaction and engagement with the organization." In contrast, only 6.7 percent of those working for enhancers scored in the top 10 percent, and 8.9 percent of those working for drivers ranked in the top 10 percent.

Chief executive Jack Zenger and president Joseph Folkman conclude, "Leaders with highly engaged employees know how to demand a great deal from employees, but are also seen as considerate, trusting, collaborative, and great developers of people."

We get more Christmas cards that way too. Be nice; it is the best compliment you can get.

CHAPTER TWENTY-TWO

A few weeks after Ahmed finished sixth grade, we decided he would go live in Yemen with his father for a year. He was about to start a new middle school anyway, and unlike his sisters, he had very few memories of Yemen. We wanted him to be with his dad and his grandparents. And I knew that this time, in Yemen, he would be in great hands.

My boy and his father were Canadian citizens. The expats lived in a compound for foreigners and dignitaries with extremely tight security. It was more or less a self-contained city. He would be safe. He would attend my beloved Sana'a International School.

All the same, the idea of him leaving home was tough for his worried mama. Was I making a mistake? What was I thinking, sending him to the same place we had left for a better life all those years ago?

Fear and trepidation filled me.

When his father promised him a dog as a reward, after years of Ahmed begging for one, I couldn't believe my ears. "You can't bribe him to go!" I yelled. "And how on earth are you going to manage a dog in Yemen? The only dogs there are the street dogs with rabies. There isn't even a vet for dogs in the city!"

Dogs are not common in Yemeni households; they are considered unclean, and I agreed with that. A dog would go outside, do his business, and come back in to sit on my furniture—it was not happening.

Adamant, Ahmed talked about a black Lab or a golden retriever—huge, sloppy, shedding, dirty, pooping dogs.

In a moment of weakness, I took him to the pet store, hoping to convince him that he wanted a hamster instead. How did I forget that he was my son, and that it would have been easier for me to move a mountain than to get him to change his mind?

While walking around the pet store, Ahmed saw a sad little ball of matted white fur sitting on steel mesh wire in a tiny glass cage. He asked the saleswoman why that dog looked so sad. She told him all his siblings were adopted, and he was lonely. There were reasons he didn't get picked: he had a heart murmur and a blocked tear duct, and he was getting older. He had been there for five months.

The sign hanging in the upper right-hand corner of his cage said "Clearance."

Ahmed sat down to greet the dog, and he didn't stand up for the next hour. This dog was his, it was clear. I convinced him to take a break to go pick up the girls and bring them back to the store, hoping they could talk their brother out of it.

Three hours later, and half an hour before the store closed, we officially became the proud owners of Kale—a bichon cocker mix of pure loving DOG. The minute we walked into the house, Kale threw up from all the excitement. I buried my head in my hands, secretly pleased for the first time that my son was going to Yemen—and taking his dog with him.

Kale slept in the mudroom, scratching at the door and crying all night, but I wasn't going to let him into the house until he got cleaned. I slept on the couch close to the back door that night, feeling like the worst person ever.

The craziest thing happened the next morning when I took

Kale to a groomer to get his matted fur trimmed and have a bath. The groomers looked dirty and all the dogs were in cages. I refused to leave him there and paid double for him to go first, so I could take him home right after. I realized I had fallen in love with the damn thing overnight.

We barely had enough time to get Kale vaccinated and neutered, and my littlest baby's head was still in a cone when it was time to fly. When we got to the airport, we learned that Kale's papers had not cleared the Yemeni Department of Agriculture's new rules, which had been set only a week before, after I thought I had cleared all requirements.

I stood at the airline desk, trying to explain Yemen society—channeling all my concern over my son into the drama with the dog. I told them this shouldn't be a problem because my father-in-law's security detail would be picking us up on the runway. Because of my husband's family, we didn't have to go through security like others did—we went from the airplane to our home.

The answer was no.

Not knowing what to do, I decided, as always, to solve the problem at hand first and then deal with the next one. So I paid for him to fly with us as far as Germany, where we had a four-hour layover.

I figured I could talk him onto the plane there—what else could they possibly do but let me take my dog with me? It took some doing, and some sprinting through the terminal, and some leaving my son with strangers, but happily, Kale was on the flight to Yemen with us.

It was gut-wrenching to be back in Yemen, knowing I would be returning to a better place while leaving my son there. Things had changed for us: we had entered the country as Canadians, which meant we had more resources and enormous security. Security at the compound was so tight that each time you left, you did so in a bulletproof vehicle with a guard and driver, which was followed by another car with two guards at all times. We were not allowed to walk on the street or get out of the car except at our destination. If I wanted to go to the grocery store, the two guards had to accompany me.

Every time I went to visit my friends, they could not stop laughing at the ridiculousness of me with my armed guards. I was ashamed to be treated as "better," or more worthy.

It seemed that our Canadian passports determined that our lives now mattered more than before. The truth is that foreign nationals were an attractive kidnapping prospect, and the company (and their insurance policy) could not take any risks with their staff.

I don't think Ahmed had grasped what this change would be like: I know we hadn't painted a proper picture of life in Yemen for him. But this was the same kid who stuck his arm out for his vaccine, bravely watching the needle go into his skin. He had the same expression when we left: his lower lip trembled, but his brown eyes were resolute.

The girls and I visited a couple of times that year, and Ahmed seemed to be settling down, making new friends, and enjoying school. Unfortunately, he did not get an immersion in Arabic language and culture, for the same reason I hadn't. Friends and family preferred to talk to him in English, so they could practice theirs.

Kale got sick soon after we arrived. But when the "vet" came, he wouldn't touch Kale—the vet was religious, and dogs were considered unclean. He asked us to lift Kale's leg and for us to press on his body, looking for lumps. I had to hold his mouth open while the vet peered in from a distance. At one point, I offered him a pair of gloves so he could do his job properly, but he declined. After that, he wrote a prescription for children's medication, saying they had nothing for dogs in the country and this would be fine.

Needless to say, Kale did not get human antibiotics that day.

When my boys finally returned home for spring break, Ahmed was home for two whole weeks, excitedly telling us about school in Yemen, all his new friends, a girl he was sweet on, and how good he was at sports. I was amazed to see how my son was thriving in Yemen in a way I never had.

Two days after the girls and I saw them off at the airport, my husband phoned early in the morning as I was getting ready for work. "We're okay, in case you're wondering," he said.

"What are you talking about?" I asked, toweling off my hair.

He calmly told me the compound had been bombed the night before and they had spent the night surrounded by the army.

Ahmed had just had his first day back at school and hadn't wanted to go down to the compound restaurant for dinner, so my husband had left him and Kale in our apartment and gone to pick up dinner for them.

Meanwhile, militias had parked a truck across the street from the compound and started firing missiles over the barbed-wire-topped wall; miraculously, the missiles struck buildings that had no one in them at the time.

As usual, what happens in Yemen is of no interest in the West, so none of the news channels had picked up the story.

My husband told me that after hearing the first explosion, he ran back to the building to get Ahmed. He found him under the main stairs of the apartment building, clutching Kale and shaking in fear. I could hear in his voice how shaken and exhausted he was.

Company officials had assigned everyone a number from 1 to 4. Those who were classified a 4, as my husband and son were, would be leaving the country immediately. They flew to Dubai the next morning, and two and a half weeks later, they were back home in Calgary. It took that long to convince Ahmed to come back to Canada. He was extremely upset and informed us that the company was not the boss of him and neither were we, and he was going back to live with his grandparents.

He also desperately missed Kale, who had the bad fortune of being classified a 1 and would have to remain in Yemen for the time being.

When Kale finally returned to Canada, five months later, he was as matted and dirty as the first day we met him.

In the years that my husband had been working in Yemen, the gym had become my place of stress release. Growing up in Yemen, I had not even been allowed to run, let alone play a sport or go for a workout. Girls in Yemen simply didn't do that, especially after puberty. We were expected to be docile, learn how to cook, and take care of the house.

Stay out of sight, don't wear makeup, don't call attention to yourself or else a good mother might not choose you for her son.

Every single move at the gym was new to me, and I discovered that I loved all of them—which was a good thing, because I needed to. My metabolism had screeched to a slow crawl when I turned thirty-five, taking me from a size 2 to a size 6 without even a brief layover at 4.

When I was a skinny kid growing up in Yemen, my mother made me finish everything on my plate. God forbid we threw away even a grain of rice. Now that I was a mother who didn't want to force her kids to eat the way I had been forced (though my kids will tell you otherwise), I also didn't want to throw food away; a diet that included polishing off the kids' plates had led to extra pounds.

I loved my standing date with my trainer and the satisfaction of pushing myself, feeling the effort in my muscles and lungs. I felt strong, and I was proud of my newly visible muscles.

While searching for fun things to do and ways to participate, I had met Jim Button, a supreme networker and brilliant strategist with a heart of gold, well known and loved by all.

Jim organized a weekly networking event called Superjocks. Every Tuesday night, a group of men and women played a different sport and then went out for a beer together. Basketball, dodgeball, floor hockey, rock climbing—you name it, we played it.

My first year in Superjocks was a series of firsts for me. At the beginning of the night, the question was always "Who has never played this before?" My hand was the only one that went up every single time. The first time I tried floor hockey, I proudly scored a hat trick, knocking over two of my teammates along the way. Some sports I love more than others, and I gleefully discovered I was best at the games where I got to push and shove.

Jim went on to build a beer brand called the Village Brewery, an incredible craft brewery in town. Their tagline is "Beer, backyards and friends," emphasizing connection, dreams, and friendship and underscoring their support of community, artists, and craftspeople. In Jim's words, "Some of the best things happen over beer. Ideas are born, friendships forged, deals struck."

He approached me to build the Village brand and be one of the company's first fifty investors, a group of people he had picked to represent the best of Calgary. I did not hesitate, and I now am the proud owner of business cards that say "Zahra Al-harazi, Beer Baron." It took me more than a few years to tell my father. I might possibly be the only Muslim woman in the world with that distinction.

Once, during one of my husband's visits to Canada, he told me, "You look like a man." The comment felt insulting, but I realized it was less about my body and more about the fact that he did not recognize the person in front of him. My membership at the gym became a new sore point between us.

I had changed, in more ways than one, and it was frightening to both of us.

When my husband came home from Yemen to visit, it was like having a stranger in the house. It was hard for me to suddenly have another adult decision-maker around, and another person making demands on my schedule and attention.

I was working hard, so I resented every single comment from him about the house, the kids, my work. He was not there; why should he have a say? I forgot that he was my husband and the children's father—that when he was living away from his kids, he was working as hard as I was.

Sooner or later, an offhand comment from one of us was guaranteed to turn into a tense conversation. Trying to discuss new interests and old ones led to argument after argument. Over the years, the arguments began to culminate in my telling him I wanted a divorce and him telling me it was out of the question.

According to our tradition, a woman cannot divorce her husband. He, on the other hand, can do what he likes; he can even take another wife—or three. The only way a wife can be free is if he says, "*Inti taleq*," which means "You are divorced." It is very similar to the Jewish *get*.

Though I felt angry all the time, I would typically be the one to back down. "The kids will hear us," I would say, ending the fight.

While my husband was in Yemen, I was calm and the family went about our daily lives. When I knew he was coming home for his break, I would start getting panic attacks. This made me feel so guilty. He was away working hard, and I should have been excited to have him home after months, but instead I resented him for coming back. Distance and time only seemed to have hardened our hearts to one another. So much for that old saying.

It Takes Change.

In Yemen, women are known by the names of the most important men in their lives: first their fathers, then their husbands, and then their sons. I was called Bint' Anwar, "the daughter of Anwar," until I became my husband's wife. This did not change when my girls were born—not until I had a son, when I became Um Ahmed, "Ahmed's mother."

For a long time, I was content being who I was told I was.

Even after moving to Canada, I carried around a lifetime of tradition, taboos, and restrictions, like a chip on my shoulder. Most were things that were told to me—not things I had considered and made up my mind about, but things I thought I must believe in because everybody said so.

My art school friend Peter opened my eyes to another way, one where I questioned my beliefs, trying to find out where they came from and whether they were the right ones. For the first time, I challenged my blind faith.

I had been given a brain. I was pretty sure God wanted me to use it. I started questioning everything—the roles assigned to me, the thoughts in my head, the words others told me—keeping what I decided I believed and discarding the rest. I made up my own mind.

I was breaking a mold that was so carefully built by generations before me. At times I felt the guilt eating at my soul. How could I be so ungrateful, so self-absorbed, that I needed to discard centuries of teaching? Like a quilt passed down through generations only to be used as a dish rag.

According to Tim Rettig, author of *Struggling Forward: Embrace the Struggle. Achieve Your Dreams*, our belief system is the catalyst for our behavior. Together with factors such as DNA, personality, and habits built over a lifetime, our belief system is what makes us do the things we do. Further, it is accumulated through every single thing around us, not just what we are taught at home.

Your beliefs are bound together. A change in one will effect a change in all, especially if it is fundamental to who you think you are; you are now tasked to put it all together again in a way that is more able to handle the next seismic shift.

My personality has always been decisive. I solve a problem and move on to the next one. I don't spend time going back, and because of that, my beliefs were set in stone.

Imagine my surprise to find out that even stones can change shape, and all it might take is persistent drops of water.

CHAPTER TWENTY-THREE

The phone rang as I read the email subject line: "You Have Been Shortlisted." I answered and heard the voice of my friend and client Andrea, who had called to explain. She had nominated me for Calgary's Top 40 Under 40 awards, organized annually by *Avenue* magazine.

At first, I was just surprised, but when I read through the email and saw I had been selected and would be profiled in the magazine, I became really pleased. I did a bit of researching and asking around, and looking at some of the past winners, and understood the opportunity: this was the best free local advertising we would ever get. The article in *Avenue* was both complimentary and comprehensive; it focused on Foundry's fast growth, the breadth of our client list, and most meaningfully, my work with our pro bono clients.

My husband knew about the award because Andrea was also his coworker and friend, but I decided not to tell him about the awards gala. He was heading back to Yemen for work, and I did not want him to go to the trouble of changing his plans. Or, at least, that was the story I was telling myself. The truth is, I wanted to have that moment without him. I was being selfish and not giving him any credit for his role and support in my award and my success.

My team, my friends, and my parents made plans to attend. In the days before he left, he asked a couple of times what I was doing that weekend and I evaded the question. Though I try to greet life's challenges with confidence at all times, sometimes cowardice shows up.

The morning of the awards, I woke up with a fever, a splitting headache, and a cellphone constantly ringing with deadlines I was missing. I had finally fallen back asleep when the phone rang again.

It was Tammy. "I have something that needs an immediate turn-around, and no one on your team is available," she said. I called my senior designer to ask what they were so busy with. They weren't, she said. She also told me she hadn't seen Tammy all day.

I hung up and immediately called Alison. "I'm done," I said flatly—it was as much fury as my splitting headache would allow. "I can't do this anymore."

Tammy and I were never, ever going to get along. We had drawn our lines in the sand and apparently could not get past them. I could not handle the conflict any longer. "Sell the company, buy me out, shut it down. I don't care. I just want out," I told Alison.

Knowing I was not feeling well and had a big night ahead of me, she kept a cool head. She told me to sleep; we would talk about it when I felt better.

At the awards party, I was at the pinnacle of my career, and yet I felt numb. Proud but not totally present. I wanted to enjoy my success on my own terms, and yet I felt very lonely.

I felt guilty about having cut my husband out of a moment that would have filled him with such pride. My body felt weak and feverish, and I had a hard time making small talk—even with the people I was genuinely excited to see.

Alison was wonderful in engaging the other team members so they wouldn't notice, and while I barely remember walking across the stage, or many of the conversations I had afterward, I do remember the tears of joy in my parents' eyes.

My parents truly enjoyed themselves at the gala—especially my mother, who was just beaming the entire time. My father had for years seemed uncomfortable about the idea of me building my own company. I don't think he had much faith in me. Was I going to lose that money? he wondered. Would it be better for me to get a good job that was safe?

That night was the first time he realized I was actually successful.

"You have made us so proud," my mother told me, with tears in her eyes. "Your father just said to me that he felt for the first time that he has a son."

It was one giant leap for a child who forever sought her father's approval—even if she did yearn for the moment he would be just as proud to claim a daughter instead of a son.

The next morning, Alison quietly pulled Tammy and me into the conference room and shut the door. By the end of the day, we had decided I would buy Tammy out.

My husband protested when I told him about the loan I had taken from the bank to pay Tammy. We had money—why didn't I ask him?

The truth is, I desperately wanted to do it myself. I had depended on my father and then on my husband for my entire life. This time, I just really wanted to depend on me.

Although I had just barely qualified for the Top 40 Under 40 award, my fortieth birthday took me by surprise. It was not the number itself—my life was very full, and I had never worried about getting old. But I woke up that morning feeling really unhappy. I was forty, and I didn't want another ten years to go by without knowing what life on my own terms was like. I wanted to make my own decisions—to feel the freedom I had never had in my nonstop trip from daughter to wife to mother.

My husband was a good man who meant well, but he did not know how to let me be the person that even I wasn't sure I had met yet.

In the middle of all the drama that was happening in my head, I was reminded that it was once again my turn to present to my EO forum group. I had kept my first two presentations pretty light, focusing on a single business problem I needed help untangling. They were thoroughly researched, polished, and safe.

I planned my third presentation in much the same vein. I had chosen Hannes as my coach this time—I appreciated his straight-forward European style and the fact that he did not beat around the bush. He turned out to be the best choice, but not for the reasons I expected.

Hannes and I talked about how my partnership at Foundry was still not working, and I told him I wanted my presentation to cover strategies for working with Alison. I looked up, waiting for the typically minor refinements my coach was obligated to make.

Instead, Hannes asked why I was in the forum. When I was too confused to answer, he told me that they had invited me to join their group because they believed I had experiences and input that would make the group interesting—that I would bring something to the table.

However, he said, "You aren't adding value and you aren't get-ting any value, either, because you're not telling us what's going on with you. We aren't stupid; we know there's something wrong. There's no point in being here without telling us. Why don't you tell me the real story?"

When I stalled, he pressed harder. Finally I told him what was going on in my marriage, and with me, but that I was not prepared to present it to the group.

He told me I needed to grow up. Then he left me sitting alone at Humpty's with my uneaten breakfast.

I put my hands down on the table and closed my eyes, hoping I would make it home before the tears came. Hannes was right. I wasn't a good member of the forum that I loved being a part of.

I felt sad, then angry at him and everyone else for forcing me to deal with what I didn't want to deal with. Then I decided to quit the forum and let them know I was done. Then I felt sorry for myself and started crying again. I cycled through cascading emotions for the next few hours, until I started working on a new presentation, one that was raw and real.

I laid out emotions and fears in stark black and white. I didn't sanitize it or make it pretty. Instead, I talked honestly about my love for my family and how I was about to break it to pieces.

The next day, as I spoke, the room was quiet. Because I had always worked hard to show only joy, this was a side of me they hadn't seen. People spoke up in response, showing pieces of themselves—big pieces—that were vulnerable. And that blew me away. I did not remember having ever felt so supported in my life. After spending most of my life twisting myself into the shapes I thought would most please whomever I was with, I had ended up in knots, and I was surprised to find out I was not alone.

My future was right in front of me now, in the form of the encouraging faces of this unexpected group of peers; to my surprise, the wind at my back was gratitude.

I believe that once you put something out there, there is no taking it back. This is partly my ego and my sense of justice talking—two extremes that, when employed together, inspire an extreme need to take action. Talking with my forum group had given me much-needed perspective on my own needs—and on my husband's, as members were also sympathetic to his side of the story. I realized it was not fair of me to keep holding back from him, or to keep arguing in circles. It was time to stop waiting.

I tried a different, much calmer, approach in the months that followed. I tried talking with my husband about what I wanted out of life and about how different we had become. I told him he deserved better than a woman who made him so unhappy.

We finally decided to tell my parents what was going on with us. He went in his own car and I in mine. I kept the windows down as I followed him, focusing my attention on his license plate, his taillights. He picked up speed, and then I did too, allowing myself to imagine an actual end to my marriage.

My mother met us at the door with a concerned look. My husband had called ahead, and it had been clear from his tone that something serious was going on. He sat down and told my parents that their daughter wanted to destroy her family. That she didn't care about her kids.

And then I completely lost it—the screaming came out of my body before any words even registered in my head. My parents looked on with shock as I turned into a person they had never met before. I *did* care about my family, I loved my children with every fiber of my being. This was not about them. As for my marriage, I had no mercy left.

"Say the words," I told him. "Say it. Say it in front of my parents. For God's sake, divorce me now."

My husband was silent. I sat down at my parents' kitchen table, the fight drained out of me, and closed my eyes.

My father asked him to go, and the sound of the door closing behind him punched a hole through me. This was real.

Hot and cold ran through my body. I sat at my parents' table and cried, as regrets, guilt, cravings, stress, and worry wrenched their way out of my body.

My mother was still on her feet, frozen and speechless. Finally, my father pulled up a chair and sat down. We began talking. My father and I had never before had a conversation like this—about relationships and feelings and needs. I told him the reasons I wanted a divorce—why I hadn't been happy for so many years.

He listened quietly and without comment, just asking a question or two. When I was finished, he nodded gravely and studied my face. "This change—leaving him—will make you happy?"

"Yes, Baba," I said, as sure as I was about anything in the world.

"Then I stand behind you," he said. "One hundred percent." In that moment, my world split open.

My mother was quiet. She would have plenty to say in the coming chaotic weeks, about how I could talk with my husband, about how we could make it work. How I should think of the children. But for this moment she had no words.

Eventually, my father called my husband to tell him I was on my way home so we could talk like adults. When I returned, there was only silence between us. Deep, unforgiving, and final.

It Takes Shame.

Aib. A word that has haunted me my entire life. It's what every generation of women in my family said to me when I stepped out of line. Even my daughters catch themselves saying it to each other and to me sometimes. *Aib.* A lifetime of feeling shame for wanting what I wanted. For needing what I needed. *Aib* means "disgrace" or "shame" in Arabic.

I should hate that word, but I don't. Shockingly, I love it because I know there is a healthy side to shame.

Healthy shame tells me that I have done something that goes against my core values and beliefs. Healthy shame makes me feel bad about my behavior, which in turn reminds me to be better.

Healthy shame doesn't tell me I am bad, but it tells me I *did* something bad . . . and teaches me self-respect and humility.

Isn't it interesting that antonyms for shame include approval, esteem, honor, praise, and pride? How do you get to those things if you have no shame?

Dave Kaiser is an executive coach who has a lot of things to say about shame and why it's your friend. For starters, he suggests that shame is a clue to your vulnerabilities. When someone's criticism holds a shred of truth, I feel the knife twist.

Eleanor Roosevelt said, "No one can make you feel inferior without your consent." "When you feel shame," says Dave Kaiser, "you are subconsciously consenting to what was said about you. It's insight into what you believe about yourself, and it indicates what you might want to work on as personal growth."

Shame also keeps your ego in check. When you've done something that hurts yourself or others, you feel ashamed. And you should. Otherwise, we would live in a world of psychopaths. Your sense of shame is a moral compass that keeps you pointed in the right direction.

Lastly, shame is actually a compliment. Dave concludes that you can feel shame only if you have a conscience and it's working. Well, check and check, so that's good. I don't get away with much, so I must be made of gold deep down.

After my divorce, my mother didn't tell her friends for over a year. A year! I took her shame as my own then. Reflecting back, the shame I felt was about hurting my family, putting my kids through emotional turmoil, and disappointing a man I had a world of respect for. If I'd made it through without any of those feelings, I wouldn't recognize myself.

There's *aib* again, keeping me on track.

CHAPTER TWENTY-FOUR

As an escape, I decided at the last minute to go to my cousin Mitul's wedding in London. I had skipped a number of other family events over the years because of distance, pregnancies, and household demands, and I had some pretty amazing cousins I wanted to know better. And, to be honest, I yearned to be close to family.

For the first time, instead of asking my husband whether I could go, I told him I was going.

It was a complicated time to leave, for many reasons. My friend Ishraq was back in the hospital, fighting off difficult side effects from her fourth breast cancer treatment. When I visited her, I told her I was getting a divorce. Her look of grave disappointment reminded me how hard I had worked to hide what was really going on, and how invested I had been, for so long, in showing other people only happiness. "Don't do this," she said. "I always thought of you as a bright, shining star—as someone who really had it together."

I wanted to tell her I understood why she thought I should stay—they were the same reasons that I argued with myself about. But instead I just gave her a kiss and told her I would be back from London in a week. I would have plenty of time to explain.

Rupa, one of my closest cousins, was the only person who

knew what state of mind I was in. Or so I thought, until my uncle Aziz surprised me by pulling me away from the chaos of the family to ask what was happening. I told him what I wanted, trying really hard not to get into details.

"Think of your kids," he said. Provoked out of politeness, I measured out words of pain as carefully as someone walking on sheets of broken glass. "Do you think that one single thought other than my kids has crossed my mind?" I told him what my kids really deserved from their parents: a life that was not lived on a battlefield.

Without taking his eyes off me, my uncle pulled out his phone and began to dial. When the person on the other end answered, I realized he was talking to my mother. He told her she needed to listen to me. "Your daughter is smart, and she loves her children. Trust her," he said before hanging up and apologizing to me. I did not know whether to be furious about her meddling or under-standing that she did it because she cared so much.

On the last day of the celebration, Rupa told me to meet her at the station at eight the next morning; we were going on a trip. She said I wouldn't need to bring much because they would have everything I needed. I got to the station in jeans and runners with my backpack, laughing when my put-together cousin sailed up carrying Hermès and Louis Vuitton bags.

I laughingly told her it seemed we were going to two different places. She took me to Marbella, Spain, where we spent three days lying by the pool and doing little else.

Rupa and I are the same person in different bodies—the only difference being that she is a decade younger and has a cute little British accent. We have always traveled well together, sometimes giving each other quiet and the space to enjoy our own company, and other times chatting up a storm. We decided to schedule an annual trip.

When I returned home, I learned that Ishraq was in a coma.

I rushed to the hospital, thinking that there was so much I still wanted to tell her. I hadn't finished explaining myself, I hadn't gotten her blessing, and most importantly, I hadn't comforted her worry about me. I was still there the next morning when she found her peace, surrounded by her family and friends.

I looked at the woman in the bed, who seemed like a stranger. Ishraq will always be, in my mind, as she was when we met: bright, bubbly, and full of life, with a smile that lit every corner of a room. Both she and I were caught between two worlds. We had not yet learned how to become who we could be—who we wanted to be.

In the end, my calm convinced my husband when my anger couldn't. He gave in. *Inti taleq.* After a victory and a tragedy wrapped up in two words, the end of my marriage was a bewildering silence.

We finally came to an agreement on how we would break the news of the divorce to the kids. We would tell the girls together, and then we would each have a separate conversation with Ahmed. However, when we sat the girls down in the living room, all our intentions flew out the window. We did not know how to handle it well, and we didn't. The girls said nothing, looking at me with a heartbreaking mix of anger, fear, and confusion.

They already knew, of course. They weren't blind or deaf—despite our efforts to fight quietly, the walls in our house were thin. And now they were looking to me to fix this.

How could I even begin to explain? I knew my decision was causing them to question everything they knew, and I was afraid it would change their entire view of relationships.

But I simply didn't know what to do to make it better.

Any dreams I'd had of an amicable separation didn't match the

Arab view of divorce, in which the other person is gone, taboo. Friendship was not an option. No joint family dinners after the dust settles; no swapping holiday greetings with our new spouses. Just nothing.

Some nights my boy would come into my room, sit next to me with his little arm around me, without saying a word, and give me a kiss on my forehead before going to bed. My son with the heart that fits the world inside it was trying to comfort me, when it should have been me protecting him from the harm I was causing.

The only thing I could do was give the kids all the love I had to give, which included trying to be the best version of myself so that, as adults, they would want the same for themselves. But that was taking the long view. For now, their world had been shattered, and, in their minds, I was the one wielding the hammer.

I lay awake the night we told them, certain that if I fell asleep, I would see my grandmother's disappointed face in my dreams again. But she didn't come.

I never dreamed of my grandmother again. Maybe she has given up on me. But I like to think she approves of the woman I have become.

It Takes Connections.

All human beings need a certain minimum quantity of regular, satisfying social interactions. Roy Baumeister and Mark Leary argue that many of the documented human needs—power, intimacy, approval, achievement—are driven by the need to belong. They tell us that the inability to meet this need results in mental distress.

We are lonely.

Connections are a side effect of belonging. They form the complex tangle of streets, avenues, and back alleys that get you everywhere in life. You never know where a friendship will lead if you take its hand. More hands, more opportunity, more inspiration, more surprises.

Most of my business came from my connections. So did my knowledge, support, and fun. I have cast a wide net of people I know around the globe. And I mean *know*. I know their kids and their business and their lives. Superficial connections will get you nowhere.

Farah Mohamed is the CEO of the Malala Fund, an organization that helps girls go to school and reach their full potential. For years, I'd admired her work at a distance. Reaching out through multiple mutual friends, I chased a lunch with her and got nowhere. She was too busy saving the world to eat for no specific reason with a stranger who wouldn't stop emailing her.

Fate intervened. One day we were both brought to the same event to speak, and I was no longer a faceless stalker. She actually said to me that she was reluctant to meet because I seemed "just too much." She felt I was intimidating. I almost fell over, because *she* was so intimidating . . . and we became fast friends.

Not long ago, I was speaking at an event in Chile and coordinated my flight to allow myself two days to explore Brazil. I have always wanted to visit the Christ the Redeemer statue, and there was a street artist I hoped to find whose work I had admired for a couple of years.

Now, I am a seasoned traveler. Over-seasoned. So forgetting that I needed a visa for Brazil until the moment I was sitting in a police holding cell at the airport in Rio de Janeiro is a low point in my traveling IQ.

Waiting to be deported, I stared at my phone and begged it to bail me out. I called friends, who called the Consulate General of Canada in Brazil. It was 10 p.m.

The consular officer was polite-ish. He listened and then asked me if I had ever been on a plane before this. Did I not know that visitors to countries probably need visas? And then he said, "Ms. Al-harazi, I've been in this situation before. I am sorry, but if I can't get an Olympian without a visa into the country, there's nothing I can do for you. Best of luck." Then a click. A very judgmental one.

Back to my phone. Who did I know that could move bureaucratic mountains? I called Farah Mohamed at 11 p.m.

Surprisingly, she answered. I explained how I had ended up where I was and asked if she could help. She paused while she flipped through her mental Rolodex, then told me to hang tight— she'd do her best.

Thirty minutes later, my phone rang. It was the consular officer. He said, "Who the fuck do you know in Ottawa? Guess what I am doing right now? I am on my way to my office to issue an emergency visa. At midnight." Another click.

Four hours later, the head of security walked to the door with me, handed me my passport with my three-day emergency visa, and apologized for keeping me so long.

The next day, the consular officer called and said, "What are you doing today? I am coming with you. I need to figure you out."

And that's how I came to spend two days exploring Brazil and meeting a consular officer. Turned out his good friend was the artist I had been trying to track down. At his studio, I bought two huge paintings that hang in my home today. They remind me of a tiny holding cell at the airport in Rio—and of friendships (old and new) that make impossible things possible.

Every single person I meet challenges me to succeed by showing me what life looks like. And my small world has unfolded into a huge playing field.

Fostering connections is about collecting people who inspire you. Internal and external barriers fall. The more people you know, the more potential the world seems to have, and the more fans you have for your own success.

A loud cheering section never hurts.

CHAPTER TWENTY-FIVE

By this time, Hanadi was already in her first year of college and Amani was in year three. I had leaned hard on Amani over the years—I guess that is the curse of the firstborn child. They are the one you depend on the most. She was the one who picked Ahmed and Hanadi up from school when I was working. She packed lunches and bought groceries. She picked up the pieces, and never with a word of complaint. And I never thought to thank her: she was part of the family, and that is what you do; we all pitch in to help when needed, right? Not once did I ask, "Amani, is this okay?" Instead, I just said, "Amani, do this."

Terrified by the idea of her going away to university, I had insisted that she go to the University of Calgary. Just as I had not been able to stand the thought of her walking to her friend's house alone, I also couldn't stand the thought of her not coming home safely to her bed every night. My girl eased her mama's worries and stayed home.

Amani is allergic to conflict. For a while after her father and I told her about the divorce, she barely uttered two sentences to me about it. The impasse finally ended during the most difficult conversation I had ever had with my daughter. All her fears came out one day, right behind her anger at me. She was scared for all of us and she worried about me. Was I going to be okay? What if I was alone forever? What if I got sick? We talked and cried for hours, and then light finally broke through the darkness gathering between us, and I felt like my daughter was mine again.

Okay, I made that sound easier than it was. It took months and years—many tears and lots of anger—to repair all that was broken. Luckily, that time was underlaid with enough love to fill all the cracks.

Remember when I said my ability to compartmentalize my feelings and frustrations was a saving grace? Well, it saved my sanity during the divorce. Every single person I loved went into their own little box and got locked up and put away until I could deal with them, one at a time.

I thought a lot, in those days, about the times when I had taken for granted those to whom I am closest—times when I had been more considerate of strangers than I was of my loved ones. The aftermath of my divorce was certainly a moment in which I needed to martial every last resource in order to survive. But I now understand that doing what it takes should never be at the expense of the people you love.

Amani graduated with a degree in oil and gas engineering, while working and paying her own way at school. After her third year, she completed an internship in an oil field in Lloydminster, just as her father had. She operated oil wells and was the only girl on her shift. She would call me with stories of her life in Lloyd. Some were funny (chasing cows out of a fenced enclosure in the middle of nowhere by yelling and waving her arms), and others were downright terrifying (having to stick her gloved hand into burning insulation material to turn off a valve).

I guess she also learned to do what it takes.

Hanadi was a different story: when it came time for her to go to university, her attitude was, "I'm out of here—I'm sick of your rules." Hanadi is sassy, independent, and strong. The more I tried to rein her in and keep her home, the more she wanted to spread her wings and take off.

Hanadi is a mini-me: she looks, walks, and talks like me. When we argue, she even juts out her chin in the same way . . . and she always wins. You can't hold that girl back, no matter how hard you try, and I gave up trying many years ago. What was the point of saying no to her, when hours later she would wear you down into a yes?

Hanadi has spirit and knows what she wants, and what she wants is to change the world for the better—and I am certain that one day she will.

She decided to go to the University of British Columbia, and the day I helped move her to Vancouver, I cried all day in front of all the other parents and kids, mortifying her, but getting laughs and lots of promises from her friends that she would be taken care of. She took a chunk of me along with her when she left.

Hanadi graduated and made the decision I knew all along she would make. She wanted to help people, the way she always has, starting in grade school, when the school created an award especially for her because she spent all her free time at school helping other kids. At university she volunteered at the Distress Centre. Then, she started working with disadvantaged and homeless youth, calling them her kids. She got attached, took them into her heart, and loved them like they were family.

I worried about the effects of her job on her and constantly tried to get her to consider a corporate job, telling her this was too much for anyone, too hard. I said, "How can you continue to do this, see what you see every day?" She looked at me calmly and said, "Someone has to."

• • •

Ahmed was soon the only one left at home, and he too was speeding through high school and growing too fast. His marks were just as high as his sisters' and his athletic awards lined his shelf.

He was great at hockey when he played in elementary school—the second-highest scorer on the team, even though he played defense. In high school, he started playing basketball instead, and he was really, really good, getting scouted for club basketball in a matter of months.

At the time, I was so busy, between work, sitting on boards and committees, and networking, that I didn't go to many of his games. In fact, I hardly went to any. But after seeing the photos other parents were posting on social media, I made an extra effort to go to the playoffs.

The first game was great, and they won, but Ahmed seemed distracted. The second game was a challenge for him and his team. I noticed that he kept looking at the bench where I was sitting. In the car on the way home, my son very politely said, "Mama, I love you, but please don't come to any more of my games." He patiently explained that since I went to so few, it made him nervous when I was there, and he did not play well. He had a responsibility to his team, he said.

I was deeply ashamed of myself as a parent and devastated to realize that while I was succeeding at every aspect of my business life, I had failed my son.

It hit me hard: I was a special guest in my son's life, not a constant. My conviction that I was a good mother disappeared when I understood that my son's mama wasn't there when he needed her to be.

I sat out the rest of the playoff games, feeling pained to miss out, and at the end of the season, I wasn't there to proudly watch Ahmed win the MVP award.

The following year, I put all his games in my calendar and tried to go to as many as I could. What made me feel even guiltier is that it was not hard to find the time, and nothing else suffered because of it. I simply needed to make my boy a priority. I finished off that year as the loudest and most obnoxious parent in the stands.

I try my best not to offer advice, but here's my one exception: do not have any regrets as far as your children are concerned. Those regrets are the only ones that matter, and the only ones that will haunt you for the rest of your life.

It Takes Calmness.

Grief is not limited to sadness. It screams at you with guilt, yearning, anger, and regret.

In 1969, Elisabeth Kubler-Ross identified five linear stages of grief: denial, anger, bargaining, depression, and acceptance. In the years I spent avoiding divorce, I raged at my husband for anything and everything. I skipped the bargaining part, and anger and depression lived side by side.

After my divorce, my son said to me, "You never get angry anymore, no matter what happens and what we do. When we were kids, we knew when you were angry and that we needed to stay out of Mama's way."

And my heart broke.

I put my children through the worst of me, and that hurts me to my core. That alone has made acceptance an easy place to live. It is a place that is healthier for my kids, which is all I need to know.

When the storm has passed, you'll be moving fallen trees and fixing your damaged roof for a long time, but it will mean the worst is behind you.

It's over.

Breathe freely, repair what's broken, and look up toward a bright new day.

CHAPTER TWENTY-SIX

My default assumption was that, since I had broken all the rules and taboos of my homeland, I no longer belonged to it. As a defense mechanism, I turned my back on my culture and my people. I cut all my ties with everyone I knew in Yemen.

However, slipping away was not so easy. Surprisingly, some people who held on the tightest were members of my husband's extended family. Texts that said "You are and will always be one of us. You are the mother of our children, and we are here if you need anything" brought tears, hope, and encouragement.

It was hard to explain to anyone exactly how fine—or, really, better than fine—I was. I felt guilty for my feelings because I had caused an earthquake in my family's life. Now, in the aftermath, it was my job to rebuild—for myself and for them.

However, I also was still living in the family home, for I had felt that leaving the house would be leaving my children. Although their father had gone back to his job in Yemen, he wouldn't be away forever. It was past time for me to find a place of my own.

I began to scan real estate listings for somewhere to live.

I wanted a porch in front of my house that I could sit on. I wanted a canopy of big trees and an older neighborhood with unique houses, not a cookie-cutter subdivision. I wanted to live downtown so I could walk everywhere. I wanted a modern, minimalist design.

I was looking for a house where my kids would love living and spending time with me. And because the emotions were still so raw, I thought that a house they loved might be a better draw than I was.

I narrowed down the field to two final choices. One was a decent option in my price range, in a neighborhood I liked, but only two bedrooms were aboveground and the other one was as small as a closet. The other house was my dream home: brand new, with a clean, modern feel, plenty of space, and ceilings that touched the sky—even the basement had seven-foot ceilings. And then there was the light: so much light in the form of skylights and floor-to-ceiling windows.

I loved everything about the house except for the fact it was listed for much more than I could spend. So I continued looking, but I kept coming back to that house. The more often I visited, the less the price became of any consequence: it seemed like a bright new future for us, and I wanted it badly.

I ran the numbers and made budgets until the mortgage application was all set. The responsibility and the satisfaction felt uniquely adult, as did the documents with my name on them.

When I signed the contract, I drained my account for the down payment. Seeing my signature resting proudly on that bottom line, I had no regrets. This home was mine, bought with money I had earned.

Not my father's, or my husband's. It was mine.

As I loaded my few belongings into boxes and arranged for movers to drop them in my new basement, I hated myself. I drove away, my kids still standing at their front door, and all of this effort felt so unnecessary. *What is wrong with me? Why can I not be satisfied with my life? Why can I not be a better mother to my children? Why am I not grateful?*

I would have plenty of time to ponder these questions from Louise's couch, as the contractors were still finishing up the last bit of work on my new house. While my art school friend had been quick to offer me a shoulder to cry on, advice wasn't really her style. What she did give me, during the five weeks I stayed with her, was even more valuable: a chance to finally feel like myself. She was absolutely wonderful—funny and distracting, comforting and hands-off, all at the same time. It felt like the old days: we lived on cheese, crackers, and wine and worked on many painting projects—hers good, mine not good.

I finally got the keys to the new place a few days before Christmas. Everyone had gone away on holiday, including my parents and all my friends. The kids were on vacation in Turkey with their father and his family. It was just Kale and me against the world.

I will never forget the moment when my key turned in the lock, the door swung open, and I stepped into my new life: blank walls, high ceilings, and floors that echoed every footstep. I felt the painful finality of twenty-three years of marriage ending, as well as all the endless possibility ahead.

I closed the door behind me and slipped off my shoes.

Now what?

Wintry Christmas nights in Calgary are particularly quiet. Snow insulates sound, and the whole town is under wraps. I dropped my bags, unpacked my toiletries, and put Kale's little winter boots on. I went to the grocery store to fill my fridge, and the only thing that kept me company was the sight of my own breath in the chilly air.

I will admit that putting the groceries away was quite exciting. It was just me, and I didn't have to deal with the kids' snack closet, which was always full of the things I hate to love and that had a bad habit of sticking to my thighs. This time, my fridge and cup-boards were filled only with fruits, veggies, protein, water, and tea.

This was my clean start.

I sat down on my unmade mattress, considered finding the sheets, decided it was too much trouble, and tried to fall asleep. Ten minutes later, I was pacing my front room, missing my kids and feeling terribly sorry for myself.

I had so many things to worry about. Money stresses were an entire list of their own. Calgary rides the roller coaster of a boom and bust economy as the price of oil fluctuates. At that moment, we were still in the middle of the bust that had followed the 2008 financial crisis. "Please, Lord, let me have another oil boom and I won't piss it away" bumper stickers were appearing around town.

Alison had told me she was ready to retire and so I had bought her out. She did not want to go through another downturn—she was thinking of her health and her home in Mexico. Business was so bad I had started paying salaries from company reserves.

Sleep continued to evade me for the next few days until, late one night, still pacing, I realized I needed to do something. Other-wise, the lack of sleep would kill me before the stress did.

I pulled a notebook from my shoulder bag.

When things are chaotic around me, I need to get organized. When I need to feel in control, I clean my desk; I sort my closet, making sure all the hangers face inward; I pull out my bucket of cleaning toothbrushes and attack my baseboards. Since I had nothing to clean in my sparkly new house, and all the boxes were already unpacked, I made a list.

Lists calm me better than bubble baths do most people. I always feel huge satisfaction as I cross things off. I'm pretty anal about it: I even write down things I've already done, just so I can cross them off.

My new to-do list included things I needed for the new house and my new life. I suddenly started to feel energized. *Freedom* echoed in my head, as it had for so many years, only this time it was an exciting reality, not a plea.

Home and car insurance, life insurance so the kids would be okay if anything happened to me. New bank accounts, automatic payments—but how much money did I actually have in the bank? How much did I really need for an emergency fund?

I needed a safety deposit box and an alarm system. Tax filing, setting up utilities, calling the cable company, changing my address with the post office and with the credit card companies. This may sound about as exciting as getting your teeth pulled, but you don't understand: this was the first time I got to set these things up for myself. Paying for them all out of my own account, by myself, and with no one to tell me to pick AlarmForce over ADT.

Once my to-do list was finished, I felt I had accomplished a lot. Why was I still not satisfied? Damn it, the list was supposed to calm me.

Then I realized the problem I had been avoiding: my children. During this tumultuous time in our family's lives, I had felt them retreating. And that had to change: my children were and are my entire world. Nothing makes sense or has value without them; I wanted their bright light back in my orbit again.

I started writing about each child: What were the red flags? What could I do to help resolve them? What was keeping *them* up at night? And how could I fix it?

My notebook was running out of paper, so the next day I bought the poster-size Post-It notes we used at Foundry for brainstorming. While at the store, I also bought smaller colored Post-It notes and black Sharpies. I even found a small pack of stickers with glitter on them and brought that home too. I stuck them at the top of every single page as a reminder of what was really important.

I started in the dining room, with a poster for each child. On each one, I wrote a plan that outlined what that child needed from me and what I needed to do.

In Yemen, we are taught that you have to respect your parents; you don't get a choice. I understood, however, that you don't just automatically get handed respect when you become a parent; you need to earn it. I was determined to earn their respect back, because I knew I already had their love.

The three posters in front of me became six, then nine. I began considering all my relationships that needed attention. I wrote down more names: the people I wished I spent more time with, the ones who needed a talking to, and the ones who had become toxic and needed to go.

I was ruthless, writing names, crossing off names, and adding some back. I was back to the old Foundry value of *Keep good company*—surrounding myself with the people I knew would push me to be my best.

I built friend lists. I had walked away from many of them, too exhausted to try to keep yet another relationship fed.

Who were the people that were going to be my support system? Who were the ones bringing me down? My friends went into two buckets: worth the effort and not.

I built mentor lists. Most of the relationships already existed, but I wanted to categorize them. What did they mentor me in? What did I need them for? They also went into buckets: personal, family, and business.

Once, when Louise was in the middle of a breakup and getting a bit weepy on the phone, I asked her if she wanted to come over for dinner and a chat. Her response was a firm no.

I felt hurt asked her why not, and she said, "You are not the person I come to when I want a good cry; you are the person I come to when I want a kick in the ass."

I am still not sure whether to like that or not, but I know she is right.

I made a list of the people I wanted in my life. Not specific names, but types of people for the types of things I wanted to do. Political hacks, fashionistas, gym rats, builders of things, and travel junkies. My kind of people.

I made another list of what I would need to do and where I would need to go to find them. I know why I wanted them in my life, but why would they want me? What value would I add to their lives?

My dining room walls started to get crowded, so I moved to the living room.

I wrote a list of words I would use to describe myself: caring, strong, outspoken, giving, energetic, determined, forgetful. A week later, I asked some friends and employees to do the same, listing the words that came to mind when they thought of me. Their words included loyal, bold, loving, strong, helping, and engaged, but also distant, distracted, unyielding, and pig-headed. I studied the lists, fascinated by the similarities and the differences. So many words describing the same trait, but in a completely different way.

I wanted the people whom I wanted in my life to want me in theirs too. To achieve that, I clearly had some work to do on myself.

Looking at the list of words, I came to realize I was building a value proposition: my core values were there, unchanged, while the things I needed to change, like being present, were doable and within my reach.

For so long, I had carefully managed how much I revealed to people. Telling them only what I wanted them to hear meant I was in control. But I needed to change that. I couldn't manage everyone, every time. It was time to stop trying to either fit in or stand out and just simply be myself.

There before me, on the Post-It notes, I had built my life team, my target audience, and my value proposition. *How fascinating,* I thought. *I had begun to build a creative brief.*

When creatives build a brand, we always build a brief first: for the team, for the client, and for the protection of both of us. A creative brief is meant to bring all parties to an understanding of what the brand needs to look, walk, and talk like. Whom it needs to engage, who its competition is, who is on its team. What does the product do, how does it function, who would want to use it, and why does it exist? Every detail about the brand and the world around it: ideas, inspirations, beliefs, values, questions, dreams, fears, and hopes.

When we build a brief, we build it to be able to sell a product or service to the audience that is willing to buy it. The ultimate goal is company growth and future viability for the people it serves.

And that's what I needed to accomplish for myself. A creative brief was the perfect vehicle for me to better understand my needs and my future.

I had always been my father's daughter, my husband's wife, and my children's mother. Now I needed to figure out who I was.

It had always been so easy, almost instinctual, for me to shift into automatic pilot. I think this is true for many people—especially women. We are the nurturers and the caretakers, so we need to keep it all together, not just for us but for those we love.

How often do we go about life without a plan and end up somewhere we didn't want to go in the first place? Step one, figure out where I wanted to go. Step two, figure out how I was going to get there.

You should understand how alien all of this was for me. In general, I make up my mind fast. I know what I want, and I chase it with determination. I don't like to explore feelings or talk about my chakras. I hate yoga, meditation, and Tony Robbins.

But here I was now, agonizing over every word, emotion, setback, and barrier. I forced myself to be honest about my shortcomings. I wrote down dreams, fears, and beliefs.

I climbed over brick wall after brick wall, peeling back layers of childhood insecurities, cultural hang-ups, shackles, and anger.

I wrote a creative brief to help me survive the next five minutes and the next twenty years.

What started emerging was messy and really cluttered. *This* was not how my life was supposed to look. I liked neat and tidy boxes.

So I started to organize. *What are my brand features and attributes, my differentiating factors? What makes me, me?* I built a passion list: things I wanted to do, taste, experience, know. (I have to admit that, so far, as quickly as I cross things off that list, I add more.)

What are my barriers to entry? What is stopping me from reaching my goals? What am I good at doing, and what am I particularly bad at? What is my brand promise? What are my values? My mandatories?

After working hard on these questions for a few days, I realized that the Foundry values I'd written years earlier, when I was a green, fresh entrepreneur, still held: they fit my business *and* they fit my life.

I drew a pie chart of what was important: family, business, friends, fitness, faith, community, and fun. How much of my pie did I spend on each thing? When I stepped back to look, I saw that the proportions were wrong.

That chart didn't correspond to my priorities or passions.

I drew a new pie chart of how I *wanted* to allocate my time.

Something very big began to emerge: nowhere, on any list, was my passion for marketing. I was coming to a shocking realization that I didn't really like my work. In fact, nothing about my work filled the part of my soul that craved purpose and a reason for being. But knowing I needed my company and its income, I filed that thought away, to deal with later.

Another slice strangely emerged: faith.

I needed to reconnect with faith, which I had turned away from for many years, first out of defiance and later out of guilt. I might not carry a photo of the Virgin Mary in my wallet, along with verses from the Quran, as my mother does, but I do believe in God.

I was tired of running away from the beliefs that had not worked for me in the past—I wanted to more deeply explore the ways this part of me could bring me to a place of peace and contentment.

What was I put on this earth to do? Why will I matter?

I wrote down my purpose statement: *I will spend the rest of my life collecting and telling stories and experiences that will change minds, perspectives, objectives, and hearts.*

It felt so right. It had purpose and heart, connection and emotion. The heaviness on my shoulders started lifting.

I began to set goals: short-term and long-term, large and small. *Within six months, I am going to fix my relationship with the kids. I am going to travel to another fifty countries before my fiftieth birthday. In three years, I am going to pay off the house and grow my company revenue to $50 million.*

The only goal I didn't write or even consider was a partner in my life. I just couldn't even think about handing any part of my life to anyone else ever again.

Notes lined the living room, the staircase, my bathroom, and the upstairs hallway. Reams of paper filled my once empty white walls.

And then, finally, I was finished.

A feeling of calm washed over me as I saw my plan in front of me.

I pulled the papers off the walls, rolled them up, and put them in the recycling bin. I already knew in my heart what they told me.

It felt symbolic of a new beginning.

It Takes Purpose.

Each of us navigates a world of dualities. My need to be me felt like it was being suppressed by a thousand different "shoulds"— sometimes valid, always frustrating—that made me into someone I didn't want to be.

I had mastered the art of the hustle: the ability to identify what I wanted and then do everything in my power to ensure I would get it. But that wasn't going to get me out of what was going on in my head. The strange unsettledness, the sense of loss after building what I thought I wanted and discovering I didn't want it anymore. Other than my children, I had no anchor, no big love for anything I could see or touch.

I needed purpose—a reason for being. What was I meant to do?

I forced myself to view my latest stumble in the dark as a chance to find a new way. They always go hand in hand, always. Adversity is always attached to a better way. Every exit is an entrance.

Out of the corner of my eye, I can see myself the way I was when I was young. I had pushed so hard and changed so much. Why? And now what?

What is my legacy? What will people say about me when I die? What will my children remember about me?

What excites me? What makes a difference in the world and an impact on other people's lives? What allows me to live my values?

. . . and what can I make a living at?

For now, I am back on track. Tomorrow might be different, but today finds me wide-eyed, hopeful, and invigorated for what's next.

Is there any better way to live your life?

CHAPTER TWENTY-SEVEN

The kids and I were working to find our new normal, and my drive was supercharged. The economy recovered, and Foundry began winning new clients again. It felt good to be back in a place of confidence.

Our streamlined team included both Kira and Laura in leadership positions, and we had our pitch meeting strategy down pat. I was the big-picture thinker, the dreamer, on the edge of my seat, waving my arms in the air and talking excitedly about our work.

Kira, with a biologist's brain, was the voice of reason. Right there in front of the client, she would gently interrupt and pull me back from the edge to talk about the practical aspects of our collaboration: the timeline, the process, and how we would report in to them.

Then came Laura, asking all the right questions, listening, learning about the client and engaging them in just the right way: What do you need? What are your pain points?

The combination of personalities was exactly right. Clients loved the dynamics of the exchange; when we went into a pitch together, it was virtually impossible that we wouldn't win it.

I took pride in the fact that we were filling the office with people who felt they could single-handedly move the earth. To draw in and nurture that talent, we built a culture that people felt really good about. We had regular team breakfasts at the corner deli, bowling nights, yoga sessions in the conference room. Everyone had two weeks off at Christmas and Friday afternoons off all summer. In our break room was a huge basket of free treats, with one catch: if you took one, you had to leave a love note. Our wall soon filled up with messages of love, gratitude, camaraderie, and new ideas.

I signed a lease on new office space for Foundry, with the same gorgeous light as in my house, in a great part of town. It was twice as large as we needed, but like my house, I had fallen in love with the building—a silver LEED-certified feat of design with a contemporary art gallery on the fourth floor and a luxury food market on the first. Both my work and my home environments became worlds that were entirely of my own making—places teeming with creativity and possibility.

My home went from empty to looking like an eclectic mishmash of cultures, genres, styles, and colors—like me. A four-thousand-year-old door from Rajasthan was turned into side tables, and a cast-iron moose head on my kitchen wall took four people to hang. Each of my incredible artistic friends had given me a piece as a housewarming gift. I was so grateful, knowing they sold those pieces for thousands. I hung street art from every city I had visited: Buenos Aires, Hong Kong, Prague, Vienna, Bangkok . . . a red parrot face mask from Panama City that was as tall as me, and another moose head, covered in wallpaper, from the Victoria and Albert Museum in London.

I often stayed in, entertaining a house full of friends, whether the occasion was an impromptu dinner party or a girlfriend who needed space during a life transition. Guests helped take my mind off the days when the kids weren't there. When Louise had to replace her floor, she moved in with me. Then came one of our clients, Lea, who was in the midst of a divorce and needed a place to stay for a few weeks, which turned into months. And then my friend Marta, who cooked *and* walked the dog.

On some days when the kids were around, the house was so full that Louise slept in my room, joking that she was the only other person I had ever invited into it.

A close friend invited me to go on a trip to Tijuana with my kids. We were going to build homes for families in need with an initiative called Homes of Hope, organized by the charity Youth With A Mission. When he had suggested the trip would be good for us as a family I agreed, thinking we needed to do something good together. Though we had been planning a family trip to Hawaii, another vacation was not going to fix things; this might be a start.

"We're going to Mexico," I told the kids at dinner. Their grins quickly turned to protests when they heard where in Mexico we were going and why. The Hawaii and Mexico trips were not mutually exclusive, I explained. This was a different kind of opportunity for our family—to be together and to give back at the same time.

Amani said she didn't want to go, and Hanadi raised an eyebrow as if to silently agree with her sister. Then Ahmed said, "Mama, that is a great idea."

That boy, my sweetness and my light, always eager to please everyone and smooth all the rough edges.

The girls shrugged and went on with their dinner, but I could see there was a glimmer of interest in their eyes.

It had been hard on my kids to grow up in the West with parents who were still holding on to our Eastern ideas. After our own strict upbringings, my husband and I often telegraphed to our kids that they should not stray too far away from our culture, which was completely intertwined with religion. We had been sending mixed messages. Live in Canada, do anything you want to do, be amazing, follow your dreams—but don't post a picture of yourself on Facebook in a miniskirt because people in Yemen might see it, don't drink, and don't go on a date.

My God, I thought, realizing for the first time that I was doing to them what had been done to me. I needed to stop. Just as I needed the freedom to breathe, so did they.

Their ties to Yemeni culture were completely different from our ties to Yemeni culture, and I couldn't force the rules of that society on them.

I am Yemeni; my children are Yemeni Canadians. The differences in our upbringing are staggering. My children were still in the process of forming their individual identities, and at the same time they were caught between two cultures: the one they were living in and the one we still wanted them to adhere to, a way of life they knew nothing about. We wanted our children to be bound by the rules and customs of our culture, but it wasn't theirs. As they grew up, conflicts around issues like dating, acceptable clothing, and curfews grew among us as well. We leave our homelands to give our children a better life and then do them a disservice by not allowing them to fully integrate.

These days I have a new message for my children: Be proud of where you are from, but be who you are.

As we got ready to go to Tijuana, I welcomed the opportunity to talk to my kids about gratitude. Yemen is a place where giving back is as commonplace as brushing your teeth—it is a pillar of faith, built into Muslim practices in both direct and quite subtle ways. The third pillar of Islam is compulsory charity, or *zakat*. Every financially stable Muslim is required to donate 2.5 percent of their wealth and assets yearly to those in need, to help them stand on their own and become productive members of society.

In Sana'a, we were constantly confronted by need: beggars would line up outside our house at dinnertime. My mother volunteered her time and mine to help others. Living in Calgary, however, we were pretty insulated from the developing world. The kids volunteered, but at the women's shelter, the high school for children with intellectual disabilities, and the seniors' home.

We packed our bags for Mexico, talking about the people we would meet. What could we bring for them? We stuffed our bags with socks and underwear, coloring books and crayons, pencils and jeans. When we realized we didn't have enough room for everything we had bought, we decided to fill a hockey bag and take it with us. One very large hockey bag turned into three, and we laughed when we got to the airport and realized that seventy other Canadians coming on this trip had done the same thing. We all brought so much with us that we had enough for the entire village.

Our group would be building a home for a mother, a father, and two kids whose current house was made of corrugated metal and rags. I took to the mother immediately, seeing in her eyes the same worries about the future of her kids, the same willingness to sacrifice, that I felt. Channeling my grandfather and his empty-handed shopping trips, I decided to ignore the organization's rules about giving money, and I carried some in my pocket, just in case I had a chance to slip it to her when no one was looking.

I saw that she was painting the back of the house by herself, so I picked up a paintbrush and followed her. We painted side by side for a while, and then I put my finger to my lips, put the bills into her pocket, and quickly walked away. I didn't want to embarrass her, and I was praying she would not make a big deal of it.

Two hours later, when we were both working on different projects inside, she ran up to me and held on while she cried. Everyone looked at us, wondering what was going on. "She knows I'm also a mother," I said awkwardly, shrugging my shoulders.

On our last day, my kids taught me a quite valuable, if totally terrifying, lesson. I had known they were working on a wooden plaque to hang by the front door with the family's name handwritten on it, identifying that this was *their* house. They had designed it themselves. What I didn't know was that the design was in the shape of a heart, and that, to finish it, Amani would be the one to cut it out with a circular saw.

I rounded the corner to see her holding the saw, every instinct screaming at me to take it out of her hands. But the look on my daughter's face, so fully concentrated on her work, reminded me that experiences like this were not solely for me to script. I turned around and walked away, my heart in my throat. The image I remember now, and will forever, is the proud and excited faces of my children as the plaque was hung on the wall by the door.

Does that mean I have stopped trying to take things out of their hands, wanting to do them myself to potentially save my kids from trouble?

Not yet. Probably never.

The mother told us through the translator that their simple one-room house, with no electricity or running water, was "a castle." We left them with hearts full, and I realized that while we were building a home for this family, we had begun to rebuild our own.

"Do you know they walk for two miles each day to get the kids to the bus stop for school?" Ahmed asked me on the way to the airport. I didn't, and I was so proud of him for asking the questions. Hanadi had a different observation. She was struggling with the experience we'd just had. She said: "The compound we stayed at was one million times nicer than the house we built. My room was bigger than the house for that whole family. I think organizations like this do more harm than good."

She was right and she was wrong. The world we live in is not built for equality and equity for all. We *can* fight hard to make a change, and she does, every single day; however, we still need to take care of those who are stuck in a spiral that will only take them downwards.

My kids had the freedom to live a life without dogma or fear, and thankfully, by the grace of God, they were able to recognize and understand those who were not so fortunate.

It Takes Adaptability.

Dr. Guy Winch is a psychologist who believes our ability to be adaptable is present from a very young age. In his book *Emotional First Aid*, he shares the following scenario:

> Three toddlers are given a difficult task to do. Each handles the challenge in his or her own unique way: one cries and gives up immediately, one tries the same strategy over and over again, and one tries different strategies until he finds one that eventually works.
>
> Clearly, the third toddler has a higher level of functioning adaptability, and as a result is the only one to successfully complete the task. Is adaptability something you're born with, or can you learn it?

Dr. Winch believes that being adaptable leads to increased happiness. "We constantly meet psychological challenges. Some of us succumb, we feel hopeless, disempowered, give up . . . and some meet challenges, take the knock and learn something from it. Our ability to have life satisfaction, to be happy, to have good relationships, really depends on our ability to adapt."

Personal happiness aside, being successful in business depends largely on how easily one adapts to change. Most companies fail because their leaders resist change. Time marches on, and the business stays stuck in a past that has moved beyond it, while the leaders wonder what happened.

Experts agree that staying competitive requires both the will to adapt to change and the foresight to anticipate it.

I believe our ability to adapt is mastered through circumstance. I learned early on how to change my behavior to be successful in different situations. This is what big brands do to gain market share. They study their target audience, research what motivates them, then build the brand to meet their needs.

In the Arabic school, I was the only one who spoke English, so I did the popular kids' English homework and helped them cheat on exams. I called it survival . . . the headmaster introduced me to his cane.

Over the years, I have grown, innovated, and upgraded who I am. Funny how we are so comfortable using those words to build our companies but not ourselves. Remaining open to new realities, new perspectives, and new ways of doing things has a lot to do with where I've made it to in life.

Do you start each day with the mind-set that you're prepared to handle whatever it may bring? That is the personality trait that determines how you respond to change.

There's a Chinese proverb that says "The wise adapt themselves to circumstances as water molds itself to the pitcher."

Life will throw a lot of shit at you. You can curl up and take it, or you can knock it down. It really is up to you. Readily embracing— and challenging—an unknown circumstance will make you interesting, diverse, and a lot of fun at a dinner party.

Or in Arabic school.

CHAPTER TWENTY-EIGHT

One of our account managers, Sarah, stopped by my desk one day to mention that *Chatelaine* magazine had opened up nominations for their Women of the Year awards. "Did you know they have a Top Entrepreneur category?" she asked. "I think we should nominate you."

This was typical of Sarah, whose great attitude and desire to make everyone happy made her a pleasure to work with. I told her I was flattered by the suggestion and her willingness to put my name forward; then I watched, in awe, as she worked to craft the perfect submission.

A few months later, she was back at my desk, thrilled to tell me I was shortlisted for the award. Some of the other semifinalists were big names in Canada, including Corin Mullins, who had made a cereal to address her husband's stomach issues, named it Holy Crap, and turned it into a $100 million business.

I did not think I stood a chance against such a lineup, but it was fun to be included—until I realized the winners would be chosen by a public vote. I had known a fashion magazine would not subject me to a financial evaluation, but I had not known it would be a popularity contest.

I wanted to throw up.

Putting myself out there like this felt like walking stark naked down the middle of the street in broad daylight. Losing is a part of playing the game, but it is a tad harder to stomach when the whole world is watching.

Shockingly, I was the winner. As much as I would like to think I held my own against some pretty incredible women, the secret to my success, in this and many other things, was my mother.

Because the vote was open to anyone from anywhere, my mother wrangled a vote out of anyone in Yemen with an email address, her extensive family in India, and everyone at the bank, the grocery store, the gym, and the hospital where she volunteered. Her book club. Everyone at the mosque and strangers on the street.

I met a new client years later who told me she had voted for me; apparently, she took a yoga class with my mother *once*.

When the magazine finally came in the mail and I sat down to read the write-up, my first reaction was dismay. I had talked to the interviewer for a couple of hours, telling her about all my business successes, yet the article focused on a rags-to-riches story about coming to Canada and getting chicken pox.

That was *not* the story I wanted to be known for—not one I *ever* want to be known for. The story I wanted to tell was positive and uplifting: Do what it takes, work hard, be successful. Take care of others. I am proud of where I come from, my upbringing, the sacrifices my families made for this life I was now living. The article made it sound as if I had succeeded in spite of them, when the truth is I had succeeded because of them.

Each season after the awards seemed to bring more invitations to global speaking events—and deep soul-enriching adventure. Every trip was an instant change of perspective, new faces and friends, endless possibilities. My Twitter bio told the world that my home base was "with any luck, on a plane." My calendar and passport filled up, my circle of friends expanded, and the weeks away turned into years.

The awards kept coming too—from the Royal Bank of Canada's Top 25 Canadian Immigrants to the Women's Executive Network's Canada's Most Powerful Women to the Queen's Diamond Jubilee Medal—and with them came name recognition for me and for Foundry.

The awards were validation, security, and acknowledgment for me. In the beginning, they seemed great for the company too—they brought Foundry visibility, credibility, and a great deal of confidence.

While I thrived on the fast pace, I was also nagged by the uneasiness I felt about my career. Was I on the awards circuit to help Foundry get recognition and, through that, more clients, or was I doing it to run away from a company I was no longer connecting with? While it is in my nature to retreat, no amount of travel could take away from the years of conflict with my partners, the recession and the realization that I was not fulfilled by my work.

I was also bewildered by the number of *women's* awards and events out there. This was Canada, the promised land in the West I had dreamed of so often as a child. I still firmly believed this was the land of opportunity—a meritocracy that transcended politics, with fair play and a level playing field for all. I was surprised, regularly, that equal pay and equal opportunity were not actually available to all. The many special awards for women could not distract from the fact that we still did not have equal representation in politics, business, industry, and working life.

I was invited to join a members-only women's club. Its website said, "From the corporate world elite to award-winning entrepreneurs, from creative artisans to the top legal minds in the country—network and grow alongside women who believe that true connections are built beyond virtual communities and the super-ficial meet and greet."

That all sounded great to me, except the "alongside women" part. *Can't women do all that alongside men?* I was so confused.

As someone from a country where women have no rights, I found the way people talked about female achievement condescend-ing; celebrating men who were "champions of women" seemed trite. It shocked me to hear the suggestion that women are capable of anything less than total awesomeness, outstanding ability, equal contribution, and tireless, courageous efforts that could change the world. By applauding female achievement as something astounding, we seemed to be selling ourselves short. Why were women ghet-toized in a country where they are legally nothing less than equal?

At one dinner, I said this to the group of incredibly accom-plished women around the table. I said it didn't matter where you came from, what you looked like, or whether you were a man or a woman. If you worked hard in Canada, you would succeed. "Don't let the thought of a glass ceiling stop you, or it will," I preached.

"Zahra, you are the boss. You're an entrepreneur, and you call the shots. You don't know what you are talking about," said Shannon, the only other entrepreneur at the table. "We are never going to understand what they're going through, because we cre-ated our own worlds. We *are* the boss," she said.

It was just the beginning of my understanding of how discrim-ination works, in even the most privileged societies. It hasn't been that long that women have held the right to vote or be called to the bar or licensed to practice medicine. Get birth control. Get a divorce. Be elected to office. Get an abortion. Not that long at all.

I understood it a hell of a lot better when I felt the pinch of sex-ism at work for the first time. A potential client who owned a golf course put out a request for proposal for an advertising campaign.

We pulled out all the stops but didn't win the contract. They later told us we had the best pitch and the best ideas. But because our leadership team was a group of *women*, they didn't think we would really understand a golf course that catered predominantly to men. My eyes were finally wide open to a truth that made me furious.

There is no problem with female ability. In fact, in the West, women now actually surpass men in educational achievement. However, despite the great gains, gender inequality persists in the workforce. Women continue to earn less than men while getting fewer opportunities and less funding.

As I write this, 40 percent of the top five hundred Canadian companies do not have a single woman on their boards. Although women now make up 48 percent of the employed labor force in Canada, just 0.32 percent—twenty-six thousand of more than eight million working women—hold senior management positions. At this pace, it will be 151 years until we see gender equality in the senior management ranks.

Now that I know about the glass ceiling, I can see its influence everywhere—even here in a land of equal opportunity.

In 2013, I had the opportunity to speak to four hundred employees of a major bank on International Women's Day. The story, as I heard it, is that during the speech, the CEO turned to a very senior member of his team and said, "Hire this woman." The job offer, when it came, felt like the ultimate validation.

I felt like I had finally arrived . . . and then I turned it down because even with the validation, I still wasn't sure of myself anywhere I didn't have complete control.

When I was young, my grandmother always told me that if I bought something with honestly earned money, it would never get lost. Since I kept losing my sense of self, I kept investing in travel. Being in a new situation always brought back old fears, but if I worked through them with honesty and an open heart, my soul came back to me every single time. The same way travel brought me freedom from the rules of Yemen as a child, it brought me freedom from a company that no longer held any attraction for me.

EO presented loads of opportunities for speaking and travel. My involvement with the organization had grown from a deep local bond with my forum group to a global adventure beyond my imagination. I was having so much fun, especially because each time I found something new to do and then did it, I could move on to find something else to fill the pit that was my insatiable demand for a new distraction.

I had turned down my first leadership opportunity with EO— or tried to. When my friend Scott, the incoming president for EO Calgary, asked if I was interested in a position on his board, I told him I would think about it. The next day, at the annual Christmas party, he announced my new position as the city's learning chair to the chapter.

He called it being "voluntold." I called it sneaky.

Little did I know this would be one of the best things that ever happened to me. Members of local boards are required to attend EO's Global Leadership Conference. My first year, the conference was in Bahrain, and it was the start of some of my favorite and most important friendships, travel opportunities, and a profile on the cover of EO's *Octane* global magazine.

That leadership position led to an opportunity to join the global communications committee. They had wanted Canadian representation on the board, and I had the right skill set.

Scott, who learned the news from a photo on Facebook, said, "How did you *do* that? Do you know how hard it is to get on a regional committee," he laughed, "let alone a *global* one?"

• • •

My cousin Rupa and I chose to spend our second annual trip together driving across California. On day one, we set off from Los Angeles in our rented white Mustang convertible, aiming for dinner in San Francisco, and almost immediately got in trouble with the law in the form of a $400 speeding ticket.

On day two we arrived in Napa Valley and found sun and more sun; our tan lines now had tan lines. We ate food and more food—drank wine and more wine, crossing the line between tasting and guzzling sometime that morning and well into the next day.

Day three brought Yosemite National Park and a stunning hike in pouring rain. That night, I lay in our upgraded "signature tent"—which featured a bear locker, access to communal bathrooms, and two narrow hospital beds—and listened to the sounds of the forest. I was so contented, thankful for my life, for choices I made and promises I kept. I wished I could bottle the feeling up for later.

Those feelings of peace lasted until about ten o'clock.

My contentment resources were rapidly depleted by the thin mattress, sharp, noisy springs, dirty blanket, and hot, smelly tent. There was no lock on the door and constant movement outside our flimsy shelter all night. The fact that we were at the very edge of the campground and both of us needed to go to the bathroom at 1 a.m. only made it worse, and the flashlights on our phones did not stop us from getting lost on the way back to the tent.

The best part of the night was watching Rupa arm herself with a "flammable" T-shirt and matches to throw in the face of any bear and/or intruder if attacked in the middle of the night.

The next morning, the not-so-inviting communal showers did not inspire us to attempt a cleanup, so two very smelly women who were wearing the same clothes we had hiked *and* slept in very thankfully drove to a day at the Refuge Spa in the Santa

Lucia mountains. On our way back to L.A., Rupa's eagle-eye gaze did not leave the speedometer except to glare at me. Did I mention I'd gotten another speeding ticket? She said I was seriously dipping into her shopping budget.

Hollywood offered star-gazing and people-watching at their very best, and the next morning, we returned to our childhood and became little kids again at Universal Studios.

The trip to California joined my already overcrowded social media posts, and as the countries and adventures racked up, my attitude toward disclosure got bolder. I had once been very careful about hiding my pictures on Facebook, worried that someone from Yemen would see a bare arm or a day on the beach. I was less careful now, less afraid of what "people" would think and more willing to risk the scorn.

Early one morning a few months later, while I was in Hawaii on my first post-divorce holiday with the kids, I woke up to several thousand new followers on Twitter and Facebook and felt my heart in my throat. My new followers were all from Yemen.

Stunned, I scrolled through the names, saw that most of them were men, and began to panic. If you are a woman from Yemen, you need to be largely unheard and unseen. You stay under the radar and don't do anything that draws attention to yourself.

I quickly found out what had happened: a Yemeni newspaper had published an article about my success and my awards, along with photos of me without my headscarf on. I felt hot and cold shivers race up my spine. I thought I was in a heap of trouble until I read the messages.

They were all from people from my country, telling me how proud they were of me, how I was one of the good things to have come out of, as one man put it, "the hellhole that we live in."

There were messages from women saying they wished they were like me and that I was a shining example and a beacon of hope for them. How they wanted to follow my path. How brave I was.

I could not believe what was happening. This was the country I thought would walk away from me, a divorced woman, one with no regard for propriety—instead, they had embraced me.

At that moment, I truly felt as if I lived in a world that I fit into. Snug and sure.

It Takes Grace.

There's an old trick employed to make fortune cookies more interesting. You add the words "in bed" at the end of your fortune, no matter what it is.

A friend asks only for your time and not your money . . . in bed. Nothing is impossible to a willing heart . . . in bed. Time heals all wounds. Keep your chin up . . . in bed.

See? It always works.

On a daily basis, I do a similar trick using "with grace."

Accept rejection . . . with grace. Delegate work . . . with grace. Call to complain about our phone bill . . . with grace.

Grace is more about style than substance, which might be why it's so hard to google it. Try and you'll get a host of religious references, zero science to sift through, and a few poems about leaves. Nothing really about being kind, generous, and forgiving.

I firmly believe that how you do something is as important as what you do. Life has a way of constantly challenging you. Address your obstacles with grace, and you'll always be a step ahead (. . . in bed).

If you're a woman with any sort of power, you'll surely be called a bitch—or worse. Face those moments with grace too. It's the best face slap I know of.

CHAPTER TWENTY-NINE

My relationships with men had always been extreme—from not being allowed to talk to boys as a child to jumping right into the business world. Now I was in my forties and single, having never gone on even one date. I had no difficulty meeting men; I moved in so many circles that someone interesting was always waiting on the sidelines. But I was like a kid on a bike with my training wheels still on. I had so much to learn.

I started experimenting, going on dates. Many dates. Has young kids? No. Wants kids? No. Not gainfully employed? No. Too religious? Too clingy? Too conservative? Double no.

I shuffled through and discarded men before any kind of expectation or commitment could set in. I kept them all at arm's length and moved on at the speed of light, too afraid to get tied down again.

After a particularly wild summer, I realized this was not who I was either. I talked to Denny, a mentor and a friend—someone I have deep respect for. Almost twenty years after his divorce, he had found the love of his life, and I wondered how he'd known she was the one.

"I made a list," he told me. "Must-haves in one column, the hills you will die on. Nice-to-haves in the next, and absolutely nots in the third. Make sure it is from the heart, and dig deep. It can't be superficial." He told me the only face he could see in his mind when he was making his list was someone he had known for twenty years—Colleen, now his beautiful wife.

I went home, made my own list, and added it to my creative brief. And then I waited, certain that the man of my dreams would immediately knock on my door.

Needless to say, that is not how it works.

Each EO conference I attended resulted in an invitation to another one. Geneva led to Munich. Athens led to Argentina. Chennai led to Singapore. London led to Washington. I mapped seven days of speaking engagements in Australia and New Zealand into a month of travel, leaving lots of time for exploration in each city.

One of EO's core values is "once in a lifetime" events, and the new friends I made in every city took time and special care to make sure I had many of them, from flying a small plane in Brisbane to surfing the Gold Coast, climbing the Sydney bridge, snorkeling the Great Barrier Reef, feeding kangaroos, and holding koalas—a lifetime of firsts . . . and new Facebook photos. Until I got to Adelaide.

I stood before an audience of more than a hundred people in Adelaide and told them how I had conquered my fear of heights, convinced it was true. "There is no lock on the cage," I said. "The only restriction you have in your life is in your own mind."

I spoke about how I jump at any opportunity to do something that takes my feet off steady ground, and the incredible feeling of success I feel afterward. From zip-lining in Costa Rica to walking the edge of the CN Tower in Toronto to Arbraska Duchesnay, an aerial adventure in Lac Saint-Joseph. My lesson to the group was push your limits, push hard, push back, and when the fear creeps in, focus on the win.

I wrapped up the workshop that afternoon, took questions, and went back to my hotel, happy to have another successful talk behind me.

At dinner that night with a few members of the board, the EO Adelaide chapter president, Dan El, grilled me. He was fascinated by the idea of fighting fear and the ways to do it. Early the next morning, I got a call from Dan. "Guess what we're doing today?" he said in a singsong voice.

It had been tough to arrange a skydive on such short notice, he told me—most places were booked solid for three weeks—but he'd been so inspired that he called everyone until he finally found a company that could take us. "I don't like heights either," he said, "but today, I am going to conquer that fear." He seemed pretty proud of himself. I froze, suddenly yearning to spend the rest of my life in that hotel room bed.

By the time Dan came to pick me up a few hours later, I had done what I do so well: I had stopped thinking about it. Giant red warning lights and alarms were screaming through my mind, and I ignored them. There was no going back.

I met Dan at the door with a composed smile.

That smile remained fixed on my face while I filled in what felt like a million liability release forms (it actually was just one), viewed training videos, and strapped myself to the human being who was supposed to make sure I went home that day.

"No one has ever died on a tandem skydive," said Mike, the very young man I believed was going to die with me in the next hour. We climbed higher, as I had told the man at the front desk I wanted to jump from twelve thousand feet. After ten feet, what did it even matter? I was pretty sure that if I didn't die on the jump, my mother would kill me for doing it.

Stomach in my throat, I suddenly remembered I had forgotten to tell my kids what I was about to do. So I quickly sent a vague "I love you, be good" text to each of them, without letting them know their mother needed a restraining order from herself. I could hear Amani's voice in my head, telling me yet again that I was batshit crazy.

I looked out the window, realizing we were higher than the clouds and the earth was round. And then it was time: I was the one who had to swing my legs out the door first, because I was in front. I was the one who had to lean forward and pull us both out of the plane. I was the one who had to release my clenched hands from the doorframe.

Here is what they don't tell you in the safety videos: After you jump out of a plane, while you are falling through the sky for forty-five seconds at the speed of a bullet, you can't breathe. Fear grips you in a chokehold, and the wind is a solid wall in front of your face. Just as I had decided I was going to suffocate and die before I crashed and died, I felt Mike tapping me on the shoulder. "Open your eyes," he yelled. "Look at the camera!"

I smiled as widely as I could, held that for a beat—long enough for my new Facebook profile picture—and then calmly told him to take the damn camera out of my face and pull the cord. The parachute went up and we floated for five minutes—the earth still too far away and me still waiting for feelings of achievement and success. And as soon as our feet hit the ground, I bent over and threw up.

Dan came down, whooping with excitement, loving every second of it. "Want to go up again?" asked the crazy bastard.

Of course, Dan was so excited to do this with me. It was the ultimate expression of an entrepreneur: *Watch me jump off this building.* And of a group of entrepreneurs: *Hold my beer, me first.*

That afternoon, on a trip to the zoo with more friends, I fell asleep for the entire safari expedition, and for the next two days, I had zero energy. I couldn't even lift my arms. I had put my body through so much stress and trauma that I was drained. And for what? What was this demon inside of me that insisted I had something to prove? Proving my worth was not a need, it was a choice—and a childish, king-of-the-playground one, at that.

I had styled myself a storyteller, and the stories I had to tell were impressive: seductive, worldly, bold. In this story, I was the adventurer I wanted everyone to see—not only on the other side of the earth but also twelve thousand feet above it. Truth is, I am scared of heights, and there is absolutely nothing wrong with that.

We are the sum of our experiences, but more importantly, we are our reactions to them. In order to get what I truly wanted out of life, I needed to push beyond the fuel-injected aphorisms.

This was when I got over myself. Hanadi helped.

Later that day on my way to the airport, when I sent the kids the smiling photo from the skydive, her wry response was "Congratulations, you've crossed another item off your midlife crisis list. Are you done now?"

The innate curiosity that had propelled me into these tours and experiences always led me to some deeper understanding of myself and the world around me. Every one of them helped shape me, even the bad ones—*especially* the bad ones. They made me braver; they opened my mind and my heart. They helped me grow into the person I was supposed to be. Where would I be without the experiences I have had and the stories I now tell? Would I be complacent? Still scared? Uneducated? Would I be lonely?

Life is not about loving only the adventure but also, as Bruce Mau has said, loving the experiment. As I have evolved, coming back to that wisdom has helped me let go of the guilt I feel around so-called failures. Challenges really are opportunities, and the way you deal with them is what defines you as a person. In other words, life will throw a lot at you. What are you going to do about it?

Although this was exactly what I had been teaching in my talks, only now did it begin to make sense in my own life. I started to love my mistakes with the same passion that I loved the wins. I began to feel less intimidated by the idea of people seeing me for who I really was, less intimidated by the truth. Less afraid of whether I would fit in. I didn't need to fit in, and I didn't need to stand out. I simply needed to be me.

And thus the kernel of an idea for a new business was born.

It Takes Money.

A report from the University of South Hampton concludes that the likelihood of having a mental health problem is three times higher among people who have debt. Depression, anxiety disorders, and psychotic disorders were among the common mental illnesses that people in debt experienced.

People who die by suicide are eight times more likely to have been in debt. People in debt are more likely to experience problem drinking and drug dependence.

About 35 percent of Americans have delinquent debt, according to a 2014 report published by the Urban Institute. A similar percentage of business owners are uncomfortable with their company debt.

Dear reader, paying off debt is a terrible life goal. Don't let it have to become yours.

We take vitamins, eat organic food, work out, and do our best to make healthy lifestyle choices. And in the end there's a solid chance we'll be taken down by our credit cards. Let that sink in.

Study after study has shown us that we do not create perfect lives by buying stuff. In fact, our stuff makes us *less* happy because every time we buy a product two things happen: First, our happiness levels start to drop the minute we have the item in our hands. Second, somebody in advertising tells us the goalposts have moved. We now have to buy the newer model to be happy.

That's what it all comes down to: our eternal search for happiness. Just charge it to a card.

And where do we put all the things we buy on credit? The Self Storage Association reports that Americans spend $24 billion each year to store their stuff. It's the fastest-growing segment of the commercial real estate industry. We are putting ourselves in debt to buy stuff that we need to pay to put away.

If you're stuck on this ride, please find a way off.

When you live smaller now, you can dream bigger for later. Start a business. Travel. Retire earlier.

These days I'm trying to launch a new business, and after that I'd like to open a nonprofit vocational school in Yemen. I watch what I spend with caution, because I know having stuff may come at the expense of my plans.

What's your debt costing you?

CHAPTER THIRTY

While I traveled the world, the price of crude oil plummeted, and Calgary's boom and bust economy followed it down. It was the same roller coaster that had been my family's personal, professional, and even political reality as long as our fates had been tied to the oil business.

Foundry had weathered the 2008 global recession with only a few bruises, but this one hurt. Dozens of projects in the oil sands had been canceled, causing a massive ripple effect. Marketing budgets were slashed, and many of our clients let go their own communications teams; surely no one would justify a brand refresh, an advertising campaign, or a new website when people's livelihoods were on the line.

Every expense was called into question—even our habit of taking clients out for lunch when we finished a project. "We can't," said a number of clients. "We have orders from up above that we can't be seen in any restaurant—especially not having an expensive meal."

As soon as I heard that, I knew we were in for a rough ride. "We hate doing this to you," I heard, again and again. "We love working with you, but . . ."

I told clients I understood, and I did. More than sixty thousand jobs were lost that year, and the sense I was getting from every side was that, on a macro level, recovery would be hard and long.

But the more time went by, the more I believed that Foundry was not what I wanted. I was tired—tired of managing people and holding their hands, tired of running a company on my own, especially one I wasn't passionate about anymore. I left brainstorming sessions with a sense of boredom and defeat, and I seldom reviewed work going out the door.

By this point, I had not been engaged with the design process for years. I was no longer inspired by the work or energized by the risk of owning my own business. I realized the passion I felt was not for my company but for financial freedom—the ability to leave my husband without waiting for a check from him every month. And now that I had achieved that, my remaining drive had flagged, and the last place I wanted to be was in my office.

I stopped showing up for work. Stopped caring. And every speaking request that came my way, I accepted. Luckily, I had an exceptional team that rose to the challenge of a missing leader.

I no longer felt passionate about building brands, as I had begun to realize that a brand is one thing and one thing only: a product that is being sold to you. It is not genuine, it is not authentic, it is not your friend. It is there to make money. Period.

Study after study has shown that we do not create perfect lives by buying brands. In fact, they make us less happy. Still, I had once been very passionate about building brands. We all want to believe that like love and hope, passion springs eternal—that it is all-encompassing and will never wane. But that is simply not true. Passion, like happiness, like any emotion, can be long-lasting or it can be fleeting. And when passion disappears, so does your sense of purpose.

I had fallen in love with design when I was in art school. Looking back, some of that love was for a skill, any skill, I could master—something that was mine alone and that could provide me with financial independence.

But if I didn't belong in the design world, then what was left? Design had been a calling, a living, and an escape route. Prioritizing design meant I didn't need anybody else. I could be rewarded for hard work, and, it turned out, I could also excuse myself from the more complicated parts of my life.

I could have tried to fix this disenchantment, to fix my company, but instead, I stepped away.

Life always intervenes, and that seems triply so with EO, which continued to be a steadfast source of excitement and adventure, no matter what else was happening in my life. Just as I was staring at the edge of the abyss with Foundry, EO sent me to Nashville for a conference.

There, I connected with new EO members from around the world, danced with Elvis—or, at least, a quite convincing Elvis impersonator—met Jessica Alba, and forgot about the state of my career. And in the middle of all that, I got a call from someone I had met while giving a speech in Toronto a few years earlier, a powerhouse I greatly looked up to and admired. We arranged to meet in Toronto on my way home.

When we sat down together, she threw out what seemed to be a lifeline: Would I like to join her team of superstars working to roll out a new Canada-wide corporate citizenship strategy?

"Yes," I said quickly.

The contract she was proposing had many benefits. I would be closer to Ahmed, who was in his third year studying engineering at Queen's University. I would finally have the corporate experience I was missing, and moving to Toronto would be a new adventure, a way to stabilize myself *and* keep Foundry's lights on until I figured out what to do next.

. . .

The second call that came on that beautiful sunny day in Nashville truly changed my life. On the other end of the line was a man who was going to become everything I never knew I needed.

"Good morning, Zahra," he said, in a deep timbre that made my heart skip a beat. He apologized for calling out of the blue and told me a story.

He said he had been divorced for twelve years, and now that his girls were adults, he was ready to find the woman of his dreams. He had been talking to a friend, describing who he wanted in his life. He told his friend, "I want to be able to see her heart in her eyes."

His friend told him he should meet me. He also said he didn't know me well enough to introduce us—hence, the cold call.

I googled him while we were talking. His voice was warm, rich, and friendly, but the photos I saw online were different. Intense, unsmiling, and very serious. In a suit every single time. *Does he ever have fun?*

Hearing the tap of the keyboard and the hesitation in my voice, he gave me an out.

"If you're not interested, it really is okay," he said.

The truth is that Mayo did not seem anything like the guys I had been most attracted to—the stormy, unpredictable, damaged ones. He seemed collected, focused, driven, steady, and stable. *Does that translate to boring?*

Three hours later, when I hung up the phone, I knew he was also incredibly smart, adventurous, strong, and exciting.

I had learned a lot about him already, and everything I learned, I liked. A farm boy from Kansas, Mayo was also a Canadian. He was a dedicated and serious athlete. He had known the only chance he had to go to university was on a scholarship, so when the other boys were drinking on a Friday night, Mayo was running a 10K, washing dishes for a dollar an hour, or studying. He got full scholarships, both athletic (for football) and academic. Upon graduation from Washburn University, he was drafted as a wide receiver for the Miami Dolphins, but he made the decision that he wanted a career, not a concussion, and left the team and his contract behind.

Twenty years later, Mayo sold his first company, which he had taken from a small, regional, almost bankrupt grain pool to the fourth-largest international agriculture company in the world. While he did that, he also devoted his life to raising his daughters—taking them with him from boardroom to racetrack to foreign lands. He packed lunches and made breakfasts. He ironed white school shirts and came home from work at 3 p.m. to take the girls to track and dance. During the time he was building his company and raising his daughters, he was also an Ironman. He did fourteen Ironman triathlons, the last one in Kona after he qualified for the world championships.

The longer we talked, the more impressed I became.

He offered to come to Calgary from his home in Las Vegas to meet me, but I preferred neutral ground. By then I had joined the national board of Make-a-Wish Canada, and I had an upcoming board meeting in Toronto. His daughters lived in Toronto, so he said he'd be happy to meet me there on the day I was free. He told me he would get back to me with a plan.

Mayo did not get back to me with a plan; he got back to me with an itinerary. A car service would be in front of my hotel at 10:45 a.m. sharp. From there, the entire day was before us: brunch, a show, and dinner later that night. A full day, with every stop carefully considered. He even went as far as booking me a ninety-minute massage at the Shangri-La Hotel after the show, sparing me both the thirty-minute drive to where I was staying and the awkwardness of freshening up at his hotel before the evening.

I walked into the Ritz-Carlton for brunch that morning in jeans and an old sweater that Hanadi had forgotten to pack the last time she was home. Mayo was wearing a sport coat, starched white shirt, and a silk pocket square.

He says he fell in love with me the first time he saw my picture, and he fell deeper in love when I walked in that morning, realizing my heart really did shine out of my eyes. *He is a charmer, that one*, I thought.

After the show and my massage, I dressed for dinner in the spa locker room. When I walked out through the lobby to head back to the Ritz-Carlton, Mayo was waiting for me. As we walked together, I spotted a boy sitting on a street corner, asking for change. He had a sign that said he had just been evicted and needed some help—and that he was willing to work for food or money. He'd written, "Don't worry about me, I am going to stay positive."

He looked so young, as if he could be my son. My heart flooded with grief for his young life.

Mayo noticed me reading the sign but didn't say anything, so neither did I. We walked past, crossed the street, and sat down for a cup of coffee. I couldn't focus. *What is that boy's story? Why is he on the street? Does he know about Covenant House?*

I needed to go talk to him, I told Mayo. "I'll be right back. I need to find a bank machine," I said. He said he was coming with me and that he had cash. How much money did I want to give him? "Enough for dinner," I said.

We crossed the street again. Mayo walked up to the boy, said hello, and asked him how his day was going. The young man jumped up, eager for some conversation. So many people walk by people on the street and don't even acknowledge or see them. He held out his hand: "Hi, I'm Liam."

The conversation got personal very quickly. Liam needed to talk, I wanted to listen, and Mayo was watching us both. His stepfather had always been abusive, Liam said. When his mother started defending her husband instead of him, he left, with his little brother. They were in a shelter for a while, but after being beaten up time and again, they had started sleeping under a bridge. He was desperate to stay clean.

Liam told us he was still in school—in a free government program for kids like him. He was training in welding and getting decent grades. "I write my thoughts down in a notebook every day," he told me. "That way, I remember to stay positive."

Mayo gave Liam a few twenties, and Liam tried to give some of it back. "Please," he said, peeling off half the notes and holding them out to Mayo. "I don't need all this." Mayo thanked him and stepped back, ignoring the bills in Liam's hand. With a lump in my throat, I wished him luck, and we walked away.

Mayo and I enjoyed each other's company so much that he offered to stay an extra day if I wanted to spend more time together. I had meetings scheduled all the next day, but I told him I would come over for a drink that night.

I was just getting out of my cab when I saw Liam, walking "home" from school. He got to the corner and sat down with his sign in the same spot as the night before.

I went into the hotel and said to Mayo, "Guess what we're doing tonight?"

"What?" he answered, with those twinkling deep-blue eyes and ready smile.

"We're taking Liam to dinner."

Liam was great company. Articulate, funny, and full of upbeat stories about school, the girl in his class he was sweet on, whom he was afraid to tell he was homeless, and his plans for an apprenticeship. He told us he had found a job that morning, cleaning floors and doing dishes at a burrito restaurant. He started on Friday, he said proudly.

When I heard that, the mother in me made an appearance: "You need to get there half an hour early and stay two hours late. Before you leave, it has to be spotless, and you need to do more than is asked of you. Be helpful, be respectful," I coached him.

When it was time to say goodbye, Liam looked at us intently and said, "I don't know how to thank you for this." I told him that when he was a successful welder and he saw a kid on the street, he should take him out for dinner.

"There is this kid . . ." Liam started and then trailed off. "I'm sorry, I don't mean any disrespect to the money you gave me. But there's a kid on the next street who I know is not using. I can usually tell. He looked like he needs money a bit more than I do. I gave him fifteen dollars and it felt really good."

My heart broke again for young lives that might never have a chance. Liam is one of the most impressive young men I have ever met, and I have no doubt that at this moment, he is succeeding at life in a way most of us never will understand. Later, as I was getting into a cab to go back to my hotel, Mayo asked me whether Liam was upstairs sleeping in his bed, and if he needed to find a new room. *Darn it, that would have been a good idea.*

As the taxi drove away, I realized he hadn't said much that night. Later, I got a text message: "Thank you for opening my eyes. I would have walked by and not given him another thought past *Get a job, kid.*" He told me that night that we were going to change the world together.

Months later, Mayo noticed I *always* gave something to people on the street, especially the young and the old. He asked me whether I worried that someone on the street would use the money I gave them for drugs.

"I don't know that they don't," I said. "But that's not the point." I told him that my intention, or *niyyah* in Arabic, was to help someone. Once the money was out of my hands, and in theirs, what they did with it was their own *niyyah*: the intention in your heart to do an act for the sake of God. I explained that the value of every deed lies in the intention behind it, not the results of the deed itself.

As much as I have always struggled with faith, it had shaped the best things about me. Meanwhile, Mayo started always carrying cash in his wallet in case I didn't have any.

It Takes Community.

There's a lot of division in the world today. People take sides on humanitarian and social issues with the same verve they use to cheer on sports teams. Our differences take center stage. Our hats and lawn signs shout which side we're on.

And then December comes around, and we all very briefly put down our verbal weapons. Maybe the cold weather invites warmer hearts, or maybe we're just tired of fighting, but it's nice. People are nice. I love December.

The things we have in common are much greater than the things we don't. When you do the math, most of us are just a few turns of fate away from being in a tough spot. When you can't eat or pay your bills or fix the car that gets you to work every day, things start to unravel pretty fast, regardless of your hat or your lawn sign. I grew up in Yemen. I know what a dire circumstance looks like.

Every religion has some version of "Love your neighbor," because every culture realizes that there's strength in numbers. No one person can really thrive in a community that's falling apart around them.

Journalist Kristine Levine summed it up best for me recently: "When you give the best you have to someone in need, it translates into something much deeper to the receiver. It means that they are worthy."

Your community is your extended family. Give your community your energy, your time, and your purpose—not just the stale no-name mac and cheese in the back of your cabinet.

Let's do good things . . . together, for each other, for the earth, and for us. There is more than enough to go around.

CHAPTER THIRTY-ONE

My second date with Mayo was in Vegas, where he lived. I saw him waiting at the baggage carousel in white jeans and a blue T-shirt, carrying a single red rose. It was the first time I saw him in anything but a suit jacket, and the first of many millions of butterflies found its way into my stomach.

As we drove up his driveway, Mayo asked me to forgive him for taking some liberties. The garage door rolled up, and there was a shiny new red bike. I have to admit, I was not too happy about it. I was worried he would try to mold me into someone else, something I had been running from my entire life.

Mayo turned to me and said, "You never have to ride it if you don't want to, but I thought it would be nice if we could go out together sometimes." He showed me the bike, which was a Specialized electric bike with the motor hidden in the frame. Unless you really knew your bikes, you couldn't tell that it was electric. He told me this way I could keep up with him without feeling self-conscious.

I think he guessed my first reaction, and without saying another word, he showed me to the guest room. There were more flowers on my nightstand and in the bathroom. To this day, when I come home after even a night away, there are always flowers by my bedside and by my sink. I unpacked and walked into the closet to see an entire wardrobe full of cycling clothes with tags still on. All in my size. Socks, gloves, shorts, shirts, jacket, and a helmet. All pink. This man was every single romance novel hero rolled into one, and he was in the next room waiting for me.

I walked out of the room to questioning eyes and laughed. "Yes, I will go on a bike ride with you," I said with a smile. That smile got bigger when I realized that while the electric bike allowed me to easily keep up with him on the road, the turbo button on my bike meant that he couldn't keep up with me on the hills.

The bank and I were settling the terms of my contract—plenty of time, I thought, to make sure this was what I wanted to do. Meanwhile, Mayo was in the middle of negotiations of his own, also in Toronto. He was in talks to take the helm of Ontario's largest electric company during its transition from a government utility to a publicly traded company.

It seemed to be the strangest of fates. All our interview and contract negotiations were scheduled by others, and yet my meetings always fell within twenty-four hours of his.

As we spent more time together, I came to realize that if I were to wave a magic wand today and wish for the perfect man—not just perfect for me but the *perfect man*—it would be Mayo who would be standing in front of me. He understands me better than I understand myself. He cradles my heart, ignores my moods, and has a great need to open every door for me, literally and figuratively. He swats away my fears with a smile that fills all my cracks like a steady stream of liquid gold, making me whole again.

"Have I told you today how much I love you?" he asks every single day. And then he tells me how much.

My need for control of my own life will never totally go away;

I fought too hard for freedom to give it up now. Yet with Mayo, it doesn't really matter how much I push him away, or how many times I tell him he can't help. He is simply there, steady as a rock, letting me know he always will be.

And I believe him.

We were both back in Toronto four times in two months. And then both of our contracts came through on the same day, sealing our fate in this new city, together.

It Takes Love.

The need to feel loved is deeply rooted. Fear of rejection can drive us to build walls around ourselves, but science tells us that reaching out with love will prompt others to return that love—and will inspire them to be more loving in general.

I know this sounds like kumbaya drivel. Please know that my cynical, sarcastic side is cringing as I type.

I will point out, however, that there is a reason that 60 percent of all the songs written in the modern era have been about love. And I am not talking only about romantic love. I have no doubt that Kale loves me just as much as Mayo does.

Some of my favorite quotes are from Marilyn Monroe, and she nails it with this one: "I'm selfish, impatient and a little insecure. I make mistakes, I am out of control and at times hard to handle. But if you can't handle me at my worst, then you sure as hell don't deserve me at my best."

Find someone who can handle you at your worst and deserves you at your best.

But first, start with yourself.

CHAPTER THIRTY-TWO

The morning of my first day at work, I was filled with excitement. I was going to a place with big budgets, lots of resources, people and mentors to learn from—all the things my midsize business didn't have. Now I wouldn't have clients; I would *be* the client. I was really looking forward to being on the other side of the table. Also, working in the corporate world would be a first for me, and I loved firsts.

I was told they had really wanted me to come on board because they wanted someone agile and bold—an *intra*preneur, someone who would shake them up, be disruptive, give them a new perspective. It sounded fantastic to me.

That first day was a shock to my system. The bureaucracy and the office politics were much wider, much deeper, and more complex than anything I had ever seen before. Each person wrapped their arms tightly around their tiny little sliver of the pie and said, "This is mine." I discovered the cost of that corporate stability: the inability to move without permission from the higher-ups.

Mayo picked me up for dinner and asked how it went. "I want to slit my wrists," I said. They had said all the right stuff when recruiting me, but that is not how it went once I was there. Large companies have the name recognition and the resources to attract top talent, but many of them prefer to maintain the status quo—embracing disruption is part of the vocabulary but not the actions.

I was determined to do well, proceeded to push past objections and resistance, and found a place where I added value. I challenged authority rather than conform to the system and the corporate rules of conduct.

One of the senior directors, Wafa, became an ally. When I had moved to Toronto, I had cold-called her the same way Mayo had called me. I told her a dozen people from Calgary had said she was amazing and that I should meet her, so here I was. She laughed and said she had heard the same about me, and she fast became a best friend and a confidante.

She was my polar opposite: patient, thoughtful, diplomatic, and well versed in corporate politics. She also was a kind soul who preferred peacemaking to conflict. In contrast, I was a shit disturber. She coached me, and I coached her; she calmed me and taught me the corporate ways, and I taught her how to let go of them.

The resources were substantial, and people to learn from were everywhere, yet I didn't belong. This time, though, I knew it was okay. I simply was not made to work for anyone else. I could not go from calling the shots and taking responsibility for my decisions to being simply another cog in the wheel. I quit my job at the bank along with my much-loved EO membership.

I decided that I did not have anything to run from anymore.

Next, I sold Foundry's assets and client list. But I did not sell the company: there wasn't one to sell anymore. I have said much, so far, about feelings of failure and loss: I had none this time, and so I let go.

When Amani asked how I felt about my decision, whether it made me sad, I surprised myself by saying I felt really good.

Foundry had given me so much. A way to leave my marriage. A way to build my credibility. Financial independence when I needed it. A way to join EO. Friendships around the globe that will last until the day I die. Opportunities to explore the world. My house. This book. Mayo. Directly and indirectly, my company served me well and left me far better off than I was before it. Monetizing it would have been the icing on the cake, but I had my unfrosted cake and it was pretty damn delicious.

During these neither-here-nor-there days at the end of my business, I began to truly understand that all I could really control in life was my *niyyah*. If I was clear about that—if I always strived to do the right thing—then I would not have to worry about the outcome.

Yes, I would still make mistakes and bad decisions, but if I could find a way to look inside myself for the confidence I needed, I could be proud even of them.

It Takes Momentum.

When there are not enough hours in the day, when I feel totally overwhelmed, or when I feel lost or helpless, I organize.

To anyone paying attention, this looks like textbook procrastination. Like I'm wasting time I don't have or simply avoiding an issue altogether. In fact, I'm taking control. I'm getting my world in order so that the panic and chaos in my brain can settle down.

In the calm of an organized mind, I move like a lioness in the Serengeti, taking down antelopes one by one. I get work done with incredible efficiency. A flood of serotonin improves my outlook and I revel in achievement—any achievement. Micro progress leads to macro progress. Antelopes lead to zebras and wildebeest. Rearranging my kitchen cupboards leads to hundred-page business plans.

Sitting on the sofa in yoga pants leads nowhere good. It's not even fair to the yoga pants.

So make a list and check things off. That last part is important—don't skip it.

Start with whatever's in front of you that's sucking your focus dry; move on to easy stuff that adds up fast: make phone calls, pay bills, put in a load of laundry, throw out the aging produce in your fridge; then attack the wildebeest.

It won't stand a chance.

CHAPTER THIRTY-THREE

My beloved Yemen is burning. It began, again, in 2014, when the Houthi rebels, who had a stronghold in North Yemen, invaded Sana'a, and a Saudi-led coalition, backed by the United States, began bombing and bombing in the hope of restoring order for the Yemeni government. As I am writing this, the bombing continues—every dairy farm, every bridge, every school. There is no electricity in the country, not even the few hours a day we used to have.

Most of the collateral damage, as they call it, is civilians—families and children. Millions are displaced, with aid used as a weapon of war. Millions are starving. Millions are dying. Nearly four hundred thousand children under the age of five are starving—so acutely malnourished they cannot survive a week without treatment. Hundreds of thousands of cases of cholera are diagnosed every day. That is what happens when the garbage hasn't been picked up in over two years, and neither have the doctors and nurses been paid.

By 2014, most of the remaining family and friends that I had in the country had left—now all, except for two of my cousins, are gone. The rest are now mostly in Egypt, Jordan, Malaysia, Kenya. Everywhere but home.

Each time I read a headline about the incredible suffering in my homeland, I feel pain for my country and its people, yet also so removed from that place I called home so long ago. The news fills me with deep sadness and a desperate desire to help. So when UNICEF Canada approached me in 2016 about becoming an ambassador, I was all in.

My mother had been a part of the UN family for such a big portion of my life; one of my earliest childhood memories is of realizing I shared my birthday with the UN: hundreds of UN officials gathered in Yemen to celebrate UN Day, with a great big birthday cake for the organization—and a little one for me. Now, as an adult, I understand how vital UNICEF services are for the more than eleven million children whom war has left in need of vital public health, sanitation, and nutrition.

The day UNICEF Canada announced my appointment, traffic to the organization's website went up by 800 percent and so did my pride in being a part of the organization.

That August, I joined a UNICEF mission to the Za'atari and Baqa'a refugee camps in Jordan. I was incredibly anxious while preparing to go. It felt almost like I was going back to Yemen— afraid of what I was going to see and how I was going to feel.

The first time I read the briefing document was at the airport. I kept stopping at words like "child trauma unit" and the instructions not to eat in public and to drink my bottled water only in the car. Some of the children we would encounter had limited access to food and drink, the document said. Try to be sensitive, the document said. Avoid situations where you are the only adult among children, the document said.

I felt raw, like my heart was being attacked. Wondering how I was going to hide my already overwhelming emotion. War exacts its most terrible price from children—not only taking their childhood but also robbing their future, if not their lives.

Their needs are overwhelming. Food, water, shelter, warm clothes, education, protection from predators, health care, sanitation, and hygiene. But they still need to be children—to be loved, to laugh and run and ride a bicycle. They need to go to sleep at night in a warm, safe bed. How would I know what to do when I saw them?

The Za'atari refugee camp is fourteen kilometers from the Syrian border, close enough for us to see the Syrian hills and hear the bombing. There we met UNICEF aid workers from all over the world, along with various other UN agencies and NGOs, all who work with so much heart and generosity to treat every child, woman, and man with dignity and care. We also met a refugee family who welcomed us into their home with warmth, hospitality, and happiness.

These people had left behind *everything*—homes, jobs, and lives just like ours. But they still had strength, resilience, and the most incredible attitudes, regardless of the adversity they were facing.

We met two other incredible families the next day—one had been living as refugees for three years, since their entire village had been leveled by bombs. Their children worked at the supermarkets and bakeries nearby to support their family, in shifts that started at 7 a.m. and ended at midnight. The second family we met had fourteen people who lived together in a tiny house; only the oldest brother, Omar, had a job—as a guard at a UNICEF center. I felt terrible drinking the tea they brought us, sweetened with sugar they could not afford, but we couldn't refuse their hospitality.

Months later, back home in Canada, the families' faces were still so present in my mind. Their hopes, dreams, and desires no different from yours and mine.

Every refugee's story is harrowing. Every face is worn out. Not one of them would ever have chosen this life or wished it upon anyone else. In refugee camps the air is thick with their pain, their exhaustion, and their need for humanity from the rest of us.

It is heartbreaking that young Syrian children know only violence, fear, deprivation, and displacement. When I went to South Africa with UNICEF recently, I had another revelation: despite the different mission, different challenges, different people, and different country, every single emotion, need, desperation, and challenge was exactly the same.

This world is a very big place and can also be a very small, sad, and lonely one.

As a mother of three children, I know there is nothing I wouldn't do to see my kids safe, happy, and healthy. I see that same love shining through in the eyes of those families.

And as someone who knows what it's like to live in conflict—to live day to day—all too well, I also know how important it is for us all to take note. This could easily be us.

Back in 2016, after visiting Amman, I had a couple of weeks before I needed to be in Bangkok for a board meeting, and Amani and I had the opportunity to travel to East Africa together. At the time, she had just completed a master's degree in sustainable energy management in Paris, and the company she was working for had sent her to Rwanda for four months, to work on a solar project in partnership with a large international NGO.

We went on a gorilla trek, spending hours with a seventeen-member gorilla family, high up in the mountains between Rwanda and the Congo. We risked our lives on the local motorcycle taxis, slept under mosquito nets, and danced to tribal drums. And then we went back to the place of my birth, Uganda.

It was the first time anyone from our family had been back, even after the government offered to give back their properties and wealth in exchange for their return, as they had with all the Asians.

I had to lie to my worried father, who told me not to go. "There is no way I'm going to take my daughter to such an unsafe country," I told him. And then we went anyway.

What started out as a fun day went downhill quickly with a blown tire. Then a late-night roadblock, after a three-hour wrong turn, meant we didn't reach our destination until one in the morning. My desire to negotiate a price when we got there rather than do the smart thing and book ahead turned out to be a bad decision. Our driver, who spoke only Kinyarwanda, had to find us somewhere to stay. The only place that would take us was an eco camp, with sand instead of water to use in the open-air toilet.

At that point we discovered that none of the banks or the safari camps would accept any of our credit or debit cards, and we had no way to pay for lodging or food.

We awoke the next morning to a leopard waiting at our door, eager to eat us for breakfast. We decided to go on safari and worry about how we were going to pay for it later. One guide—who was fascinated by two crazy women with no money who wanted to go on safari—agreed to take us . . . and then come with us to the next town, where there was a bank that would accept our cards.

I hadn't been sure how I would feel going to the land of my birth again, and the truth is, I felt nothing. I had no connection to this place and no desire to try to find one.

It Takes Chaos.

I like planning. It gives me the sense that I'm in control and that the world is an organized place that makes sense.

But, as uncomfortable as it might be, there is no greater catalyst for success than chaos.

There's a lot to be said for slowly making your way to the top rung of the ladder, putting in your time, and impressing all the right people at all the right events over many years. I respect that path, but it is painfully slow.

If you can spot a moment when your situation is fluid and the future is unclear, you'll have a brief and powerful window to take advantage. In uncertain situations, you can jump ahead in leaps instead of steps. It's like finding that shortcut in Ikea that bypasses the lighting and rugs and brings you swiftly to the checkout.

These are called inflection points: moments when a person can modify the trajectory they are on.

Such is the thinking in a new book by Eric C. Sinoway on the teachings of Harvard Business School professor Howard Stevenson (*Howard's Gift: Uncommon Wisdom to Inspire Your Life's Work*).

Stevenson says that if you want to jump from employee to business owner or take your company in a new direction, you need to strike in a moment of chaos and uncertainty—when the structures are removed and the rules are suspended. A moment in which you can reflect inwardly about what you want, and then act to redefine the situation in such a way as to help you accomplish it.

For Foundry, this happened when I bought out my business partners. I could see them waffling about our future together, about what they wanted, about how difficult they thought it was to work with me, and so I forced their hand. I borrowed a scary amount of money and turned their internal conflict first into an uncertain future for my little company and then into a decade's worth of business progress.

So keep an eye out for inflection points, and skip the lighting and rug departments.

Progress may be closer than you think.

CHAPTER THIRTY-FOUR

I was so eager and so terrified for Mayo to meet my family. I waited a while for the introduction, but once I met his girls for a family dinner, I knew it was time.

I told my kids I had met someone. "Really?" said Amani, with a grin. "We didn't notice." *When did my kids become such smart-asses?*

It seemed I was the only nervous one. My kids wanted me to be happy. Mayo, too, was calm and collected. He had asked me a million questions about the kids over the course of the week leading up to our visit, and when he met them, he remembered every detail and won them over easily and graciously. I am not surprised that my kids genuinely like and respect Mayo. There is nothing *not* to like about that man.

Recently, Amani's friend Maha came over for dinner, and the next morning, Amani called and told me, laughing, that Maha had a new goal in life: "To find someone that will look at her the way Mayo looks at you."

Winning over my traditional, conservative Muslim parents was, shockingly, just as easy. My parents have only ever wanted my happiness—and my happiness could not have been clearer to them if I had shouted it from a rooftop.

I had learned to stand firmly enough in my own identity to present my decisions with confidence, and to trust that the ones who love me most would recognize that confidence and support my decisions.

My growing sense of contentment with my life did not erase all the regrets and unresolved feelings of the past. I did not see Wan for many years after the divorce, and my family went two separate ways. But when one of Amani's best friends got married, she and Wan were both in the wedding party.

I knew Wan was doing great—he had finished university and had a great job that was steadily giving him promotions and raises. But I had no idea if he wanted to see me, and I was nervous about going. Hanadi, who was home for the summer, came with me to the wedding. As we walked through the door together, she told me, with worry and sadness in her eyes, "Wan is not going to talk with you, and it is okay if he doesn't."

I told her I understood and accepted that. And then I saw him walking toward me.

He gave me a hug and walked back to his friends. I could feel my heart expand and then settle down in my chest. There was a familiar ache, of the love I always had for him, and with it, a kind of opening too: finally, some forgiveness for myself.

It Takes Experimentation.

We are creatures of habit. The world holds billions of unique experiences, but we like routine. We stick with what we know.

Well, let me tell you, there's nothing like emotional trauma to make you willing to try new things. Perhaps it's to jar yourself out of a numb state, or maybe life seems suddenly shorter, or then again, you could just be searching under rocks for your true self.

And maybe your true self likes motorcycles and skydiving. You should probably have a look.

My mother loved dinner parties. She would cook a feast for days, and her presentation skills were phenomenal. She is a great chef, but she drove my father and me crazy with preparation. The one thing she did that I never understood then was try new things . . . all the time. Some worked, some tasted terrible. We would always tell her to just cook the things she knew how to do well when company came. Why experiment on them? She just laughed and created the next masterpiece . . . or disaster.

Years ago, when I was going through mental overload, I took an entire month off work and bought five new cookbooks. For thirty days straight, I cooked my way through them. Results were mixed, but that's not the point.

I love dinner parties and cooking just as much as my mama, and I have 128 cookbooks in my pantry to prove it. And while I have a few tried and true favorites that I make often, every time I have people over for dinner, I try something new. A few are masterpieces and some are disasters. *That* is the point.

I tried something new.

Lust for life is a contagious phenomenon. Jump out of an airplane and watch how many people suddenly ask you to lunch. People will start asking to spend time with you again. Good friends will support you through trying emotional times, but it's not exactly fun for them.

Larry Alton, a journalist for HuffPost, believes there are three big benefits to leaving your comfort zone.

You'll overcome fear—the thing that holds us back most in life. Your mind tends to exaggerate what can go wrong. Commit to an adventurous spirit, and fear will cease to be a paralyzing factor in your decisions.

Your creativity will skyrocket. Your brain will get a workout. When it's flexed and challenged to really think, your creative side is stimulated, which affects every area of your life.

You'll learn about yourself. No matter your age, if you've been living the same day on repeat for many years, you're probably missing out on some of your unique likes and dislikes. Consider that you don't know yourself as well as you could. As you experiment, you'll naturally recognize who you are and who you want to become.

So live a little. Do some things that are out of character, and risk loving them. They might be delicious.

CHAPTER THIRTY-FIVE

I was still very much trying to get my bearings in Toronto when I heard that a young woman named Sarah Katyal had suggested I speak at an upcoming women's conference.

Her name sounded familiar to me. When I looked her up to thank her, I realized we had appeared in the same *Chatelaine* issue. Back then, Sarah had been recognized as a voice for young entrepreneurs, a top 20 under 30, and she was clearly a bright star—driven, connected, constructively honest, and full of ideas.

I invited her out for a coffee, and as we were getting to know one another, our conversation turned toward ideas we really wanted to see come to life. I told her about RedBalloon in Australia, a company that allows people to gift experiences, like sky diving or food-and-wine tastings, instead of giving "stuff." I told her how much I wanted to design a company like that—a marketplace where people could seek out experiences and learn from them.

By this point, I had given significant time and thought to this idea: I already had a name and website designed and the start of a business plan. I had even secured all the domains and social media pages. When she expressed interest in the concept, I hired her to put together an investor pitch for me. As we worked on the pitch, the plan slowly changed into something that truly inspired us both, and Sarah came on as a partner in the new company.

We were a team from the start: brainstorming, pressure-testing, iterating, and reiterating. The idea of the company changed form again and again, but we remained just as thrilled by what was emerging: an online marketplace for in-person learning. Tinder for learning experiences, if you will.

Sarah and I were baffled by the lack of innovation in learning—and by how hard it was for most people to access a better future. We did not focus on fixing traditional education systems but rather on improving access to knowledge and, in so doing, disrupting the world of how we learn.

We know that each of us, as an individual, is defined by our experiences and by the skills we've acquired through them. This combination determines who we are, what we know, what we do, and how we do it. The knowledge we acquire through skill-building contributes to more than just ability—it creates resilience, confidence, access. So Sarah and I have set out to create a place where knowledge can be transferred, shared, and celebrated. It's called Skillit. Our mission is to offer skills training to low-income seniors, students in debt, and single parents who need an advantage in the workforce, delivered through the power of a huge and invested population.

This mission is deeply meaningful to me. I know the person I am today is the result of my stretching my wings and trying everything and anything. This was not always pretty. I broke rules and confidences, and more often than not, I faked it until I made it. But I had the incredible example of my mother, who is still pushing out of her comfort zone and making connections—cultural and spiritual—that have given so many a unique perspective. And there is also Hanadi, who has a lot of her grandmother in her. Her passion for young people and investment in their future inspires me to no end.

Sarah and I believe that a part of giving young people access to a better future includes making sure we don't leave anyone behind.

That is why every person who sells skills on our marketplace must donate a skill to someone in need for every ten they sell. We also plan on spending 1 percent of our revenue buying skills from our makers to add to the pool of donated skills.

Sarah is both brilliant and eager—a delight to mentor. She is also a textbook millennial. I don't mean to say that like it's a bad thing; it isn't. It's just a generation gap to bridge, like so many that have come before. But at times, this gap feels even wider—particularly when someone from the younger generation looks me in the eye and confidently tells me they are going to do it their way.

We argue; we push back on one another's ideas. We are both so passionate about this company that an outsider looking in on one of our conversations might think we're about to come to blows . . . but we never do. We each have such a clear understanding of who we are and what we want from our shared future and from this company. And as much as we are willing to fight for what we believe, we are also willing to listen.

It is so gratifying for me to see the ways in which the most talented people I know are coming together to help us build the new business. Louise came up with the name for the company, and Jon designed the brand. Tara, who worked on my personal PR in the Foundry years, tracks our social media. Wafa and my good friend Shari are advisors. We've even hired Nicolle, who for years worked for Foundry as a copywriter, but under the pseudonym Kitty Wong because of her day job. (I did have her boss's blessing!) After a couple of years of that, Nicolle laughingly informed me that Kitty Wong was kicking her ass on the awards circuit.

One of the biggest pleasures has been stepping back to let Sarah run the show. At this point in my life, I have earned the freedom to decide which parts of the business I love and which parts—namely dealing with HR, finance, and operations—I am more than happy to leave to others. The benefit of truly knowing who you are is the ability to seek out the opportunities where you will flourish. It also helps to know she is fabulous at it.

As we build this company, it feels, in some ways, like I am back to my teaching roots. Only now, a world and a generation away from where I began, and thanks to the power of technology, I can make a difference I was not able to make then. My dad was right: computers are the future.

What excites me most about the work is that it is a total embodiment of everything that has brought me to this point in my life—a final combination of all my learnings, lessons, experiences, and passions. From the heartwarming ways in which people are sharing of themselves and giving back to the way Skillit is all about making you the best version of yourself, about building confidence and success, and about improving lives. The team and how we came together; my amazing relationship with Sarah . . . even my children doing the research and sending out countless emails for us, Mayo helping us at every turn, and my parents proudly telling everyone about Skillit. Everything about this company makes my heart so happy.

As I spend so much of my day thinking about skills and experiences, I can't help but reflect on how much the world has changed since I was a cloistered teenager who thought that marriage was my only ticket to freedom. The Yemen of my childhood is gone, sadly. But technology has shifted some of the limitations that geography and circumstance once imposed on girls like me.

The truth is that my teaching career did not stop at YALI: I have had so many opportunities, thanks to hard work and more than a little luck, to recognize that I do have skills to share and stories worth telling. I am confident that by building this company, and sharing my own experiences with others, I can teach people to recognize their own expertise—and, in turn, to pay it forward.

I feel so strongly about all this that it almost does not matter if Skillit achieves the success that we want. In the busy world of start-ups, which fail at a dizzying rate, I believe that our team, and this company, has already succeeded. And beyond that, beyond work, is where my life truly begins. For I now have complete faith in my incredible support system, which exists in spite of—no, scratch that, *because of*—all of my extremes.

"Babe, you are so organized, precise, focused—I am a hurricane within a tornado," I once told Mayo. "So how do we work?"

Mayo smiled, looked at me with those warm blue eyes, and said, "You are my alter ego, Zahra. You are everything I had been trying to suppress for sixty years."

I am still not sure that is a compliment, but I will take it anyway.

EPILOGUE

In every family's history, there are stories in which the agreed-upon endings have different beginnings, and nothing makes this more apparent than trying to weave together all those stories to make a book. While working on this book, and during a private conversation, my cowriter asked my father the same questions she had asked me about my childhood. Our answers were the same, with one very important exception. He had wanted to send me to university in London, he told her, but instead, I wanted to get married.

When I heard this, I drew in my breath, the same way I had during the initial conversation with my father more than thirty years earlier. And then I picked up the phone and called him.

"Baba, that's not right," I told him with a catch in my throat. "You told me I couldn't go." My father seemed just as surprised to hear my recollection as I was to hear his.

As we talked, it all became clear. My father had been as invested in my higher education as I had been, but caught between two worlds, he needed some time to think through his plans for me. He needed me to convince him.

I had not given him that time.

From my very earliest memories, I was constantly making up my own mind—insisting on a way to be on my own, if even for just one minute. As a teenager, I repeated what many women before me had done: I settled for marriage as a means to escape patriarchy without hurting anyone. That is what my seventeen-year-old life came down to, convincing my soul that it needed to be quiet for a bit while I figured it all out.

Hearing from my father that a different path had been available, or even preferred, was confounding. All I had ever wanted—a life of my own making—had been already within my reach had I just stopped for a minute. This pattern has been repeated throughout my life. I jump in with both feet and run toward conflict and strife with the same passion as I run toward love and experience.

The even more powerful realization, at that moment, was that none of it mattered anymore. I was no longer angry about the past. My parents have given me every single ounce of their love. Not only did I want for nothing, but I would not change a second of my life to get to this point.

For so many years, I fought for what I thought was complete freedom—in relationships, in life, in work. I hated being told what to do, and from the time my parents' tight hold made me desperate to be "bad," I pushed back. Now I can see how past relationships define your behavior in your new ones if you let them, and if you do let them, then the other person still has control over you and they still win.

Life is never going to be perfect. There will always be bumps and roadblocks. What it takes to be free is knowing, with conviction and confidence, that we are well equipped to handle them.

My journey has been full; I can't think of another word to describe it. There have been countless hard lessons, but those don't matter in light of the things I cherish most in this world: namely, Thing 1, Thing 2, and Thing 3 . . . my children.

What that journey has taught me is that true freedom is a life free of regret and anger.

What it took is loving with abandon, experiencing with real pleasure, and appreciating the ride with a whole heart.

I can now look at myself and find dignity instead of shame. I am strong instead of fearful. I find love instead of rejection.

And that elusive place of belonging, for which I had been searching for so long, was there all along.

I realize now that the person I am today is the same person that got me here.

True fulfillment cannot come from a plan, any more than it can come from a product, a book, or even a strong work ethic—although the latter certainly helps. What it takes is faith that we can each find our way forward through our own unique challenges. And doing so with gratitude—the most important life lesson I learned from my mother and grandmother, and what I now see through the eyes of Mayo and my kids.

Gratitude. A way for us to appreciate what we have instead of always reaching for something new in the hopes it will make us happier. An opportunity for us to refocus on what we have instead of what we lack.

These pages hold some of the qualities I've collected on my journey. You will need to figure out what to bring with you on yours.

Alhamdulillah.

ACKNOWLEDGMENTS

This book has been a labor of love by a lot of people, not just those who helped it come to life, but also those who held my hand, taught me about life, changed my outcomes, and brought me home. Thank you.

My children, the loves of my life, the best thing in this world. They amaze me, fill me with pride, and overwhelm me with my love for them.

Amani, my smart, angelic firstborn child who is as stubborn as the rest of us and just as determined to do it her way. Amani has the strength of a lion, the heart of a saint, and a smile that will knock your socks off the minute you meet her. She is smart, sassy, capable, fiery, and just as much of a bulldozer as the rest of us.

Hanadi, my super-independent, feisty little "Do I look like a gender studies student?" fireball (translation: middle child). The woman with a heart that is too big for her body, who never stops wanting to help anyone in her line of sight. My child who never takes no for an answer and will move mountains—just watch her go.

And last but not least, Ahmed, my sweet boy, dedicated, serious, handsome, smart, loving, thoughtful, hardworking, and the most caring heart you will ever see . . . and you *will* see it because he wears it on his sleeve.

There is a saying in Arabic that roughly translates to "Even a monkey looks like a gazelle in its mother's eyes," and I know that is true. I am very biased about my kids, and I look on with wonder at the lives and personalities they are crafting with ease and passion. They are well on their way to creating their own powerful destinies, and I proudly have a ringside seat.

My loves, I can't wait to see the places you will go and the things you will do. I love you with every fiber of my being.

My parents, who not only gave me life but gave me this life. Thank you for your support, guidance, kindness, and love despite how differently I want to do things and how far I venture from the path that family, culture, and obligations demand I be on. I love you.

The father of my children. Thank you.

Rupa, thank you for being the little sister/co-conspirator/sometimes big sister that I always wanted. I love you.

Al-harazi girl cousins, each and every one of you is a force to be reckoned with and has a story that needs to be told. I am so proud of you all. Hayat, Hanan, Rupa, Sabiha, Alifia, Sahara, Yasmin, and last but not least Fatima. I love you.

Suzanne Brandreth, my agent and my friend, it has been one heck of a journey, hasn't it? We only made it because your belief in this book and in me never wavered even for an instant. I love you.

CookeMcDermid, my agency, the ones who took me on and stayed by my side, especially Dean Cooke, Sally Harding, Ron Eckel, Paige Sisley, and Leah Shangrow, and at Cooke International, Hana El-Niwairi and Carolyn Buszynski. Thank you.

Speaker's Spotlight: You signed me on so early in my career, and it is thanks to you that I even have a book deal. Thank you, Melanie, for being my "keeper" and doing it with so much style, beauty, and grace (and for being my baked goods dealer). And to Farah, Martin, Marnie, Brenna, Kelly, Michelle, Aya, Jennifer,

Donna, Tami, Dwight, and all the rest of your amazing people, thank you.

My girlfriends: the ones who have always been there, whom I can count on and trust. Who have laughed, raged, and cried with and at me. Ishraq, I can feel your smile from heaven. Louise, my vault and partner in crime . . . I am your biggest fan. Wafa, sister of my heart, steady as a rock and always there. Noni, with a huge, giving soul and a spirit full of love, laughter, and sunshine. Sarah, Nicolle, Susan, Kimberley, Shari, Shriti, Emma, Chai, Seba, Andrea, Theresa, Laura, Amanda, and Zabeen, the powerhouses in my life who shake the earth that they walk on. Redha, Hana, Najwa, Ghada, Nahla, and Eman, my childhood sisters. I love you all.

The Sarahs in my life: Sarah Katyal, my fellow starry-eyed dreamer and believer, business partner, and cofounder, I love watching your journey into the person I know you are. Freelance editor Sarah Wight, who crossed my t's and dotted my i's and took a canvas and helped turn it into a work of art. And last but not least, Sarah Robbins, my cowriter, who patiently spent hours upon hours listening to me talk about myself incessantly and took that and turned it into beautiful words on a page. Thank you.

"Kitty Wong," who jumped in at the last minute with piles of memories and her amazing writing skills, which I have always stood in awe of, to help me with the themes in this book. Thank you for spending an entire weekend sitting in your "car office" and writing magic the way you always do. Love you lots!

Norm, you have been there, through thick and thin (mostly thin), and stuck with me no matter what section of quicksand I was standing in on any particular day. Thank you, and lots of love to you and your little munchkins for giving up many weekends and evenings for me.

Brad Wilson, my editor, who stayed staunchly in my corner through six name changes, three cowriters, and four completely different drafts of this book. Brad, I can't believe we (you) pulled this off! Thank you.

HarperCollins: what an amazing team to work with! I had my pick and I chose you because you impressed me the most, and you continue to do so. Zeena Baybayan, Cory Beatty, Kate Cassaday, Michael Guy Haddock, Alan Jones, Leo MacDonald, Iris Tupholme, and Noelle Zitzer. Thank you. My thanks to copyeditor Patricia MacDonald as well.

And Mayo . . . the love of my life. My protector, my knight in shining armor, my soul mate, my cheering squad, and my rock. You make me a better person. I love you more than all the stars in the sky, all the sand in the deserts, all the water in the oceans, and all the air in the universe (and yes, I will always win this *I love you more than* . . . game).

You once laughingly told me that "together we add up to twenty, maybe two hundred, maybe two thousand . . ." I say that together we add up to everything. I love you so much.